Rajkumari Amrit Kaur

Rajkumari Amrit Kaur

The Dedicated Gandhian and Health Minister

Dr. Shiv Gajrani
Dr. S. Ram

Commonwealth

Rajkumari Amrit Kaur

First Published : 2012

ISBN 978-81-311-0362-3

Published by :
COMMONWEALTH PUBLISHERS PVT. LTD.
4831/24, Prahlad Street,
Ansari Road, Darya Ganj,
New Delhi - 110002
Ph. : 23272541, 23257835
Fax : 91- 011- 23257835
e-mail : commonwealthbooks@gmail.com

Laser Typesetting by :
Dimple Computers
Delhi

Printed at :
Roshan Offset Printers
Delhi

Preface

Rajkumari Amrit Kaur was born on the February 2, 1889 in Lucknow to a princely family of Kapurthala. She gave away all the worldly pleasures and focused her attention on serving the society. Throughout the freedom struggle of India, she worked in close association with other freedom fighters.

The ruthless killings that took place in the Jallianwala Bagh Massacre of 1919 motivated her to join the freedom struggle. Eventually, she worked together with Mahatma Gandhi. She went far away from materialist life and began leading the life of an ascetic. She came to live in Mahatma Gandhi's Ashram in the year 1934. She also raised her voice against inhuman acts like ill treatment of Harijans.

After the Independence of India, Rajkumari Amrit Kaur joined the Jawaharlal Nehru's first Cabinet. She was the first woman to hold a cabinet position. She was made the incharge of Ministry of Health.

She played a pivotal role in the task of conceptualizing and laying the foundation for the establishment of the All India Institute of Medical Sciences in New Delhi. For this, she secured aid from different countries like New Zealand, West Germany etc. She and her brother even donated their ancestral property that was made the holiday home for the staff of the institute.

She served as the Chairperson of the Indian Red Cross society for a long period of fourteen years. She made an immense contribution towards the development of the tribal groups of India. She held the position of health minister till 1957. Thereafter, she took retirement from the ministerial activities, but still remained a part of the Rajya Sabha. Till she was alive, she held the presidency position of AIMS and the Tuberculosis Association. She also served as the chairperson of St. John's Ambulance Corps. This great soul departed for heaven on the 2nd October in the year 1964.

Authors

Contents

1

Contact with Mahatma Gandhi

I

The ideology that Gandhiji preached became so much a part of our philosophy and our way of life that it is difficult to realise from what small seed it grew. Gandhiji planted it several years ago and tended the delicate sapling which today has taken under its full-grown shelter not only the people of this country but even from many other parts of the world. It is only those who were with him in the twenties and the thirties of the century that saw its gradual evolution.

In this article, written during the Mahatma's life-time, Rajkumari Amrit Kaur draws a vivid pen picture of the impact of this ideology on her own thoughts and way of living.

GANDHI—THE TEACHER

A teacher affects eternity; he can never tell where his influence stops.

Henry Brooks Adams.

The late Shri Gokhale was an honoured friend of my father and often used to stay at our home. I may say that the flame of my passionate desire to see India free from foreign domination was early fanned by contact with him. He once said to me, "One day soon you will, I hope, see a man who is destined to do very great things for India." With this at the back of my mind I seized the very first opportunity I could of being presented to Gandhiji. This was in 1915 at the Bombay Congress when Lord Sinha was presiding. It was the first Congress I had the privilege of attending. Gandhiji was more or less an unknown factor in the political life of India at that time. The tumultnous ovation went to the great Tilak who had just returned from the Andamans. Gandhiji spoke a few words about Indians in South Africa. With no loud speakers in those days his speech was more or less inaudible except to those on the dais or in the front rows of the audience. But there was a quiet strength, an earnestness and a deep humility about him that went straight to my young heart; and I feel I have owed allegiance so him and his way of life ever since, even though circumstances did not permit my actually joining him till much later.

He came to Jullundur after the massacre of Jallianwalla Bagh. By then he was the idol of the people The undisciplined crowds had trodden on him. At 6 p.m. he was suffering from a badly bruised foot and high fever. My doctor brother, who happened to be the Civil Surgeon there, begged of him to postpone his journey by 24 hours, "How can I break faith with so many who are waiting for me at various places?" came the quick reply. "And I assure you I shall be free from fever by 10 p.m. which is when my train leaves". I sent him a hot water bottle and begged of him to take it with him for the journey. The next morning the bottle came back with a note of thanks written by Mahadev Desai in which he said "You will be glad to know that the fever actually went before he left Jullunder so he had no need of the bottle afterwards".

His second visit to Jullundur the same year brought him to see the because he had heard I was ill. He asked me to give all my 'foreign finery' to him to burn and take to 'Khadi'. I stoutly denied having much 'foreign finery'. I said I now bought only Swadeshi. "That is finery too". I pleaded that burning was quite wrong. His reply was : "Not even when these things stand for the chains of our slavery? But if you will not burn, at least give it to me, and I will send it to poor Indians in South Africa and you take to spinning and Khadi". Alas! that his words, at that time, fell on more or less stony ground. I tried to wear Khadi but found it too coarse for my fastidious tastes. In those days there were none of the fine Andhra or Bihar muslins such as there are today. Because his words carried power in them, however, I learnt how to spin and used to give my yarn to be spun for cloth for a poor child or woman. I began buying Khadi for dusters, towels and for any rough use in the house.

Afterwards Gandhiji said to me : "Many people have used Khadi as a door mat but they do not realise how they have thus wronged it and all it stands for!" Later when the realisation of what Khadi embodies dawned upon me I understood what he meant by calling any cloth that was not Khadi as part of that which was contributing to keep us slaves. Years later, when I came to live with him in Maganwadi, he saw or sensed, perhaps, my inability to rid myself of some of the comforts to which my sheltered life had accustomed me and how understanding he was! He would not allow me at first to sleep on the ground. I was not made even to wash up my own plates etc. I was willing to do everything and pleaded with him to be allowed to do so—but Gandhiji, while he has the enivable capacity of drawing people to him, has also the even greater capacity of keeping them with him. It is because he leads gently over the rough places that he evokes complete loyalty from all and sundry.

It is in the very nature of things that people of all sorts and conditions come to him from the four corners of the earth. It is the old story of the maimed, the halt and the blind coming to someone who can give them succour. And just as I have seen and felt his gentle hand bringing relief to a fevered brow, just as I have seen him taking infinite delight in washing a leper inmate's sores or ministering to other sick folk—so do his words of love and sympathy bring solace to many a stricken heart. But those who are nearest to him sensed in him also the hardest of hard task masters. Which of us has not come under the castigation of his righteous indignation? On such occasions tears do not move him. "Tears are not the expression of the sorrow that should be yours", he once said to me "they are a token of the pride and anger in you. You do not understand the first principle of non-violence which is infinite humility".

It is from the trifles in one's daily life that Gandhiji teaches big lessons. My thermos had broken. We were leaving Delhi for Wardha and Gandhiji had said he wanted to take his evening meal on the train. I had to take hot milk as well as hot water for him. It was difficult to manage with only one thermos which was left to us. Shri G.D. Birla, seeing my difficulty, gave me a brand new one which he happened to have got only the day before. I willingly took it. When I poured out his milk from it in the train he at once saw that it was a new article for he has an eagle eye. Had I bought it? I told him the whole story. He was bitterly disappointed in me for having taken the gift so readily. Was I a pauper that I should make anyone spend money on me? It did not matter that the friend who gave it could afford to do so, but I should have known better. Money is a sacred trust with those to whom God has given it, and not a penny of it should be spent on him who has no need of it or on anything that was not needed. Mahadev, who was returning to Delhi from the station, was told to return it. Afterwards it became Mahadev's property and how often when I used to see that flask did I recall to mind the fifteen minutes' salutary lesson that it had given me!

"Never try to wean me from doing that which I like and which gives joy to others." This was in the early days of Sevagram when I felt that helping more than a dozen persons with food was too much for him. That he can no longer serve out the food or take a part in preparing it or not even eat in the common room is a sorrow to him. But I must realise my limitations.

"Why do you waste so much of your time on the personal affairs of the mad inmates of your Ashram?" Quick comes the response to this oft-repeated question: "I know mine is a mad house and I am the maddest of the lot. But those that cannot see the good in these mad people and blind". I am again and again remined in his dealings with human beings of the great prophet of Nazareth who came, not to be ministered unto, but to minister. "They that are whole need not a physician but they that are sick".

"You are very unfair to your own people. If it is a case of Hindu versus Muslim, it is always the Muslim whom you favour. If it is either against the Harijan, you will be on the side of the Harijan, and as for women you will always take their side." No one had a heartier laugh than Gandhiji over this remark, made by a valued co-worker in jest and yet with so much truth in it.

Children have a special attraction for Gandhiji. He is as a child with them. "Little Kanu, by insisting on making me tell him stories is making me an expert in the art. For you know it is an art and a marvellous way of impating all kinds of knowledge to children. All the instruction I was able to give to my own children was during my walks from Phoenix to Durban. I had no other time. I did not send them to school, and they have a grudge against me, perhaps, for not having given them the opportunity for passing exams and receiving the so-called higher education. But I consider that I imparted to them far more than they would have got from school or college". That is the reason for Gandhiji's insistence on the quality of the teacher in his scheme of basic education. "Textbooks are really not necessary if the teacher is, as he should be, a storehouse of knowledge".

It is alleged that women talk more than men. At any rate, perhaps, they gossip more. Commenting on this overindulgence on our part one day he said to me : "Of course, you know the English proverb, 'silence is golden'. Have you ever probed into the depths of this truth? If you have, you will try to set an example in this regard to the younger members of your sex who surround me. I have long since realised that one should not utter one word more than is necessary. "Even my jokes (and he has an endless fund of Kumour) are meant to bear a lesson within them. The moment one speaks more than is necessary one veers from the truth, and you know that untruth and violence are twin sisters. My own habit of weekly silence for 24 hours sprang just as much from the desire to discipline my speech as to give myself rest and more time for quick despatch of my work." Recently he said to me, "You do not know how I strain myself to keep my thoughts pure. I believe thought is more potent than speech. For achieving my object I have perpetually to dive down deep into the well of truth. That alone can wash away impurity." It had happened that morning one of our party had said something to annoy him. "I should have corrected her, of course, for her error, but I had no business to be angry with her as I was".

Nothing annoys him more than being called a 'Mahatma'. "I should not be a seeker after truth if I had stopped growing". Vital decisions are taken overnight, as it were, and adhered to with all the courage and faith born of deep conviction. This was so when he decided to move to Sevagram. Hut or no hut, rain or no rain, road or no road, he went to live there in June. The same applies to the recent lightning decisions to start a nature cure clinic in a village and to live in Harijan quarters in big cities. No entreaties can move him once the decisions are taken, and since such are arrived at through worship of truth and non-violence, they are basically correct. To watch him at Uruli—his latest venture—conducting a roaring nature cure practice among all and all sundry, men and women, rich and poor, is an invigorating exercise. Most people are frightened, after a certain time of life, of breaking new ground. But Gandhiji at his advanced age starts with all the vigour and ethusiasm of youth. His zeal is infectious, and when I see with my own eyes these men and women with simple faith in his healing powers, I wonder why most of us are incredulous when Gandhiji prescribes Ramnam as the panacea for all our ills, whether physical or mental.

A foreign friend meeting him after many years asked : "What news of your family?" Without a moment's thought came the reply: "The whole of village India is my family". And I was reminded of an incident which Ba had related to me of how once, when some sweets were being distributed to children in Sabarmati Ashram, she had given an extra portion to two of her grandchildren and had properly earned the wrath of Gandhiji whose love is too universal to admit of comparisons or differences in his mind, however much those near him may indulge in petty jealousies. Woe betide any inaccuracy in work by those who are working for him. He will take all the pains possible to teach, he gets work out of everyone according to his or her capacity, but I am sure many like myself have often incurred his displeasure for looseness or lack of thought, for he cannot bear inaccuracies or thoughtless speech, writing and action. I had accompanied him to a meeting, and he had given me a slip of paper which I had been commissioned to give to—, I did as I was told and the person concerned read the same and talked to Gandhiji about it. On arrival at Sevagram I was asked for the slip. I said I had handed it to—who had read it, said what he had to say, and imagined he had either kept or returned the same. I thought my responsibility had ended with handling it over to—.

The next morning I received the following letter : "Amrit, an ideal secretary keeps her chief straight where he is going astray. She hovers round him and watches all the movements about him, picks up his papers even torn—lest he might have torn important ones in mistake—collects all she given him if it is to be found anywhere. therefore she leaves after him and seeks what he has left behind and, if not owned by anybody else, collects it. Now I was right in correcting you yesterday but wholly wrong in showing disappointment or irritation. Forget the wrong and treasure the right. What I have said is by way of indication. Follow the spirit of this note and you will be an ideal secretary."

"This is my birthday present which goes loaded with all the good wishes that I am capable of conceiving. Love, Bapu."

I doubt if anyone can possess more unique and treasurable birthday gift.

Nothing is more delightful than to hear from Gandhiji first hand of many incidents in his early days in England and South Africa. They are probably all related in his Autobiography. Many are the stories against himself related with roars of laughter, but he makes them live again by his graphic description, and his narrative always has a bearing on the matters being discussed in order to give practical instances. "It has been a rule in my life never to ask anyone to do anything which I have not tried out in practice myself."

I had the privilege of being with him when the sad news came to him of Shri Chhotelal having out an end to his life. It was a cruel blow that one who had given up his belief in violence and served faithfully for so many years should end his life by a violent act. And while he restrained his tears the wound was deep, and he was in quiet thought for some time. Was it a heart-searching as to why he had failed to keep Chhotelalji from violence? He has often said : "I can never forget Chhotelal", I was with him too when Jamnalalji went. He arrived there very shortly after the sad event. The family was naturally distraught. The blow was sudden, the loss irreparable. But with the arrival of Gandhiji a deep calm came over the mourners. "What room is there for tears when he know that death is but a passing into life?" Nevertheless while he has schooled himself not to weep, he is human enough to enter into the sorrows of others and strengthen them with his love and sympathy. At prayers in the Ashram at Sevagram that evening he talked of the loved co-worker and told us how he would miss one who had brought him to Wardha and to whom he turned for everything he wanted. "I feel today as if my right hand had been cut off."

Truth to tell, however, Gandhiji has the capacity to carry on his work with or without his immediate helpers. This was amply brought home to each one of us the other day when he suddenly felt that he should go to Simla unaccompanied by any of his staff.

"I want to be alone with God as my sole support. I am going on very important work. I am preaching every day to people that God is our only help, I am asking them to rely on Ramnam and not on medicines for the curring of their ailments. I must put my own faith to the test. And why should you worry? There will be many others who will look after me and who know my wants." I similar decision was taken yesterday in regard to going from Mussoorie to Delhi in a 'bus rather than in the comfortable car in which Shri G.D. Birla had sent him up there. All pleading on our behalf that he would be less tired in the car, that he needed all the rest he could get in view of the heavy work and the heat awaiting him in Delhi, met with the stern rebuke that not one of us was able to understand the inner meaning of his decision. With Gandhiji it is ever a case of scaling more and more difficult heights. I am reminded again and again of the true pilgrim's progress towards that self-realisation which is the goal of all high endeavour.

The harder the task the greater in form does it find him. While honourable and reasonable compromise is in the very marrow of Gandhijis bones the grim determination never to cede principles is always there. "Fear of consequences may never deter the believer in non-violence. For non-violence knows no defeat." Sometimes when he has not been able to bring his point of view home to co-workers, he has said : "I must be content to plough a lonely furrow rather than resile from a position which I am convinced is the right one." I remember so well his saying this to Mahadev on returning to his hut in Sevagram in 1939 on the outbreak of war after a meeting of the Congress Working Committee. But failure to carry conviction invariably makes him turn the searchlight inwards. "There is something wrong in my presentation of the non-violent aspect and not the fault of those who will not agree with me."

"How are you feeling in spite of the heat and the strain you are undergoing these days.?" "I am very fit as you can see. Everyone is really jealous of me. But I am not as well as I should be because I get irritated very easily and that is a sign of ill health. In me raised blood pressure too is often a result of anger."

To the thousands that come to him for solace and advice Gandhiji gives a listening ear with all the understanding of a man able to put himself into the shoes of another person. "I felt, if I was to be a guide to friends, co-workers and seekers, I must cultivate the art of listening."

And so, those of us who live with him find in him a teacher who instructs big things from very small happenings, who chastises "as a father the son in whom he delighteth" and who inspires one and helps one to grow. And this applies equally to old or young, man, woman or child. It is the power of handling aright individuals and groups that contributes to success in the every day life of the Ashram or village no less than in the big events that concern the country.

"I want to live to be 125, if I am able with God's help to live as I should to attain that age, I want to live so long not merely to see India politically free but also to see how I can help to bring about the Ram Rajya of my dreams whereby she can make that contribution for which the world is looking to her."

Few people can speak with authority on Gandhiji or present us with intimate glimpses of the Mahatma's everyday life or of the way his mind worked. Of these select few Rajkumari Amrit Kaur was one of the closest to him. In this revealing talk to an American audience, Rajkumari analyses the secret of his appeal.

II

Wardha,
14-10-1934

Dear Sister,

I have your letter. You were quite right in writing to me as you have done. It may be most difficult to give two hours to the artist friend. But I shall see what is possible. I look forward to your sending me a copy of the photograph of Charlie Andrew's head.

The rumour you have hard is correct. I am trying to retire from the Congress. But that does not mean a life of quiet for me. Indeed I do not know what is to happen to me after the Congress session is over. But I should love to undertake the mission you would like me to. I do not know what is expected of such a mission. As you know, I took up, among several other things, woman's cause also when I began public life. And my love for that service has persisted throughout all these 45 years. I would like you to sketch for me what you would have me do, and if I feel up to it and have the opportunity, you may depend upon my taking up the mission.

Yours sincerely,
M.K. Gandhi

Rajkumari Amrit Kaur
Simla

Wardha,
21-10-1934

Dear Sister,

I have your very frank and precise letter. I regret to know that you are in frail health. I want a band of persons who would devote themselves fully and their time to the work, move about and will go the villages and try progressively to supply their own needs through the villages unlike as we do now. I see that I must not expect these things from you and must therefore deny myself the privilege of your close association. Nevertheless, I will avail myself of your offer to do whatever you can in the Punjab. Do you keep yourself in touch with what is being written in the pages of Harijan? If you do not please let me know and I shall see that you are supplied with copies.

I fear I shall not be in Karachi at the time of your Conference. I shall however hope that having come all the way from London Dr. Maude Royden will not leave without seeing me but I wish you could come with her.

Yours sincerely,
M.K. Gandhi

Delhi
17-1-1935

My Dear Sister,

I must dictate if I am to write to you at all today. You must not overwork yourself. You must give yourself proper rest and build up your body to the extent it is possible. As a confirmed believer in the natural mode of living, I think that we can rebuild shattered bodies by conforming to the laws of nature. Very often I have known persons who have succeeded in getting better where medical assistance has failed. This is no reflection on the doctor brother.

I hope you got copies of the A.I.V.I.A. constitution and have sent in your form to Kumarappa.

I would like the Raizada to convince me that it is proper for ourselves to prosecute poor Harijans for breach of the Sarda Act. In the meantime, I am certain, we must not undertake these prosecutions. Prosecutions must be preceded by educative propaganda.

Love.

Bapu

Rajkumari Amrit Kaur
Jullunder City.

Harijan Home, Delhi,
21-1-1935

Dear Sister,

I have sent in your application to Kumarappa. You shall be your own junge as to the enforcement of rules 9 and 10 in your own person. What I expect you to do is not a visit to every village in your district, but acquisition of a right knowledge of the villagers' wants and organisation of the effort to meet them. For this you are fully fitted in spite of your dilapidated body of which we must talk when we meet.

I leave on 28th which is my silence day. Come if you easily can between 26th and 27th.

The cold spell has meant more than the loss of a crore or rupees for the starving millions.

Love.

Bapu

Wardha,
2-2-1935

Dear Amrit,

Here is my message for the Harijans who are troubled about child marriage :

"In these days of self-purification, Harijans ought to know that they are to avoid all the bad customs of caste Hindus. They should therefore avoid child marriages. But reformers may not be impatient. Sarda Act is, in my opinion, a wise step. But it may not be strictly enforced against Harijans when it is very laxly enforced against caste Hindus. There should be effective enlightened propaganda by Harijans among fellow Harijans on the evil of child marriages and the bearing of the Sarda Act on them. And then when it is made certain that people wilfully ignore that Act a few prosecutions may be undertaken. But even then, they must be the sole concern of Harijans. They may not ask for or receive even financial assistance in this matter from caste Hindus. In any case at least one year should be given to concentrated propaganda."

If this is not the message you want you may withhold publication and let me know what you want.

There is no cold here. We have been having rains instead.

I hope you are better.

Love

Bapu

Unrevised

Wardha,
18-2-1935

My Dear Amrit,

Your letter of 5th instant is still before me.

A parcel of envelopes was sent to you the other day.

The writer's cramp is still there. I wrote today for Harijan and a few brief letters. But that was about all I could do for the day with the right hand.

I know that your entry and that of women like you into the village movement will make it artistic and attractive.

I take it that Shummy's name may now appear on the Board of advisers. Never mind his ignorance. It takes a wise man to own his ignorance. And have not doctors to unlearn many things if they would serve villages? Please tell me his full name and title for the Association Register. My love and thinks to him.

I am glad you have commenced your visits to villages. I wish it were possible for you to lesson your desk work and increase concrete village work. But I see you have a special gift for writing work. Your organisation perhaps can't do without the quantity of work you are giving it. Only, please take care not to overwork yourself by reason of your having taken up village work.

I have passed on your message to Kumarappa. You are quite right in not taking members' pledges indiscriminately.

Here is my message to Harijans :

"Please tell Harijans that in the movement for self-purification that is going on at present, they are expected not to copy the vices and errors of the so-called caste Hindus. I was therefore distressed to find that child marriages were as common among them as among some caste Hindus. It is a cruel custom having nothing of good in it. They should also know that it has been declared illegal by special legislation. I hope therefore that Harijans will make a great effort to rid themselves of this evil custom."

I hope this meets your requirements.

Mira had a bad motor accident. All her companions were hurt. One of them was very badly hurt. She was the least injured. The car was smashed to pieces. They were all thrown up in the air. It was a miraculous escape. The one who was seriously injured is lying in the local hospital. He is out of danger. No one dies without His will.

Love,

Bapu

My dear Amrit,

I have your two letters. Yes, the Khan Brothers are truly servants of God. I am glad you were able to go through the book at a single sitting. You should get some copies from Devadas, free if you like, and send them to your English friends.

The paper I that Jugal Kishore has sent you, has the defect you point out. I am making investigations to see, if improvement can be made. Envelopes should present no difficulty. They can be neatly prepared by the hand. The making of them may by itself become an occupation. Do the ones I have sent you lack the finish?

You may not wait, for adopting Khaddar, till you have used up all your mill-made saris. There is any amount of beauty to be found among hand-spun stuffs. Of course, hand-spun silk is

Khadi.

Please give my love to Maharaj Singh and his wife. You may not know that my second son is Editor of a S.A. paper called Indian Opinion. He is a good young man. He did not like Maharaj Singh's policy and attacked him fiercely in his paper. Andrews and I reasoned with the boy for the manner of his attack but we failed to convince him of the error of his method. He is an obstinate boy. I told him I did not mind his criticism where he disapproved of a policy but I reasoned with him as to the manner of his approach. I am still trying.

I remain unconvinced by Mrs. B. Nehru's arguments. My point is that we as reformers may not do the work of prosecution. The Sanatanis will pay the fines and put up the Harijans against us. I am quite clear in my mind that we have to begin with the so-called higher classes who are the real culprits. That Harijans know sometimes that they are contravening the Sarda Act does not affect my argument. They are still ignorant of the wrong doing. Mere defiance of law his ceased to be a wrong in itself. My argument holds good even for the women's organization. You may show this to Mrs. B. Naturally, if my reasoning does not convince you, you will ignore it.

I must inquire about linen.

You will come whenever you can. The earlier the better.

Love,

Bapu

This paper is specially bad. I hope you can decipher the writing.

Wardha,

26-5-1935

My dear Amrit,

I have now got your yarn. It is not bad. You should now learn to make properly twisted strands. If you do not the yarn becomes weak. I see you have sent a lot of razor blades some of which are quite new. They make up for the postage spent on the yarn. Now you should collect a fair quantity before you send a parcel.

Did you get the packet of envelopes and notepaper? The expert has (not) yet commenced paper-making. I put him on to making notepaper etc. out of the stock brought from Indore. When he does make paper you shall know.

Yes, I began about the market in Simla. I suggested your personally visiting it and studying the local vegetables and fruit and their quality from the health point of view and at the market knowing the poor who come from distant hills to sell their produce. You can also sell paper, Khaddar and the like among those who will congregate in Simla.

I hope you have both already felt the effect of the mountain air.

Andrews should be here during the week.

Love,

Bapu

Borsad,
2-6-1935

My dear Amrit,

I reach Wardha on 3rd instead of 2nd. I shall send you more note paper and envelopes after reaching Wardha.

I hope there is no after-effect now left of the accident.

How about your slivers?

Yes, I know tho Khambattas very will indeed. They are both very good workers. I am eagerly looking forward to Charlie's letter about them. Please send me their address and have the enclosed delivered or posted to Khambattas.

Mira says it is like a furnace in Wardha just now. It is much better comparatively in Bombay.

Love to you all.

Bapu

Tell Charlie, Khan Saheb sends his love to him.

Wardha,
7-6-1935

My dear Amrit,

I see why your body wears itself out. You insist on doing everything thoroughly. Of course, it is the right thing for any seeker. But there is no warrant for any seeker taking over more than he or she can well manage. I wonder whether I was right in letting you come into my movements. God will take care of you. You must cut down the social functions of Simla even though it may involve some seeming sacrifice of the good you might do to the movements you may be in. No movement designed for the multitude will suffer by your conserving your time and energy by cutting down many social functions.

Now for Khadi. All Punjab shops are not run at a loss. The Simla one has always been. Management is no doubt defective. But the people in Simla look down upon Khadi and there is a class that is afraid to wear it. The wearers become marked men. Your idea of having a Swadeshi Mart on the Mall is attractive but its execution is risky. However good Swadeshi articles may be, they must suffer in comparison. And I doubt the utility of aiming at gaudiness. I differentiate between art and gaudiness. What one sees in fashionable shop windows is by no means all art. To produce things or real beauty and hope to put them side by side with the showy things of the Mall in Simla is an expensive ambition which we had better suppress at least for this season. Do what you can with the shope as it is. Convert it into something better. Let there be Swadeshi article in it. Arrange it after your taste and gain experience before you take expensive quarters. We must have this as one of the topic of discussion when you come down in July or August—the earlier the better.

You will read what I have felt and done about the Quetta disaster. You will read my letter to Charlie. He should know that one swallow does not make a summer. He will have to trace me in Orissa or some such place when I take up walking again. Meantime I accept 12 miles on the Hills as a fair beginning.

I am waiting for the analysis of falsa.

Note : Paper and envelopes are nearly ready. Some slivers are also ready. I want to put together a fair lot. I hope to give you the cost price of every thing, at the time of sending the articles. I have kept no count of what has been already sent of you of paper or slivers. Nor need you worry about these.

Love,

Bapu

Wardha,
13-6-1935

My dear Amrit,

Your letter brought tears to my eyes. God will certainly bless service so conscientiously and selflessly rendered.

I would have joyously taken you both to Quetta if I could have gone. But it was not to be.

Yes, you will convince me of the necessity of removing the Khadi Bhandar to the Mall.

I can't write much, as I am writing with the left hand. The right needs rest.
Love.

Bapu

Unrevised

Wardha,
19-6-1935

My dear Amrit,

The frank admission of one's proved helplessness does not make one a coward but may be the beginning of bravery. I am taking you at your word and dictating. Writing with the left hand is a pleasure to me but I cannot do it with the same ease and quickness as with the right hand.

Charlie has duly handed your letter. I am returning the photo prints with autographs in the manner suggested by you.

I cannot remember Krishnalal Goswami. It may be that he was in the Ashram during my absence. Charlie says he has distinct recollection of having seen him an Ashram. Mahadev has not. What he has said to you about Charkha seems to be correct and shows that he knows something of the art of spinning. Slivers I am sending with Charlie. You well tell me how you find them. You should have the spindles locally made. If you cannot secure good steel they can be made of any iron. So long as they are true it does not matter much. A weak spindle spins as well as any other, so long as it remains true. But in an inexperienced hand a weak spindle will go wrong more frequently than a steel spindle.

I am sending you also 450 note paper sheets and an equal number of envelopes done up in 9 bundles. I was about to have packets to 50 each pressed and nicely covered in some blank paper, of course handmade, when your letter came telling me that I was to send the sheets coverless and that you would have them dressed up for the windows. You ask me to give you the price. The bundle that is coming to you with Charlie and the one that was sent previously to this were made out of paper which has cost me Rs. 12. Odd sheets that were saved were used up by me. There still remain 150 sheets with me. The labour of making these I have not counted, nor the price of material specially prepared for making the envelopes. The price of the latter can only be trifling. The price of the former cannot today be estimated. Two or three workers have been at it for some odd days. I did not ask them to keep record of all the time that they gave to this work. Now I have given you enough material to put your own price on the note-papers and envelopes. The least you have to sell them for is Rs. 12. But you are at liberty to do what you like them. Of these slivers I can say nothing because all I have to pay for is the cotton purchased from the Khaddar Bhandar. But I have kept no account of what has been sent to you. The raw material could not have cost more than a rupee and a half.

As to the Quetta relief I have asked you to reserve for the time being what you collect. Letter on I shall be able to guide you. The relief will last for some time. Of course, this advice has force, so long as you have no definite idea about its direction. Immediately you know where you would like to spend your donation, you will not hesitate to do so.

One thing I cannot help asking you to collect for and that is the Harijan Wells Fund. You will note what I have said about it in the ensuing number of the Harijan.

About the photos you will do what you like with them. They are your property. I think this covers all the points raised in your two unanswered letters. There is nothing wrong about the right hand. It will be all right after due rest.

Love to you both.

Bapu

Wardha,
4-7-1935

My dear Amrit,

I have your letter. Your letters to me are love letters, each time I suppose not less than an hour's effort even for you—a ready and fast writer. Now that we know each other so well, you can certainly save your time by writing only when you must. Though I treasure your long letters. I would be satisfied with a mere postcard telling me of important events.

You have your work cut out for you at Poona. Are you coming to Wardha on your way to Poona or on your way back or both ways? The whether is much cooler just now.

I have shared your letter with Kumarappa. If you can establish contact with rickshaw pullers, it would be a great thing. They can easily spin, weave and add to their meagre earnings.

I am sorry Krishnarao is leaving you. Of course ultimately you will have to rely upon yourself. Though your arms may not be strong enough to work at the bow, it is good that you will know the process of carding. That would enable you to regulate and control carding by others. If your girls learn spinning, you will insist upon their carding. Unless they do, they will never spin regularly. And it is a bad job to depend upon others for slivers. If they form a kind of spinning-club, they can have a division of labour. Some may gin, some others may do the carding, many can make slivers, and all will spin.

The clothes you have for Quetta relief, may be sent to Dr. Gopichand for the refugees in the Punjab, unless of course there are refugees in Simla itself, in which case you can distribute your clothes among them. Only I fancy that in Simla you will have the most well-to-do refugees, whereas in Lahore the poorest must have congregated.

I shall hold on to the money. It can be sent where they have spent what is being collected now. There is always in such calamities an ample fund in the beginning stages.

You need not get out of your 'Ville' to sell those papersheets and envelopes I have sent you. I am in no hurry to have the price of them. And ultimately even if they could not be sold there, there would not be any difficulty in selling them here, without any loss. I know we cannot make the profits that you can, but you must not give undue labour to their sale.

The slivers I have sent you, should give you at least 25 counts, as they are capable of giving 30 counts.

Please hand over the enclosed letter to Andrews.

Love

Bapu

Rajkumari Amritkunvarbehn,
Manorville,
Simla.

8-7-1935

My dear Amrit,

These are the remains of the paper sent to you. Never believe what the papers say of me unless you have confirmation from here. I did howl from pain for 45 minutes. When it was over, there was no weakness felt, no weight lost. It was an overdose of neem leaf. I was trying its maximum capacity. Such experiments must be tried on self. My experiments have never done permanent harm. I have made rich discoveries for myself and companions. In the early days my teeth suffered. But there too, there was nothing wrong with the experiment. It was my ignorance of early days. If our doctors knew the properties of indigenous food and drugs, the way of persons like me would be simple and easy.

I shall have more paper made for you.

Believe me I am quite fit.

I had to do the writing myself today. Monday?

Bapu

Wardha,
1-9-1935

My dear Amrit,

This paper is the waste of what is now being prepared hereby apprentices. I am sending it for you to see the colour and the thinness. It lacks finish. Presently we shall produce the finest paper made in India at a reasonable cost. Devadas's coming to you will be earlier than I had expected. I am sending your love letter to Devadas, Kumarappa may leave Nagpur on 4th and be with you on 6th.

I have sent you a bag of rice with A. It is very good though cheap. I have paid double railway fare for the goods train would have meant a month's waiting and the risk of damage. I wonder if I did right. The rice should keep good in Simla though unpolished rice must not be stored for long. If the quantity sent is too much for you, you should sell it. I hope to send you the bill herewith if it has not gone already.

The takli also went with A.

If Devadas does come, you should use him for Khaddar propaganda. He knows spinning.

We are crowded here just now. We have the members of the Harijan Board.

Janakiprasad finished his seventeen days under extraordinarily good condition. He broke it on honey, lemon and water.

I was not able to take your apples. I have so many who are in greater need.

Love to you both,

Bapu

Wardha,
4-9-1935

My dear Amrit,

This is thinnest paper made here. You can write on both the sides as you can see. He has prepared the blotting paper too. And he promises to make considerable improvement. This paper industry may prove a veritable boon. If it does, it will be a proof of what a combination of talent and labour can do for the village. I am hoping to get with your assistance, more than over 8 annas per day for the makers.

Avinashilingam has got your rice with him, he says, as he could not find your place. He would not let me pay the railage. The cost of the bag is a trifle as you will see. The railage twice the price of the article!! I wonder if I did right in spending you all that quantity. Perhaps you did not know what a bag would contain. There are bags and bags!

Having asked you to accommodate K. and D. I am not going to say more than I have done. I only hope that they will not prove a source of burden to you. Of course you are not expected to give any time to them. It is monstrous for poor people to think of going to fashionable hill stations. You are responsible for the mischief. My poverty is only so-called.

Shummy must not forget the real poor. I must have the analysis of the neem leaf.

Love

Bapu

Wardha,
6-9-1935

My dear Amrit,

Your daily post has commenced even before the patients are there! This is like your rehearsal of Shakuntala. Next time you come, you will teach something of your art to the girls, if a little time can be saved from your secretarial work. I suppose your rehearsal there was in English? Whose translation was it? Who were the actresses?

Yes, you will have the salesman and present rent paid for a limited period if you will guarantee purchase of a definite minimum of Khadi and not stock mill cloth. You can sell all other Swadeshi articles. But my anxiety is for you not to add to your already heavy burdens, financial and administrative. Run the Swadeshi enterprise by all means if you have the right stamp of men and your financial responsibility is rigidly fixed. The undertakings with which I am connected are so vast in their scope that they can absorb fortunes. That they have never yet done so is because I have never allowed them to go out of hand. And as there is protection from within, there is little chance of personal gain. All I want therefore is your great ability, constancy and purity dedicated to the service of the lowliest and the downtrodden. That, thank God, I already have.

I return Vijaya Singh's letter. I do not like it over much. But I have no right to judge. You will insist on a proper accounting of every pice spent.

Madadev has gone for a day to meet Jawaharlal. I fear however that he must have missed him by a few hours. J. flew earlier than he had expected.

I hope you are not overworking yourself.

Love

Bapu

Wardha,
9-9-1935

My dear Amrit,

Just a line whilst I use the right hand. I see that I must rest the right hand except during the silence day, if I am to retain its use for that day for some years. This is merely a precautionary measure.

I am eating your apples. But you won't issue preemptory instructions with each consignment you may be sending. I assure you, I shall not deny myself fruit when I need it.

Khurshed is acting as Secretary, Mahadev having gone to Allahabad only to miss Jawahar and now having gone to Sardar at his bidding. She is giving full time and is slaving today even as you had to that terrible Monday.

Amtul Salam has just risen from sick-bed to find Mira taking her place. And it is pouring cats and dogs today! I hope however there is nothing serious with her.

Ba and Devadas must have come to you today, I do hope all this party won't be too much strain on you. Shummy will give me his professional note on both Ku. and D. pleace.

I wonder how long the bag of rice will last you. Next time you should import paddy from the nearest place and instal a husking chakki. That would be the cheapest method and in keeping with the village spirit.

Love to the ever increasing family.

Bapu

Wardha,
19-9-1935

My dear Amrit,

I am not going to worry about Ku.'s temperature. He is absolutely safe under Shummy's care.

I do not remember having suggested your name to Rajendra Babu. If you really do not feel equal to the task, say 'no' unhesitatingly. If it is from the Congress standpoint that the pamphlet is required, you must not undertake the task. If is from the woman's standpoint, I do not know anyone who can do it better than you. But I myself dread your undertaking fresh burdens. Therefore whilst from the latter standpoint I would like you to shoulder the burden, you shall be the judge as to whether you can spare the time. It need not be a book. A pamphlet of 25 pages octavo size compactly written would be quite good. Of course, you may write more if you feel like it.

You shall have the paper as soon as possible. The samples not yet received.

Did I tell you yesterday that Mira was on her back? She has just been transferred to where Ku was pleaced. Amtul Salam, tell Ku. has now got her job and is now up and doing. She has forgotten that she was sick only yesterday. Please tell Ba, Laxmi is to be put up at the Bungalow.

Love

Bapu

Just received wire about Devadas. Thanks God.

Wardha,
14-9-1935

My dear Amrit,

Your unfailing full letters are a blessing to me. With the two patients under your care I have no anxiety about them. Please tell Pyarelal I have his letters. I take him at has word and save time by not replying just yet. Mahadev has not yet returned. He may not before Monday.

Your reply to Dr. G. is quite correct. I am destroying the letter as desired by you. You must resolutely refuse to carry burdens you cannot bear.

Mira is still not out of the wood. She had another restless night. Nevertheless the fever is abating though slowly.

Rajaji is still here. He will probably leave on Tuesday. Laxmi and the new-born are well. Tara still has recurring fever. And so has Manu. They are all at Jamnalalji's Bungalow.

Tell Ba and Devadas I got no time for writing to them. My letters to you must serve the purpose of separate letters.

Love to all,

Bapu

Wardha,
16-9-1935

My dear Amrit,

Your dear letters never fail me. God bless you. You must not tax your eyes overmuch and then spoil them.

With the doctor in the house, I must not say Devadas should not be pressed to eat more than he wants to take. Better to let him go slow. That is the lay man's tip to be taken for what it may be worth.

Here are two letters.

Love to all,

Bapu

Mira is free.

Unrevised

Wardha,
23-9-1935

My Dear Amrit,

Your letter to Chowdhury has told. He has taken it in the right spirit. There was no occasion for apology. And if you cannot call a spade to your own people in your own home, which Maganwadi is, where could you do so? You must repeat the performance, whenever the occasion arises.

This size is specially prepared for you. But you will give me your criticism on it. For the stinking lot you have to pay nothing. Has the stink gone with exposure to the sun and the air?

Puri should send his detailed criticism without delay. He must not wait for the time when he comes here. I must not be kept in darkness.

I am eating your apples with vengeance. And I needed them. They and musambis have acted like medicine.

Mira is free from fever. But she is still terribly weak and the digestive apparatus does not respond as it should. In spite of big doses of Eno's Fruit salt, she has to take the enema in order to get a clearance. But there is no anxiety on her behalf.

You won't get full marks as good nurse, nor Shummy as a good doctor, unless between you two you make P. take milk and your excellent butter.

Has Shummy anything to add to what I have given in Harijan on snake-bite? Is there an easy way of distinguishing a poisonous from a non-poisonous snake? Does he recommend any book on it?

When does he think Ku. can be discharged?

Here are some letters for your guests(!)

Love

Bapu

When do you descend to the plains? You may not overstay your time in Simla for the sake of the convalescents.

Wardha,
6-9-1936

My dear Rebel,

All these few days I was in no mood to play. Hence I had forgotten that you were a rebel, Idiot &c. &c. Now I am somewhat composed. You have still to send me the news that there is reconciliation between you and S. If you have not gone to him, you must do so at once.

I told you I did not like that eruption on the thumb. You must not doctor it yourself. You should see a competent doctor, if Shummy will not attend to you. Nor can I guide you from here as to your food except in a general way. The bath is all right. You are right in raising its temperature. It is enough to have it at least 5 degrees below the temperature of the body.

I must tell you later what I consider was the cause of your breakdown. This is being written after 8 p.m. So I must write more.

Mahadev has kept you fully posted about the health. Hence I need say nothing more except that I am Al.

Please thank Shummy for the book on snakes of which I saw some beautiful live specimens yesterday.

Much love from,

Robber

7-9-1936

My door can never be shut in your face.

Wardha,

10-9-1936

My dear Idiot,

I had the physical capacity to write to you all these days. But I have been so busy talking things that I have not been able to do any writing except on Monday. I hope you got my letter written that day.

Now too I am writing this before retiring for the night.

Yes, I had a good letter from Shummy. I do not agree with you that Segaon climate had nothing to do with my malaria. Indeed Segaon is noted for its malarial climate. It is for me to conquer it and not shun it. I hope to be there on Saturday. The plate will be taken tomorrow. It will decide my fate.

Your letters received with extraordinary regularity have been a rich treasure. You must not trifle with your eczema or the eruption on tho thumb. You must put yourself under a competent doctor and do as he tells you. So long as you take eggs, I do not think anybody will insist on your taking meat. I would like you to write to me saying you have called in skilled assistance. Consult Shummy on the point. You must not be obstinate on the point.

No more just now.

Love

Bapu

Segaon, Wardha,

12-9-1936

My dear Idiot,

Well, I am at last in dear old Segaon, without Ba, Lilavati and Moti. Amtul Salam is here for a few hours and she goes back to Wardha. Lilavati is in M'wadi under discipline and Ba has remained there out of sympathy. All is quiet here and looking nice. In front of me are two live snakes in the cage caught yesterday. Your green soap bit is there in its place. It will give a few days work still.

You will be glad to learn that your thermos was broken to pieces after giving a night's good use. The door of the cart suddenly opened and the thermos fell out. You are not to replace it any more. I must do the best I can with improvised things. You know by this time that I am shameless enough to ask for thinks I need. And such a thing is a real good magnifying glass. But this at your leisure and not by post. Tell me what was the const of the thermos broken today. It is pure curiosity that prompts the question.

I hope you have listened to me and taken expert advice about your eczema. It is a thing not to be lightly treated.

You won't be anxious about me. I shall take every care of myself.

Mira is now in her cottage.

Love

Tyrant

Segaon, Wardha,
13-9-1936

My dear Idiot,

As you want me to destroy your letters at once, I have always to write from memory. Yes, S. wrote a sweet letter which I am going to acknowledge, though he does not want me to.

Here is my diagnosis of your illness. You left in the midst of nature treatment. As it was not completed, there was a reaction in a radically changed climate. It would be called a healthy reaction, if it could be treated as a nature cure method. This not merely hip baths. There are steam baths, light baths &c. But this was not to be. I was not alarmed over the reaction but over the just resentment in the family. They cannot sympathize with nature cure methods.

Have I made myself clear? Thank God, now there is peace in the family.

But you must not trifle with your eczema. I would certainly treat you if you were with me. But that cannot be certainly not for cure. You have to go through the orthodox method, the quicker, the better.

Yours is a departure from the orthodox routine. You may not therefore resent the criticism of the family. You will justify your rebellion only by your large-hearted charity, ever increasing inner joy, equableness and possession of good health. Rebellions can only be justified by success. If you will therefore be patient and wise in your changes, all will be will.

Please give my love to Tai, if she is still there.

You need not now give me daily letters if you are pressed for time or too lazy to write. Writing to me must be no tax on your mind or body.

Cartloads of love,

Robber

Segaon,
18-9-1936

My dear Idiot,

Just a line only. Your apples have been eaten by all with relish. Not an invitation to send more.

Khan Saheb was most grateful for the attention given by you to the girls. He wants you to go out of your way to befriend them and direct them the right way. Here is his letter.

I am glad Shummy is now attending to you. You will now get will quick. Obey him willingly like a good idiot that you are.

Cartload of love,

Tyrant

Segaon,
20-9-1936

My dear Rebel,

You are in danger of losing caste even with Tai, if you persist in defending my non-violence so long as it has not become your very own. That the savage in us may get the better of us when we are tried, does not affect our position, if we even while we are savage know that we are doing wrong. The fact is that in this age of doubt, we are never sure of our ground. Some attractive argument which we cannot answer baffles us instead of humbling our pride in our intellect. These questions of non-violence birth-control, and the like are eternal problems. So it might be better for you in the long-run, never to seek to defend my views. When it is your own views. I know you are more than able to hold your own. I do not want your great ability to be discounted because of your association with me. Rather would I like it to be said that neither your body nor your mind had suffered decay after you began to come to Wardha.

I am glad S. is now treating your eczema. You must not be touchy about the feet. Is it not better that what is in is now coming out. The only thing to have a remedy that results in elimination, not suppression.

I hope you will have no difficulty in deciphering the leaf 4. You will have none if you will treat this as part of it. You know what I mean.

Even among closest relations some can be shameless. I belong to that class. Therefore don't send me a thermos, till I call for it. I assure you I am getting hot enough drinks. On that score you need not worry.

I entirely-agree with you that women are better nurses and more to attentive details than men. Whether it is so for modern women or not, you can speak with greater authority than I can.

Your recent letters make me feel, uneasy. You seem to be overdoing things again. Learn to say "No", when you are physically or mentally too tired.

Ba and Manu went to Delhi yesterday. And Lilavati is still at Maganwadi. Mira has no temperature today as yet though this is the day for it.

Your apples were eaten with great relish by Khan Saheb and me.

Sufficient for the day.

Love

Bapu

Segaon, Wardha,
21-9-1936

My dear Idiot,

Your eczema has to go, I do not know how. Will Shummy approve of gently steaming the part affected, then applying ice poultice? If you think you can discuss this with him you should do so. But at the same time you must not fret because it is a skin disease. You will be well earlier, if you will cease to think about the trouble. How I wish I was by your side at the present moment! But that cannot be.

Please tell Fielden with my regards that he is working himself to death without a just cause. He ought to take leave and get well quickly. Of course, the effect of malignant malaria is said to be very bad.

I wonder if Mahadev passed on to you the yarn that I was to have died of heart failure at 10 a.m. on Friday last. This was sent by a learned man in all seriousness to Jamnalalji. He told me all about it. And though he made light of the information, he could not help posting poor Mahodaya here for the night. Though he was deprived of the privilege of last rites, he came in handy as Mira happened to have high fever that very day.

I hope the access of visitors has not proved a real strain on your scanty resources. I wish you could hide yourself somewhere during the cold season. Any other hill will be better than Simla. It is impossible to try Mahabaleshwar or Ooty?

Love

Robber

Segaon, Wardha,
24-9-1936

My dear Idiot,

This is a left hand effort just to give the right a little rest.

You do seem to be overworking yourself. You ought to find a way out.

The newspaper cutting is funny. They cannot live without lies. Presently they will reduce you to thin air!!! Then you will fly about everywhere without any escort and I shall need to provide no corner for you, when you choose to waft yourself to Segaon. The only difficulty will be how to make you out—a mere airy nothing. Well, by the time you become nothing. I shall have grown a sixth sense enabling me to recognize beings or no-beings of the air.

Don't you think that I have nothing else to do but to write nonsense. I wanted to chat with you. I don't want to be always lecturing to you on your eczema. And the wretched cutting gave me the text for this letter.

The apples have come in again. Are they still from your garden?

Love

Robber

Segaon, Wardha,
26-9-1936

My dear Idiot,

If the unbreakable thermos comes, I shall not return it. As I destroy all your letters. I have inadvertently destroyed the Mahmudabad address. Please repeat it on a separate sheet.

Surely it is idiotic to pass summer in Simla merely because you possess a house there. You ought to select another summer resort where you can really recoup yourself.

Remember one of the attributes of non-violence. It seldom speaks, it simply and silently acts. It appeals not to the intellect, it pierces the heart. The more it speaks and argues, the less effective it becomes. Therefore do not hesitate to let your case be lost by default. Apparent defeat may be the hour of victory. Speech is often a sign of weakness.

You will please give a trial to meat if S. says it is necessary. Your vegetarianism will be on surer ground for your yielding now, if yielding becomes a duty.

Love

Robber

On the train,
16-4-1938

My dear Idiot,

We are moving towards Wardha. I am in a fit condition. I have started the day with 160-4/98 an unusual thing nowadays. And mark you, up to Gwalior the crowds won't let me rest. They would shout in my ears, as it were.

Mahadev I have sent to the Frontier to see things for himself. He should be there 3 or 4 days.

It was a nice chat with the Viceroy. Quite inconclusive. It was not meant to be conclusive. It was an exchange of ideas. More when we meet.

You must take yourself fit in Simla. You must take the hip baths and exercise. It is criminal to tie yourself to the desk. Play tennis daily, if it suits you.

Sushila has remained in Delhi. She must have written to you.

Love

Tyrant

Segaon,
22-5-1938

My dear Idiot,

A letter, addressed to me at Calcutta in which you wrote about a young graduate, went from place to place and was received only yesterday. Your letter written on the train was duly received and was easily readable. And now has come yours of 19th.

I feel better and rested after reaching Segaon. I want mental rest. The mind has been overworked. I can take that rest only here; so I find from experience.

The heat is no doubt trying. But I feel the joy of being a co-sharer with the other inmates. I propose presently to take daily silence for a few hours.

My weight was found to be 106 yesterday–not much of a loss for retaining the health I was able to keep.

Yes, the Mysore communique was distinctly good. You must have liked the W.C. resolution. It was good you went to Mysore.

I shall gladly revise what you may send.

What do you say to my exploit about Prithvi Singh?

I must send you a copy of what happened between Jinnah and me. He is a very tough customer. If the other members of the League are of the same type a settlement is an impossibility. But there is a way out for a unilateral undertaking. Settlements can be unilateral. I do not know that a unilateral undertaking will not be in the prevailing atmosphere a better mode of handling the situation. But every attempt must be made to arrive as a mutual understanding.

I have not yet written to the Mirza. I shall do so in a day or two. As for myself you are right. You and others can help me only through prayer. I feel that the cloud is lifting. What is happening to make me feel easy, I do not know. And why should I worry? God's ways are mysterious.

I had an hour's good chat with J.L. on 19th. Your diagnosis is correct. The European visit will do him good. Of course he is at heart religious, though he denounces religion, He reads the Gita. He sports a Buddha head in his bedroom. Whatever he does and wherever he is, it is well with him.

Did I ever tell you that I did not deliver your letter to Jinnah? I did not take it. It should have made on mention of me but should have confined itself to the question itself. But it does not matter.

How are you doing? What about the eczema? And the throat?
Love

Tyrant
Segaon, Wardha,
17-6-1938

My dear Idiot,

I have ever liked the idea of our women seeking foreign aid in their fight for freedom. Hence I do not want the League to inquire into the position or condition of India's women. This kind of propaganda turns their attention from themselves. Their fight is not even against India's men. It is and must be among and against themselves. I have never relished the fight put up for women at the Round Table Conference. Such being my radical views you can understand my indifference to what the League does or does not do. But if I have to examine their viewpoint. I refuse to read colour prejudice where are other cogent reasons to justify a particular course of action. I wonder if this is plain of you. You may not agree just yet, though you will in the end. For I am quite sure of my ground. The women in S.A. rose at a bound by their own action. And have not they, the village women done likewise even here?

I had a long chat with Ashalata about Parkinson's note. I think she has grasped my point.

Love

Tyrant

Segaon, Wardha,
23-6-1938

My dear Idiot,

My idea of boycott is that it can be a perfectly non-violent measure. When it is that, it becomes a duty. Hence boycott of Japanese goods does become a duty for those who consider Japan to be wholly in the wrong. And when it becomes a duty, it takes no count of consequences. And duty has to be performed whether one has company or not. Have you seen Stanley Jones thesis on the subject?

No more today.

Love

Tyrant

Segaon,
8-7-1938

My dear Idiot,

What a question? Of course, you pass though W. on your way to B. That means you may be here when the W.C. meets. And here you will find yourself in a crowded room. But that you don't mind.

How you manage to lose your voice from time to time? You must go to a place where you can't be pestered. It is not Segaon? And now I can build for you also to your design!!

J.S. letter to S. you have now. I hope the talks have stopped of course. The reply has to go from W.C.

Yes, J.I. is having a grand time. He is raising India in the estimation of the West.

It is perphaps as well that you will be the only member of your peace Brigade. This work does not need thousands. True immolation of a few will do the trick.

You are wrong. I began work among women when I was not even thirty years old. There is not a woman in S.A. who does not know me. But my work was among the poorest. The intellectuals I could not draw. My appeals have always been from heart to hearts. I have felt like fish out of water in the company of intellectuals. Hence you are wrong in laying down the sweeping proposition you have. You can't blame me for not having organized the intellectuals among women. I have not the gift. And then my method of organizing is out of the ordinary, not necessarily superior. All I mean is that I have nothing to show on paper. But just as I never fear coldness on the part of the poor when I approach them. I never fear it when I approach poor women. There is an invisible bond between them and me. And why do you miss the agony I am passing through? Is it not for womankind? I am wringing my soul for adequate purity to enable me to render greater service to them and through them to the whole of humanity. Ahimsa, which is my sheet-anchor demands all this.

I expect your next letter to tell me you are well.

Love

Bapu

My Dear Idiot,

What a sad and wretched letter, yours of 11th. I am enjoying myself and you are sorrowing for nothing. When you come here, you will laugh at your own folly. My misery is superficial if there is any yet left. My peace cannot be permanently taken away by anything or anybody. You simply do not know me if you think that my experiences have undone me. If there is real attempt at purification, it must strengthen me and make me more joyful. But how can I help you if you must allow your imagination to run riot?

You have to apologize about women. I could not organize intellectual women as such. I have not organized intellectual men as such. But this thing does not end itself to argument. I simply cannot subscribe to the charge that there has been any neglect on my part about organizing women. It may be that I have not had the qualifications for doing better. But that would be no charge against me. However I do not mind our complaint. I rather like it. It show that there are things in which we look at things differently. And why not? True affection does not demand identify of outlook. But I do not even on this point despair of convincing you that I could not have done better than I have. My passion for brahmacharya has that meaning. I must be wholly pure, if I have true love for womankind.

Love

Tyrant

I believe apricots did arrive—all rotten. Apples have come. I shall certainly eat them. You must be well quickly.

New Delhi,
21-10-1946

Chi. Amrit,

Your two letters came in together.

I am sorry for your sufferings. Let them do you good which they would if you interpret them correctly. Physical suffering can be and should be transmuted into spiritual joy. It is difficult process but has to be gone through if one is to be truly rich. This forced illness should be used for enriching one's thoughts.

That Shummy is not angry with me shows his nobleness, not the care I should have bestowed on you. On the first sign of the boil I should have insisted on your going to Simla. This place is not made for nursing patients like you. It is its unavoidable limitation.

Love

Bapu

V. cannot be sent for as you suggest. I know him much better than you do.

New Delhi,
23-10-1946

Chi. Amrit,

Your letter. It would be tragic if you couldn't go to Paris because of the obstinate boil. The doctor in attendance can't say even that much! I am sure a good Vaidya or perhaps better still a Hakim could prescribe and innocent ointment which would bring it to a head and open it nicely and close the opening within the limited time. Ramanama is the sovereign remedy by it cannot be prescribed. It has to come of itself, if it comes at all.

J's wound is nothing but Badshah's is bad. It was a narrow escape for the three.

Love

Bapu

Calcutta,
4-11-1946

Chi. Amrit,

Your packet just come. Am over head and ears in work though this is silence day. Bihar has shaken me to bits. I have been for the past six days on spare diet (milkless) principally for health. Now Bihar will send me to complete fast if things do not radically mend. There will be no time limit. Do not agitate yourself but be really glad that I feel I have the strength to go through the ordeal and live up to my creed.

Do not interrupt your Paris programme. If that programme is not to come of at all, and if you are strong enough, you are at liberty to join me.

Love to you all.

Bapu

Kazirkhil,
Ramganj, P.O.
Noakhali District
18-1-1947

Chi. Amrit,

I have your letter. I indulge in the luxury of dictating it as our friend Rangaswamy has volunteered to do all shorthand work that may be necessary. Parasuraman having gone, let us hope only for the tome being. Of course, if he retains his strong oppostion to some of the things I stand for, naturally I do not expect him to return. He is such a good man that I have left it open for him to return if ever his mind is clear and he wishes to come back.

Whatever opportunity for serivce that may be offered to you and which you feel you should undertake, you will always have my approval. You know my own reaction to the visits to the West. At the same time I do not altogether discount the service of those who feel that they have a mission abroad. Of course, the condition is that you keep well and do not work yourself to death. I hope that Sardar will take care of his health.

I enclose herewith a letter from Madelene Rolland received by Pyarelal. It has reference to you also. In any case you would like to see the letter. You can return it to Pyarelal after you have read it.

Bapu ke Ashirvada

Not revised

Kazirkhil, Ramganj P.O.
Noakhali District,
22-2-1947

Chi. Amrit,

Just as I am dictating to friend Rangaswamy I get your letter and I have interrupted the dictation in order to see your letter. I have, now read it and hasten to dictate my answer.

I have received all the letters referred to by you and I have sent replies also. I can't recollect just now but I will see if I can give you the dates. I do hope that by the time this reaches you, you will have recovered your voice fully.

Of course, there is every chance of your getting back your Hindi and Roman-Urdu dictionary. I don't think I carry it with me. I will enquire and send it to you, care of Sardar, as soon as I trace it.

There is no cold here but there is still a freshness in the air. Real hot weather has not set in. Nights are quite cool and I use all my blankets. But there is no need to worry about me. I am keeping good health and have been able hitherto to go through my programme with clockwise regularity.

The second stage of the pilgrimage ends in Haimchar on Monday, the 24th inst. It is Thakkar Bapa's headquarters. I want to watch myself for a few days in Haimchar before resuming the third stage. It may also be that I might have to hurry to Bihar. Sardar Naranjan Singh Gill, who was in Bihar for three days, gave me the impressions of his tour and had strongly recommended that I should go to Bihar if only for a few days. I have put myself in communication with the Prime Minister of Bihar and await his reply.

I begin the pilgrimage every day at 7.30 or 7.35 and the stages are so divided as not to require me to walk more than one hour and fifteen minutes at the most. The least I have been called upon to walk is thirty minutes. Once and only once his it been one hour and thirty minutes.

I see that this dictionary business cause a lot of worry and takes away much of your time. Would you like to be relieved of that work? If you would, I would then like to keep your dictionary for the time being.

I am glad that the licensing clause in regard to Khadi has been removed. How I would love to think that you have carried convinction to the Prime Minister of the Punjab about vanaspati. Pyarelal is in his village now about twenty miles from here and doing excellent work. Sushila has gone to Sevagram in order to put matters straight about the maternity home and hospital.

It is growing by leaps and bounds and has, become very popular. She may return to her village work here as soon as she has finished her work in Sevagram. Renuka is here with me at the village. Her village is less than two miles from here. In appearance she looks just as she was. She has had to take great care of herself. But she is all right otherwise. Only this morning she enquired about you. I told her that I heard from you fairly regularly but that you were trying to save my time as much as possible. She asked me whether you were ever coming to this part of India. I told her not whilst I was moving from day-to-day but that if I stayed for any length of time in one place and if you are well and available from your work in the Assembly or otherwise. I would like you to come for a few days, and she was happy. She is doing her work steadily with her little band of workers.

Manu I have reserved to the last. Everybody here knows everything about her. Therefore I would love to say a word or two for your information. But I must forbear for it is now towards one o'clock and I must have a little bit of rest and grease on the soles of my feel.

Love

Bapu

Patna

20-4-1947

Chi. Amrit,

I have your letter. I am quite clear that Dr. Ambedkar's demands cannot be conceded. Please look up what is known as MacDonald's Award at the Round Table Conference which was born of a wicked conspiracy against Indian Nationalism. For the first time it created a division amongst Hindus and Hindus while granting separate electorates for the so-called scheduled classes. It was against this vivisection of Hindu society that I had prophesied revolt. As result reservation of seats was very considerably increased and primary elections were separated but the total separated was undone. In my opinion this was the utmost that could be conceded to the separatist tendency and the attempt to break up Hinduism. The opposition and the influence of caste Hindus in joint electorate is in my opinion nonsensical. Joint electorate means the influence of the party with which the electorate becomes joined. Such evil as there is in joint electorate can be obviated only by right type of education and enlightenment. If Dr. Ambedkar's objections were upheld for any length of time, be it ever so little, it would undermine Hinduism. The fear of boycott, therefore, should produce no consternation.

Love

Bapu

2

Views on Gandhi

I

I was privileged to learn a great deal during my long and close association with one of the greatest men the world has ever seen. I speak or write about him, however, with a sense of both reverence and reluctance. Reverence because he was truly worthy to be revered; reluctance because I wonder whether I can really claim to interpret him aright.

I first heard of him from a great patriot whom Gandhiji used to call his Guru or preceptor. Mr. Gokhale, a great friend of my father, referred to Gandhi as a man who, when he came to India, would revolutionise the country. My young heart remembered those words and shortly afterwards when Gandhi did leave South Africa for good to return to his native land, I did my best to get into touch with him. Event followed event in quick succession, very soon after his return, when he took over the political leadership of the country and I, along with thousands of others, was drawn to him and his way of thinking. When he called on Indians to join his army for the freedom fight, he stressed that women would be just as acceptable to him as, if not more so than, men because he needed moral courage far more than physical prowess. This was, I felt, an irresistible call to my sex and something which threw a new light, as it were, on how, whilest fighting for our freedom, we should also, under his leadership, be able to fight against many of the excrescences that had crept into our society, including the subjugation of women. Indeed, political freedom for him was only the first step towards the building up of a new order of society.

Now Gandhiji was seemingly a man with no outward attractions and yet I have never come across such a magnetic personality who draw into his fold all sorts and conditions of men and women. This was due entirely to his deep love for making and an amazing understanding of human nature.

History records no parallel to the following Gandhi commanded even beyond the borders of his own country. He was born and bred in a religious atmosphere and the impress of his mother—a profoundly religious woman from his own description of her—never left him. It was she who first sowed the seeds in his young heart which helped him to develop that worship of truth and love which were the hallmark of his character and the guiding star of his life. When punished for non-attendance at a gymnastic class at school because the master would not believe that having no watch the cloudy weather had deceived him, the young boy wept in anguish, not at his punishment, but at the mere thought of having been accused of telling an untruth. When he was tempted stealthily to eat meat by his schoolmates, the knowledge that he was deceiving and lying to his parents was always gnawing at his heart and it was this hurt to his growing moral stature that finally made him decide to abstain from meat-eating. Again it was the innate love of truth which sent him as a boy of fifteen to make the touching confession of having committed a theft to his father.

The lattre's tears of love and sublime forgiveness made the boy's repentance complete and have been described by him in his autobiography as an objectlesson in pure Ahimsa. Early in life the Ramayan of Tulsidas made its impress on him thanks to the opportunity of listening to religious conversations between his father and his friends. He got a grounding not only in Hinduism and its sister religions, but in other faiths also which inculcated in him a spirit of tolerance and respect for all religions. Of those boyhood days he writes : "But one thing took deep root in me—the conviction that morality is the basis of all things and that truth is the substance of all morality. Truth now became my sole objective. Truth began to grow in magnitude every day." Later on his conception of truth widened to "Truth is God". *Pari Passu* with this passion for seeking truth he wrote : "A Gujarati didactic stanza likewise gripped my mind and heart. Its precept 'return good for evil' became my guiding principle. It became such a passion with me that I began numerous experiments in it. Here are those (to me) wonderful lines:

"For a bowl of water give a goodly meal;
For a kindly greeting bow thou down with zealt
For a simple penny pay thou back in gold;
If thy life be rescued, life do not with hold.
Thus the words and actions of the wise regard;
Every tittle service ten-fold thy reward.
But the truly noble know all men as one;
And return with gladness, good for evil done."

With the religious background of his home and with the early realisation by this outstanding moral genius of the spiritual values of life, it is small wonder that Gandhi decided early in life to choose the straight and narrow way—the path of renunciation, the path of suffering, the path that leads to eternal life. Opportunities of leading a life of pleasure backed by the capacity, to earn wealth did not tempt him. A burning passion for reform within, an irresistible urge to give up all to serve his fellow men became the motivating power behind all his actions, once he had found his highest self in South Africa. When he came to India, having left South Africa for good, he had immense experience in contacting human nature in all its phases, in leadership, in organisation, in administering public funds, in training the young, in journalism, in ministering to sick and suffering humanity, in dealing with government and, above all, in self-restraint and suffering. Through this experience his faith in truth and non-violence, as the key to all moral and spiritual progress and the only means of attaining man's deepest aspirations, had taken firm root in him.

Luminaries like Gandhi are sent once in an age by providence to dispel the darkness with which humanity, through its own weakness, envelops itself from time to time. They bring hope and cheer in place of despair; they are pointers to those who have seeing eyes and understanding hearts. It was India's good fortune that she had a man of his moral and spiritual stature to guide her in her righteous warfare against the oppression from which she had been suffering for centuries. It was only natural that a man of his calibre should at once come into the arena to raise suffering Indian humanity from the mire into which it had fallen. The Indian struggle in South Africa had lasted eight years. Satyagraha had been applied for the first time to masses of men and had won through. "A Satyagraha struggle is impossible without capital in the shape of character, wrote Gandhi. Not all the gold of Sheba would have made it successful if the participants had not been prepared for self-purification through self-suffering and had not been self-reliant. The ways of Satyagraha and Ahimsa were Gandhiji's richest gifts to India, and through India to the world. As he said : "The world rests upon the bed rock of Satya or truth. Asatya, meaning untruth, also means that which is non-existent, and Staya, or truth, also means that which is. If untruth does not so much as exist, its victory is out of the question. And truth being that which is, can never be destroyed. This is the doctrine of Satyagraha in a nutshell."

Throughout the freedom struggle this was the supreme lesson that he tried to instil into our minds, that means and ends are convertible. "Violent means", he laid down, "will give violent swaraj (self-rule). There is no wall of separation between the means and the end. Indeed, the Creator has given us control (and that too very limited) over means, none over the end. Realisation of the goal is in exact proportion to that of the means. This is a proportion that admits of no exception." To cling to truth, to invite suffering on oneself, never even to think of injuring the opponent is surely the highest way for man, if man could only rise to his full moral stature. This is what he believed and lived up to. He claimed Satyagraha (insistence on truth) to be a complete substitute for armed revolt. But to the end of his days he said that it had not been tried out on a really mass scale. His faith in this creed, however, never faltered and he believed that the kingdom of God could never be established until and unless man gained the necessary moral victory over himself. Professor Joad truly wrote : "Gandhi is a moral genius and his method belongs to the coming generation. He had announced a method for the settlement of disputes which may not only supersede the method of force but, as man grows powerful in the art of destruction, must supersede it, if civilisation is to survive."

I believe that Gandhi's greatest contribution to world thought was his insistence that truth and non-violence must prevail in politics, no less than in any other sphere of activity. “My politics”, he avowed, “are not corrupt. They are inextricably bound up with non-violence and truth”. It was this bond which made him non-cooperate with evil in whatsoever form it seemed to him to exist. His non-violent non-cooperation—and I well remember how this phrase took India and the British Government by storm when he first used it in 1919—was, however, always “a prelude to cooperation”. Behind it there was invariably the keenest desire to cooperate if there was even the slightest change of heart in the opponent. He once wrote : “I am by instinct a cooperator. I have presented non-cooperation in terms of religion because I enter politics only in so far as it develops the religious faculty in me.” Again : “Religion should pervade every one of our actions. Here religion does not mean sectarianism. It means a belief in the ordered moral government of the universe. It is not less real because it is unseen. This religion transcends Hinduism, Islam, Christianity.

It does not supersede them. It harmonises them and gives them reality”. Gandhi saw life as one indivisible whole. He owned kinship with all God’s creation and therefore in his vocabulary there were no such words as caste, communalism, narrow nationalism, sedtarianism or racialism. All his strivings, as a seeker after God (Truth) had their beginnings in, and were permeated with, the idea of establishing the Kingdom of Heaven on earth. The Ram Rajya of his dreams was not mere political freedom. He once described it as a “perfect democracy in which inequalities based on possession and non-possession, colour, race or creed or sex will vanish. In it, and state belong to the people, justice is prompt, perfect and cheap and there is freedom of worship, speech and the press—all this because of the reign of the self-imposed law of moral restraint. Such a state must be based on truth and non-violence and must consist of prosperous, happy and self-contained villages and village communities. It is a dream that may never be realized. I find happiness in living in that dreamland, ever trying to realise it in the quickest way.

It follows, there, that Gandhiji’s contribution was greatest in the realm of the social and moral regeneration of India. None knew better than he how hard was the way of non-violence and truth and yet he believed that it was the way of salvation for mankind. He felt that it was possible for India to adopt it by reason of her past traditions and rich spiritual heritage and he hoped that if she could rise to the heights which he expected of her, she might be able to give a lead to the world. I fell that the path this great leader wanted us to tread is best summed up in the eleven vows which we of his Ashram (retreat or hermitage) repeated every day during morning and evening prayers. These eleven observances, namely; non-violence, truth, non-stealing, continence, non-possession, bread labour, conquest of the palate, perfect fearlessness, equality of all religions, swadeshi, removal of untouchability, were to be carried out with inflexible resolve and utter humility. Let us try to understand them one by one.

Non-stealing must be taken in a far wider sense than non-stealing of what does not belong to you. Stealing includes spending more on yourself than you need. It embraces time wasted which might have been given to service. Indeed waste in any form is stealing.

Non-possession signifies complete surrender of yourself as well as your wordly goods to the service of humanity. Every thing we have is a gift from God and bequeathed to us as a trust.

Continence is something far more than mere celibacy. To quote his own words : "It means complete control over all the senses and freedom from lust in thought, word and deed." Again : "The ideal that marriage aims at is that of a spiritual union through the physical. The human love it incarhates is intended to serve as a stepping-stone to divine or universal love."

The control of the palate in again an essential of self-restraint without which there can be no self-realisation.

The high calling of bread labour was a discovery, as he so often said, which came to him almost overnight after reading Ruskin's "Unto this last." The moment he discovered that the life of the tiller and the handicraftsman was the life worth living he "arose with the dawn, ready to reduce these principles to practice". "Search for the real is not a sparetime occupation. Work is part and parcel of it. Not the drudgery at a machine, of course, but the happy sunlit work in the field or the garden or amongst friends and family".

"Fearlessness", he wrote, is of course the first requisite of spirituality. If you want to follow the vow of truth fearlessness is absolutely necessary. Cowards can never be moral."

Swadeshi was conceived by him as a religious principle. He described it as "that spirit in us which restricts us to the use and service of our immediate surroundings to the exclusion of the more remote". He held that the love of "foreign finery" was responsible for the gap that divided the educated from the masses, as also for the grinding poverty of the latter.

The removal of untouchability was a living passion with him, for was it not a blot on the fair name of Hinduism, for which there was no religious or moral sanction? Untouchability was a barbarous symbol of violence, without the removal of which India was doomed.

The equality of all religions was part and parcel of his concept of religion. While for himself Hinduism was all sufficing, his respect for other faiths was unbounded and real. This is what he said in this regard : "I believe that it is impossible to estimate the merits of the various religions of the world and moreover, I believe that it is unnecessary and harmful even to attempt it. But each one of them, in my judgement, embodies a common motivating force, that is, the desire to uplift man's life and give it purpose."

Now none of the above mentioned observance could be achieved with any degree of success except by a votary of truth and non-violence. "I want to see God's face", he once wrote, "God, I know is truth. For me the only certain means of knowing God is non-violence—Ahimsa—love". In other words, if there was in man a desire to seek God, he had to perceive that God is truth and that truth and non-violence are inseparable. They are, as he often used to express it, as the two sides of a coin. In recent years he used to say, "Truth is God".

Many used to question the morality of the several fasts that Gandhiji undertook during his long years of service. Was there not coercion in such fasting, however thinly veiled it might be? But Satyagraha, or insistence on truth was something that had on occasion to demand even life from the believer. The threads of love and truth were inextricably woven into the fabric of the way of life of the Satyagrahi. Therefore, fasting and prayer, just as non-violence and truth, were inseparable in his concept of the search for God, "I believe that there is no prayer without fasting and there is no real fast without prayer", he once wrote.

This did not, however, mean that he ever believed in the intherent merit of mortification of the flesh. On the contrary fasting to him was a joy, a communion of spirit with his Creator. The call to fast came invariably as an inner urge. It was never meant to coerce; it was always for purification of self and others and in order to remove distress and injustice by means of soul force. For those of us who had the inestimable privilege of living with him, it was common knowledge that on every day of rejoicing or remembrance, Gandhi fasted. He called on the entire nation to observe "hartal" (complete cessation of work) on 6 April, 1919 and a hartal included a 24-hours fast, because *pari passu* with the outward demonstration against the policy of authority, was the inner symbol of heart-searching and dedication to duty.

In fact the latter was far more important because, without self-purification, all action however peaceful outwardly, would not be free from violence. From then onwards, April 6th to April 13th, Jalianwalla Bagh Day, has been known as 'National Week'. We of the Ashram always fasted both on April 6th and April 13th. Krishna Jayanti (Janma Ashtami) was not observed as a day of feasting. It was observed as a day of fasting in order to return thanks to God for the message of the Gita—and how can the message of the Gita he assimilated unless there is inner purity? I well remember his saying to me once that he wished the festival of Christmas were preceded by a period of prayer and fasting in the same way as Lent precedes the joyous festival of Easter, which signifies victory over death. Independence Day was another day of fasting and when I fasted, as nearly all of us used to do with him, there was an amazing sense of inner calm. I put it down to the richness of prayer which hallowed every action of Gandhi and which had an effect on the entire atmosphere.

If therefore he resorted to fasting on days of rejoicing, what wonder that there was in him an even greater urge to fast in times of mourning? The reverence for all religions being a basic belief, it is not difficult to imagine the hurt caused to him by communal strife. All the fasts that he undertook during his service of India were taken after days and nights of egony of mind and spiritual communion with God. All were undertaken with one aim and one only, namely a ceaseless heart searching, a ceaseless waiting on God, a ceaseless prayer that he himself might be parged of any shortcomings that he had that he might be shown the way, so that he might lead those who looked to him for guidance and, if his stand in God's eye was correct, that those against whom he was waging moral warfare might be converted to seeing the error of their ways. Fasting was in his opinion a most potent weapon in the armoury of the Satyagrahi. There was no mortification of the flesh in it for the man of faith. Nearly always Gandhiji used to suffer from nausea on the third or fourth day of a fast and he invariably said that this was due to lack of spiritual strength in him. If there was complete faith in God then he held that fasting should never cause any weariness or discomfort of the flesh but that the Satyagrahi should be able to go smiling into the arms of his Creator Puny human beings as we were in comparison with this spiritual giant. I often used to wondes at Gandhi's extreme humility. But then he held that unless man reduced himself to a mere cypher, he could never even begin to understand the meaning of non-violence.

The partition of India was a colossal blow to Gandhi, for he just could not understand why Hindus and Muslims, blood brothers, could not live together. Having said that India was or should be "fitted for the religious supremacy of the world", how could he bear to see her house divided against itself? How could he atone? By fasting and prayer, was the only reply.

And now a few words about Gandhi, the man. What drew men and women and children to him? I have no doubt that it was because he just radiated love. Life with him, however simple, however austere, whatsoever hard work it meant, was always happy because of the warmth and comfort of the love with which we were surrounded. He never asked any of us to do what he had not carried out in practice himself. Now what struck me most as a member of Gandhi's family was the care and attention he bestowed on each one of us. He was father and mother to us all. The food we ate, the amount of sleep we had, the work we did or were capable of doing, our mental and physical well-being were just as much his concern as ours. Such personal interest could only be born of an abounding love for all who had entrusted themselves to his care. These contacts undoubtedly enabled him to have an insight into our characters and gave him an overall picture of the Ashram which would otherwise not have been possible. A morning round to see the sick, a nightly round to see that everyone was comfortably in bed, a walk round the environs to see that the sanitation and hygiene were as he would them be an inspection of the kitchen, of the living rooms, all seemed sometimes to my small mind as things which took away from him precious moments which should have belonged to bigger national issues. But they were of considerable import to him. And now, as I look back on incident after incident of his loving kindness, of his attention to detail, I realise that in being faithful in small things he was perpetually seeking to make us see truth and was thereby being faithful to Him who had called him to such great things.

Just as he was father and mother to all of us who were privileged to be members of what he called his inner circle, he was the most wonderful listener to all who sought his advice on matters, whether personal or impersonal. Here again some of us used to try to prevent him from giving undue time to those who were in our opinion not worthy of it, who we considered were cranks or obsessed and certainly had no right to take him away from his real work. But invariably he resisted these un-understanding efforts of ours. "The world would be poorer without such persons. They are God's creation, affected for a purpose. In extending sympathy to them we raise ourselves. In ignoring them we show the littleness of our character." This is what I learnt from him again and again. And therefore it used to be a source of inspiration to see or sense Gandhi giving himself so utterly to the work in hand. Surely there was no need for him to learn the maxim, "whatsoever thy hand findeth to do, do it with all the might."

In spite of his gigantic stature his humility was quite astonishing. He often said that the seeker after truth has to be a learner to the end and that humility was the first step in the path of non-violence. The love and adoration of the masses which was his in such measure was an urge to give himself more and more to them, never an urge to be pleased with himself. For women he had a special attraction. And why? Because he entered into their feelings as no man can ever do. He often used to say that women were themselves to blame for the social injustices under which they were labouring. I do not know if any other man has ever acknowledged in such terms the equality of status of man and woman, "the companion of man, gifted with equal mental capacities". In the moral sphere he always gave her a higher place and his faith in womankind never faltered. "If non-violence is the law of our being, the future is with woman." He called her the "incarnation of Ahimsa". Ahimsa means infinite love. Let her transfer that love to the whole humanity, let her forget she ever was or can be the object of man's lust. And she will occupy her proud position by the side of man as his mother, maker and silent leader.

It is given to her to teach the art of peace to the warring world, thirsty for that nectar. She can become the leader in Satyagraha, which does not require the learning that books give, but does require the stout heart that comes from suffering and faith." If women over the world will take to heart these wonderful words of encouragement and dedicate themselves to follow them in thought, word and deed, "the Kingdom of Heaven" or the "Ram Rajya" of Gandhi's conception could certainly revolutionise life on this planet of ours. But can we? It sounds ever so easy, but is in reality ever so hard. The way of Satyagraha and Ahimsa will for all time remain the priceless gifts which this great seer gave to India and through India to the world. All his activities were motivated by religion, not the religion of narrow dogma or ritual but the religion of truth and love, which impelled him to dedicate to service all his amazing talents. And so he lived and died, fearless, devoted, incorruptible, a spiritual giant, the like of which is seldom born. Nearly a decade has passed since the martyrdom of Mahatma Gandhi, but in the hearts of all true Indians he lives for ever. Many are the intimate stories of his everyday life that are recounted to us by those that came into close contact with him. Those that Rajkumari Amrit Kaur relates here bring out the essential humanity of that super-human being, his ability to be at one with the highest as well as the lowest, the riches and the poorest, the mighty and the helpless. The following sketch was written specially at the request of the Illustrated Weekly of India and appeared in their Diwali number of October 20, 1957.

II

Hath he not always treasures, always friends,
The good great man? Three treasures—love and light;
And calm thoughts, regular as infant's breath;

Himself, his Maker, and the angel Death.

Samuel Taylor Coleridge in "The Good Great Man."

To live with Gandhiji for even one day, not speak to him but just listen to what he said to others and watch his actions, was to learn a wonderful lesson of how one should conduct oneself. He often used to say that thought is more potent than action and now as I grow older and older and ponder over many things, I have come to believe that the less one speaks and the more right thinking one indulges in, the better is one's contribution towards the creation of an atmosphere of understanding and goodwill.

There is no gain saying the fact that in our country today we are passing through a very critical phase. Most people think in terms of money, whether it be internal resources or foreign exchange or foreign aid, when they talk of a crisis. I myself learnt from beloved Bapu that always the emphasis should be on the moral rather than on the material values of life. We, who had the immense fortune of learning at his feet, day in and day out, did begin to realise that he paid very much more attention to the spirit in which we carried out any work that he asked us to do rather than on how good that work was.

We learnt from him how important it was for man to dedicate himself entirely to the cause which he had espoused and the first step in the development of a spirit of dedication was to give devoted attention to the smallest duties of daily life. Living as we did with him in surroundings wherein persons of varying temperament and drawn from various walks of life had come to learn from Gandhiji, the first essential was to develop a spirit of friendship and toleration. Bapu maintained that caste, creed and nationality could or should never over-ride the bond of humanity. Hence it was that he put the removal of untouchability as the first plank in his work for the salvation of India.

It is true that today to practise untouchability is to offend against the law but, as he often used to say, "it is our hearts that have to be cleansed from the sin of untouchability" and we have therefore to ask ourselves how far our hearts have been cleansed. One the many long and eventful train journeys that one undertook with him, the collection of funds for Harijan work was a positive duty. Crowds collected at every station for his 'darshan' and always in addition to his smiling countenance the people could see his hand outstretched for their pennies to pour into it.

These collections, made up mostly of annas and pice and some one—rupee notes, amounted generally to thousands of rupees at the end of the year. Those who were in charge of the collections had to note down the name of and the amount collected at each station. Gandhiji was a stickler for correct account keeping and I remember being rebuked by him once for asking as to why he could not be content with just a total of all the monies collected during a journey rather than such a detailed reckoning. "Would not those who had collected at a particular station and who, perhaps, had waited there for hours, not be grateful to have the name of the place registered?" Always the thought was the happiness of the many and not the work entailed for a few.

"My Ashram is a 'menagarie'", he once smilingly remarked, "and I am the keeper of it;" and at another time, "My Ashram is an asylum and I am the chief madman." These were in response to some of our remonstrations with him as to why he paid so much attention to matters seemingly unimportant and to those who were a burden rather than an asset to society. The world would be the poorer without them, he used to say and "you must never grudge to those in need the little happiness and solace that I am able to give them." Indeed he was giving every moment of his life and when one sees today the mad rush always to "get", one wonders how far we have travelled from the path he trod, and would have had us tread.

Because of his amazing ability to put himself in the position of the person who was pouring out his woes to him, Gandhiji made the best of listeners. Never once did he interrupt and only when the seeker after guidance or comfort had finished did Gandhiji tender solace or advice in his inimitable manner, and send the visitor away a happier and a wiser man.

This same solicitude for his immediate circle made him an excellent doctor and nurse. Believing as he did that man fell ill because he had disobeyed one or other of the laws of nature and must therefore turn in penance to nature to be restored, he had made a real study of and experimented with himself and others with water therapy, message, and packs, dieting, including refraining from food and I must confess that often and often during my tenure of office as Minister for Health have I longed for our doctors to turn to such simple remedies for simple ailments rather than to the wonder drugs that have taken the profession by storm, as it were, today.

In any event many of us learnt how to nurse and how to prepare invalid food, mud packs etc. and appreciate the benefits of simple food; and none of us will ever forget how soothing was his touch on a fevered brow or aching head, and how much his morning and evening visits cheered the sick. I have never met anyone who in daily life literally practised the axiom of "cleanliness is next to Godliness", as did Gandhiji. In the poorest of poor surrounding he would not tolerate uncleanliness. I received my first lesson in scavenging from him and after that this work had no terrors for me. Never did he ask any of us to do something which he had not tried out himself and that is why he was able, not only to command obedience and loyalty but he was able invariably to inspire. Untruth, untidiness, intolerance, uncleanliness, unpunctuality were all forms of violence and were a reflection of the inner self of the person who was unclean in mind, dirty or disorderly in person, or had no conception of the value of time, or of one who was conceited, for Gandhiji maintained that intolerance was a child of ignorance and those who think too highly of themselves are blind to their own failings.

I remember one evening, while Gandhiji was writing something important with his own hand before retiring to bed that I was enjoying myself chattering away to Prabhavati Jaiprakash Narain. When he had finished—I believe it was an article when had to go the first thing in the morning for 'Harijan'—he admonished me very gently for what he called a mere waste of words. And, as always, whenever he wanted to bring home a truth to one he said that one of the virtues he had from early years tried to cultivate was not to say a word more than necessary for the purpose. I am afraid I have never been able to live upto his advice but I did realise how very advanced he was in the art of both speaking and writing briefly and to the point.

"If I had not been blessed with a sense of humour I would long since have been dead" is what Gandhiji said on more than one occasion. There were some of his intimate colleagues like Sardar Vallabhbhai Patel and Shri Jamnalal Bajaj with whom there were endless sallies of wit and roars of laughter which all of us enjoyed greatly. And no one laughed more heartily or enjoyed a joke more than Bapu himself. One really never had a dull moment with him.

We nearly always slept under the stars; and all around Bapu, all sleeping on the floor, were the woman of the Ashram. The loveliest end to the day's work was for us women, to crowd around him before he want to sleep and listen to some story or other of his many experiences, full of humour and yet pregnant with meaning. I still smile as I recall his narration of how he had to cut his own hair because no barber in South Africa would cut a black man's hair and how after his first "exploit", as he called it, on himself, when he went to court, a brother lawyer had asked him how and why he had allowed rats to get at his head! How he laughed himself when he related the story! Much of the old experiences which he related were to be found in his autobiography but the stories were never stale and became for more vivid when retold by him.

It is strange how often sentences or words uttered by him come back to one's memory now as if they had been engraved in some corner of the mind. He was such a wonderful teacher that one never forgot what he tried to teach. How little, of course, one is able to live upto his teaching is something of which one ought to be ashamed if one is honest with oneself. Perhaps few people are aware of how fond Gandhiji was of astronomy. After one of his first sharp attacks of raised blood pressure, before we had moved out to Sevagram and were living in Maganwadi, Wardha, he was ordered a month's complete rest. When the stars came out he used to bring two little books on astronomy as also the latest newspaper chart and lying in bed look at the sky and initiate those of us, who wanted to learn, into the names of the stars and the mythological stories, both Greek and Roman, as well as Indian related to them.

It was during this time, sleeping on the roof of Maganwadi, that he woke me up one morning, very early, and showed me the Southern Cross which lovely constellation up till then had been a mere name to me. Absorbed as he always was in work, he was by no means unaware.of the beauty of nature. The mountains, the moon, the stars, the lovely sunsets we used to have during the monsoon season in Sevagram were always a joy to him and constant reminders, if any reminder for such as he were needed, of the existence of God the Creator.

Gandhiji loved the beauty of language too and always appreciated a well written article or letter. He was meticulous where his weekly articles for 'Harijan' were concerned. They were always given in the first instance to one or other of us to read and suggest any verbal or other amendments, and then finally edited by himself before being sent to the press. And when I sense the futile controversy that today exists in our country in the matter of language I wonder again how far we have wandered from what he would have wished for the development of Hindi-Hindustani, as he used to call the simple language which he wished to develop into the Rashtra-bhasha.

Over-Sanskritised or over-Persianised Hindi were an abomination to him for he felt that there by we would be adding to the cleavage between Hindu and Muslim. Nor did he never dream that the languages of the States would divide Indians from Indians. I remember so well, when someone asked him why he had elected to live in a Maharashtra village rather than in a Gujerati one where he would probably be able to propagate his message and achieve results in his work more quickly than elsewhere, his unhesitating reply was that in the first place he never thought of himself in terms of being a Gujerati, and secondly precisely because he was a Gujerati it would be wrong for him to settle in a Gujerati village. Once he resolved to write for 'Harijan' in nothing but Gujerati and Hindi and we were to translate what he had written into English.

I personally was sad and begged of him to write at least one small note in English because his English was quite remarkable and his writings will certainly in years to come be included as a valuable contribution to English literature. But he was adamant. However, after a while letters from abroad came pouring in and in the end he could not resist the impassioned plea of his foreign readers to write original articles in English in the 'Harijan'. I am one of those who would like English to be included as one of India's languages. The knowledge of it is far too goodly a heritage to lose.

It is difficult to know where to end when once one begins to talk about beloved Bapu. I have tried in this article to stress some of the lessons he taught which we are in dire need of remembering today.

> To banish the evils of caste, communalism, and provincialism, to live simply and cleanly, to think well for thereby alone can we act well, to devote oneself utterly to the work on hand, however, insignificant it may appear to be, to be truthful at all times—surely these are the things, this is the spirit of work for her that India needs most today.

As we celebrate Gandhiji's birthday this year, as we rejoice at Dussehra which story denotes the triumph of good over evil, as we light our 'divas' for the lovely festival of lights, let us rededicate ourselves to keep alive and undimmed the message that Bapu left with us and the torch that he lit for the salvation of India and indeed of the world.

As one of his most devoted and true followers, Richard Gregg, has said, "In that way Gandhi's way—lies hope."

TO GANDHIJI

> Thine was the prophet's vision, thine
> The exaltation, the divine
> Insanity of noble minds.

H.W. Longfellow

Bapu! what offering can I, who was not worthy to touch the latchet of your shoes, lay at your shrine in this the hour of your greatest triumph?

For you the veil has been lifted. You always spoke of Death as a friend and told us not to fear him. You taught us many things, us your erring children. You showed us the way of life by walking yourself along the narrow, rugged path which the saints who have gone before you have trod. You showed us how to love where there was hate. You taught us that Truth is God. You demonstrated that perfect freedom lay in His service.

It was so easy to struggle along by your side when you were with us. Your faith, your love, your courage and your strength upheld us. We laid all our burdens on you and you bore them willingly. You forgave us much because you loved us greatly.

Now God, in His infinite wisdom, has called you to His bosom and we, weak mortals as we are, feel helpless and orphaned.

Without you our hearts ache, our eyes are blinded with tears, fear possesses our minds, our faith is weakened, for you have left us at a time when we fell we needed you most. The hour of your greatest triumph is the hour of our greatest defeat, for it was one of our brothers, one of your own erring children that strayed from the path and brought shame to our land. But weakness and fear were never in your vocabulary. You knew them not. You were an unremitting fighter against the forces of evil. These forces of evil—for what are hate and violence except twin daughters of evil?—are stalking the land today and we stand in danger of losing our souls. The political freedom you won for us was just the first step towards building the Ram Rajya of your dreams.

And so we too, inspite of human frailty, inspite of the gloom that today envelops us, must shake off all fear and continue the struggle with the matchless weapons of truth and love. Only thus will we be fit to be called your children. Only thus would you have had us act. Only thus will be able to got sustenance from the power of your atoning love.

May the music of your dear voice still be heard by us from out of the Great Silence, may the fragrant memory of your words and deeds and thoughts, when you were with us on earth, still refresh and inspire us; may your love overshadow us perpetually, may the radiance of your illumined soul still light the path for us and may your unseen presence ever be near us to lead us gently over the rough places and sustain us.

To dedicate ourselves anew to such service as you tried to train us for is the only offering that we, who believed in your way of life, may dare to offer you.

In this broadcast talk delivered in July 1948 on the Swiss Radio network, Rajkumari Amrit Kaur explains the basic principles of Gandhian philosophy.

THE BASIC TENETS OF GANDHIAN PHILOSOPHY

Let us hear the conclusion of the whole matter : Fear God, and keep his commandments; for this is the whole duty man.

The Old Testament
Ecclesiates XII : 13.

I was one of the fortunate ones who had the privilege and rare joy of being closely associated for several years with Gandhiji.

Often he spoke of his visit to Switzerland in 1930, when he came here specially to see his old friend Romain Rolland, and he never forgot either the warm welcome the residents of Geneva and Lausanne gave him or the beauties of nature with which Providence has so richly endowed this lovely land.

I was drawn to Gandhiji very early in life. He drew men and women of all sorts and conditions to him by reason of his boundless love for humanity and his immense understanding of human nature. No one was too small or insignificant for him. Position, sex, colour, race or community made no difference to him. While he loved his own country he loved the world no less.

In fact, as he always said, he felt that if he could truly serve India, and if India could really take to heart the age-old message of Truth and Non-violence and build up her structure of society on it, he would be serving the entire world through her. To those of you who have read his autobiography, "My experiments with Truth"—, it will be apparent that Gandhiji was a seeker after Truth, from even when he was a child. Laterly he often used to say "Truth is God, If I, therefore, seek Truth I seek God." He held that Ahimsa, *i.e.* non-violence, was not possible without Truth and likewise Truth was not possible without non-violence. In other words, these two essentials were like the two faces of a coin. It is necessary to understand his unshakable belief in Truth and Non-violence if we are to understand fully his life and teachings.

Early in his South African life he realised that non-possession was essential for a truly non-violent man. He had gone to South Africa as a laywer and had soon begun to make a mark for himself there. The moment the realisation dawned upon him that he must give up worldly possessions if he wanted to serve his people truly he did so without a moment's hesitation. This capacity to act straight away on an inner conviction and to stand by it at all costs was one of his many great qualities. He never asked anyone to do anything which he himself had not done or tried out successfully. Truly he was a born leader of men. From that day onwards he adopted the simple life. His wants were reduced to a minimum and that remained so to the end of his days.

Strict adherence to non-violence, truth, non-stealing, non-possession, conquest of the palate, bread-labour, removal of untouchability, recognition of the equality of all belonging to one's own country, fearlessness, celibacy, were the eleven vows which his followers repeated every day, morning and evening, at prayer time. His day began with prayer at 4.20 a.m. and whatever his pre-occupations or in whatever important task he might have been engaged he never missed his evening prayer to which he welcomed as many persons as could come.

He often told me that he loved worship in the open air best just as he also loved to sleep always under the canopy of the stars. Gandhiji was a profound student of the Bible as also of the scriptures of other religions and hence he insisted on equal respect for all faiths. One of the Bible stories he liked to dwell on most was the which referred to the rich man who went away sorrowful "for he had great possessions." Gandhiji's belief in the conquest of the palate signifies that a man must eat only in order to live and, therefore, his food should be of the simplest. Our fare in the Ashram consisted of steamed vegetables, milk and milk products, bread made from wholemeal wheat, handpounded rice, salads and fresh fruit.

I am sure all experts in dietetics will admit that the above is a wholesome diet. No one, in Gandhiji's opinion, could claim to be fed, housed and clothed unless he did something in the way of manual labour. Therefore all of us had to do scavenging, washing of our clothes, helping in the kitchen, gardening or any healthful activity which contributed to our community life and to mutual aid.

Gandhiji believed in our villages, because India is essentially a land of villages, being able to produce all their requirements themselves. He always felt that wars would cease if cut-throat competition in trade and the lust for seizing world markets could be avoided. Hence his emphasis for Indians to spin and produce their own cloth and to grow enough food for their own requirements. He believed in handicrafts and their proper development, as against large scale industry to which he was opposed, because it led to unemployment and an unseemly competition between nation and nation and also because it contributed to an uneven distribution of money.

The removal of untouchability in India was an article of faith with him. He held it to be an evil custom which, like so many others, had crept into Hindu society and for which there was really no action in Hinduism. That it was through his insistence on this Truth, that the citadel of untouchability has been broken in our land, will always stand out as one of the most eternal monuments to Gandhiji.

All of Gandhiji's life was devoted to the service of the poor and to the removal of injustices. He could not bear injustice in whatsoever form it existed anywhere. For woman he had a special regard. He looked upon them as embodiments of Ahimsa or non-violence, if only they would realise their inner strength. No physical might could overpower them if they girded themselves with non-violence. That was his firm belief. He led India to her goal of political independence, through the way of non-violence. That she strayed from the right path immediately after she became free was a matter of poignant grief of him. Whatever wrongs, whatever cruelties had been perpetrated on non-Muslims by the Muslims of Pakistan, he never wanted the Hindus to retaliate. When some of them did, he raised his voice in protest and met his end at the hands of a fanatical youth.

For such as Gandhiji it was a fitting end to a life of utter service. Non-violence means self-suffering and he firmly believed that there was no other way or salvation. It was the way of Buddha, it was the way of Jesus Christ. He always said he was preaching new. The great thing about him was that he was full of human sympathy and understanding with a heart over-flowing with love. He was no visionary as his life shows. He lives for all time and I hope not only India but the world will reap the benefit of his example by trying to live up to the ideals for which he lived and died.

Reproduced below is the Presidential address delivered by Rajkumari Amrit Kaur on December 1, 1949, at the inauguration of the World Pacifist Meeting held at Santiniketan.

ON NON-VIOLENCE

Non-violence implies voluntary submission to the penalty for non-cooperation with evil.

Mahatma Gandhi

I am sure all present here today are aware of the genesis of this gathering. In a world where in spite of two world wars in one generation mankind is still thinking in terms of a third and what must be a worse conflagration, it was only natural that those who had worked and suffered for peace in other lands should seek to come to Gandhiji and learn further from him. From before and during the war years and after, he alone had been as a lighthouse, standing out serene and unharmed by the storms that beat around him. When he was taken from our midst doubts arose in many minds as to whether it was any use holding a gathering of this nature without him.

But I for one am glad that our friends from far and near have come. After all Gandhiji is only not with us in the flesh. His spirit lives and is always there to bless and guide. On behalf Dr. Rajendra Prasad and the Committee over which he has presided ever since the idea of the Conference came into being, I welcome you all very warmly to India.

Man is peaceful by nature. Life could not exist for one moment if he were not, and yet it is a sad commentary that even today the vast majority take it for granted that there is no solution for our problems other than armed conflict. There must be something wrong somewhere and it is towards trying to set right that something wrong that gatherings like this can contribute.

Gandhiji showed us a way of life that would militate against war. If we study closely the eleven vows that we repeated in his daily Ashram prayers we will see clearly the way of the man of peace. All his creative activities in this country were based on non-violence, *i.e.* the work of these organisations was essential to the creation of a non-violent society. "Truth is God" he said and "Truth and non-violence are inseparable". It is for us to consider whether what he tried to build up here is not the way which the world should adopt for the attainment of world peace.

I venture to submit that it is. Our friends from other lands have come with their own experience. We shall hear of these from them. It is only by pooling our resources, both mental and moral, that we can hope to create an atmosphere for and a will to peace amongst fellow men. The path trod by the saints and martyrs, who have been sent by God from time to time to enlighten our darkness, has always been a hard one. I believe that Gandhiji went as he would have liked to go, laying down his life so as to make it easier for others to live.

We are meeting in what is known, and what other speakers have already referred to, as the abode of peace. It is difficult in these lovely surroundings to believe that the ugliness of hate and war can exist. It is meet that this gathering should have taken place here and later go to Sevagram from and to where both these immortals lived in order to bring light and love where there was darkness and hate, and also strove for that international goodwill which, alas, does not exist today.

I cannot do better than quote from what is one of the gems of Gurudev's inspired writings. May this prayer be in the hearts of each one of us as we deliberate in the coming days.

"Give me the supreme courage of love, the courage to speak, to do,

"To suffer at Thy Will, to leave all things or be left alone

"Give me the supreme faith of love, the faith of the life in death, of the

"Victory in defeat, of the power hidden in the frailness of beauty, of the

"Dignity of pain that accepts hurt, but disdains to return it".

Poppy Day 1949, a day of remembrance of the Armistice day of the 1914—18 Armageddom, was perhaps the most appropriate one to bring out the theme of the failure of force and the new hope of peace in the weapon of non-violence. Rajkumari Amrit Kaur, steeped in the Gandhian ideal, proves herself the best fitted to preach it.

NON-VIOLENCE—THE ONLY ANSWER TO THE ATOM BOMB

> "Nothing could have been more obvious to the people of the early twentieth century than the rapidity with which war was becoming impossible. And as certainly they did not see it. They did not see it until the atomic bombs burst in their fumbling hands."

H.G. Wells in
"The World Set Free" (1914).

"Since wars begin in the minds of men, it is in the minds of men that the defences of peace must be constructed".

UNESCO Constitution

I feel extremely diffident about writing or speaking on the subject of non-violence because of the realisation within me of how very very far I am from being non-violent in thought, word and deed. But having lived in close contact for many years with Gandhiji and having drunk deep at the fountain head to his inspiration I have, within me, with all my personal weaknesses, the conviction which grows with the passing of time, that there can never be peace in this world of ours unless mankind adopts non-violence as a creed. I will, therefore, quote liberally from Gandhiji's own words. "Truth and Non-violence were inseparable. There could be no non-violence without truth and no truth without non-violence."

Ever since the dawn of history man seems to have been forced generally to decide issued by means of armed conflict until it has come to be taken for granted by the majority that war is just as inevitable for mankind as occasional illness or any other misfortune. Indeed I have heard people say that war is send by God. While admitting that it is a calamity while it lasts because of the suffering is entails, they believe that in the long run it is good for man to fight it out with fellow man and it is moreover one of nature's solutions, just as epidemics are, for over-population. Two world wars within the memory of one generation, however, and the horrors of the atom bomb have begun to make people think; and it is as well that this should be so.

The world has been narrowed down to such an extent of recent years that it is impossible for an armed conflict anywhere, however, small its spark, not to spread like wild-fire and envelop the entire globe. The horrors of bombing, the inflicted on civilian populations and the incalculable maiming of mind and body of all that has life, which the last war brought on human beings, have definitely instilled fear into the hearts of men.

The atom bomb, the last word in the armoury of destruction today, is casting a dark shadow over the entire world. There is a race for armaments again, a race in further scientific discoveries even more potent than the Hiroshima bomb. The ways and means of manufacturing these poisonous weapons are a closely guarded secret and so the unhappy story goes on. For it is an unhappy commentary on man's nature that he should be unable to find ways and means of living at peace with his own kind and be forced to resort to wholesale destruction in order to live.

Ordinarily speaking, man does act non-violently towards his neighbour. Society could not exist if men were unwilling to abide by certain codes of life. "I have found that life persists in the midst of destruction and therefore there must be a higher law than that of destruction" said Gandhiji. It is, therefore, to that higher law that man has got to turn if he is to find peace. Non-violence is an active force; it is, as Gandhiji so often termed it, "a weapon of the strong". It is the law of love and therefore there is no fear; for fear and love are contradictory terms. Love seeks nothing for itself, envies not, gives all and asks for nothing in return and thereby gains everything. To quote Gandhiji, "The law of love will work as the law of gravitation works, whether we accept it or not. And just as a scientists works wonders out of various applications of the laws of nature, even so can a man who applies the law of love with scientific precision. For the forces of non-violence is infinitely more wonderful and subtle than the force of nature. The man who discovered for us the law of love was a far greater scientist than any of our modern scientists . . . The more I work at this law, the more I fell the delight in life, the delight in the scheme of this universe. It gives me a peace and a meaning of the mysteries of nature that I have no power to described. For me law of Satyagraha, the law of love is an enternal principle." He interpreted Satyagraha, literally insistence on Truth, as Truth-force, Love-force or Soul-force.

There is no gainsaying the fact that if man could be impregnated with this force he would be able to withstand all violence. But equally there is no doubt that such spiritual strength is immensely hard of attainment. Non-violence connotes a way of life. It is the strait and narrow path which demands infinite patience and sympathy, a capacity and a willingness for self-suffering for the vindication of truth, superhuman courage, renunciation of this world's goods for personal gain or enjoyment and an all-embracing love for everything that has life. Gandhiji maintained that it was a force that could be used by individuals as well as by communities, by men, women and children alike.

It was the answer to domestic as well as to political disputes. He claimed that its universal applicability was proof, if proof were needed, of its permanence and invincibility. "This force is to violence and therefore to all tyranny, all injustice, what light is to darkness," he once wrote.

Gandhiji was an idealist. What he said may be logically true but then all men are not the spiritual giants that he was and therefore has teachings are impossible to follow for the average man, say the doubting Thomases of this world. Such comments come from those who are weak and oppressed with fear. It is only when man realises that there is something in him which is superior to the brute within that he can aspire to become a Satyagrahi and be armed with a weapon against which the might of all the atom bombs in the world cannot prevail.

I have already said that non-violence is a way of life. If an individual, a family, a community, a nation or indeed the world wishes to live at peace that way has got to be followed. Here in his own homeland Gandhiji prescribed many things to us for the attainment of the Ram Rajya (the Kingdom of God) of his dreams. The fundamental requirement of Satyagraha is the strength to endure the uttermost suffering without inflicting any suffering on others.

If the prescribed spinning and the use of Khadi (hand spun and hand woven cloth) for us and the promotion of all other cottage industries it was because he believed that these were the main plank in village regeneration without which India could not live. If he preached the removal of untouchability and the uplift of women it was because non-violence and suppression in any form could not live side by side.

If he lived and died for Hindu-Muslim unity it was because he knew that India could never take the lead in world peace unless she had cleaned her own house of prejudice and hate. He always said he was not preaching anything new. The message of Truth and Love had been given by the saints and sages of old and all religions proclaimed it.

But man had fallen away from the Truth and hence all the world's woes. He wanted society so to purge itself that there would be the least need of government. That State is best governed which is governed least. But he know that nothing purged so well as self-suffering and there could be no freedom without perfect surrender to service. Gandhiji was convinced that it was wrong to multiply one's wants as was happening in the West. Centralised production through mills and factories, large scale industry in other worlds, meant unemployment and a cut throat competition for world markets. Exploitation and war were acordings to him, the natural concomitants of the civilisation adopted by the Western world as has been proved in this century and Gandhiji was profoundly anxious for India not to go the same way.

To the end of his days he hugged the hope that India would chosen the path of non-violence and demonstrate that it was far stronger than any weapon of destruction that man's ingenuity could manufacture. His way is a hard way, trod by him and trod in their day by the founders of all the great religions of the world and all the saints and sages and martyrs that God ends from time to time to lighten our darkness.

There can be no life without death. In order to fight the atom bomb mankind has to be prepared to suffer to the uttermost but not inflict suffering. That we have to work for this noble end is obvious; for the greater the violence we enact, the greater the violence we breed. War is no solution to any problem. If it is not, then no atom bomb or even something more destructive can save any nation.

Which of us or how many of us are willing to choose the path of self-suffering and remain true to the God within us is the problem that faces both individuals and nations today. On what we choose depends whether there is peace or not in this world. If we choose aright the atom bomb will be ineffective.

Universal fellowship and the brotherhood of man are ideals that have become deep-seated convictions in the hearts of true Christians. Rajkumari Amrit Kaur has not only voiced these but has abided by them in public and private life. How she applies these to the politico-social situation in the India of the early thirties, is best seen in her address to the Fellowship Guild at an after-meeting session held on June 18, 1933 in London.

THE BROTHERHOOD OF MAN

"A new commandment I give unto you.
that ye shall love one another."

The New Testament, John VIII/134.

"Behold how good and how pleasant it is for brethern to dwell together in unity."

The Old Testament, Psalms.

I am exceptionally fortunate, for she (Dr. Maud Royden) has spoken of brotherhood, a subject which has the profoundest meaning for us in India today. As you know, India is struggling to find the ways and means of self-expression and I feel that perhaps today, when this atmosphere of brotherhood and love has been created in this form, I may be able to convey to you something of the underlying spirit that is moving India today.

You know that for the last three years the governments of India and Great Britain have been trying to frame a new constitution for India, because they felt that India had got beyond the stage of the old one. I am not going to speak in detail of the problems that concern the Round Table Conference. As I say, I should like to be able to convey to you the underlying spirit in India; why they should want self-government. India is a land of heterogeneous people; it has been called a continent and not a nation, a fact looked upon as a potent argument in their favour, by those who wish to stand in the way of India's advance to self-government.

We who live in the North of India are certainly different in race, in language, in custom, from Indians who live in the South, in the same way as the people of Bengal are different from the people of Bombay and so on, but believe me when I say to you that there is no difference betwen us where the real spirit of nationhood is concerned. It exists not only amongst the educated classes India, but among the illiterate and ignorant women and, working as I have been among these women, I have found even in the humblest homes, in the villages, this same spirit. India has awakened from age-long slumber almost, as if by magic and she is progressing so rapidly that I, as an Indian, when I have been away perhaps for six months, find myself out of touch with the trend of events on my return.

What has been the cause of that awakening? Undoubtedly we must attribute it to world causes and, in particular, to the contact with Western civilisation which, though not so ancient, has nevertheless taught many India lessons.

India realises today that in order to reach her desired goal she must give up many of her ancient customs and ideas, which have clogged the wheels of progress. She is today standing at the parting of the ways, and a very heavy responsibility indeed rests on the shoulders of rulers and ruled in a joint endeavour to map out a true course for her on hitherto uncharted seas.

And then we must ascribe this awakening to another factor. India has learnt in the school of hard experience that to have the fullest and freest scope for self-expression she must be mistress in her own house. Great as have been the blessings and privileges of British rule in India, the spirit of my country today is vibrant with the feeling that there is no longer any ground for their continued political subjugation; but in this very natural desire of hers to throw off the fetters which she feels are binding her and preventing her from fulfilling her mission in the world, India is conscious of her own weakness and, therefore, yearns the more for that true heart-to-heart co-operation of the great British race.

I feel sometimes that there is among the general public of England a very great ignorance—born perhaps of apathy—towards the spiritual revolt against a system of government which India feels has failed to help her to rise to her full stature, and not only against the system of government, but also against a mentality that has refused to recognise her common humanity. This spirit is a living force in India today, and is more intense, perhaps, amongst the women, because I think that women are by nature more patriotic and more willing to sacrifice for a cause, than men. The communal dissensions which are so rife among a certain section of the male polity have not, I rejoice to say, found a place in the hearts of my Indian sisters. We are striving to stand by moral principles which alone can give us the national solidarity for which we yearn, and without which there can be no peace or happiness for India, and if not for India, surely not for Great Britain either.

It is heart-rending for us to be told by these responsible for framing the constitution of India that, because the male population—or a certain section of them—cannot come to an agreement, we women, who form 45 per cent, of the population, must also be brought into this welter of communalism which has wrought such havoc in India has been responsible for keeping alive the spirit of separation.

I cannot believe that these facts are unknown to those in authority in this country. Like it or not, as we may, no part of the world can retain the illusion of separateness and Nationalist India is, therefore, insistent in its appeal to the Governments of both countries to exercise this demon of communalism, root and branch, from the body politic of India. You will agree with me, I think, that a spirit of separation, once fostered and allowed to grow unchecked, can lead nowhere save to a country's ultimate ruin, and surely that is the negation of the doctrine of brotherhood which it is the bounden duty of each one of us to inculcate in the minds of all. And so today the question I went to place before you is this : is the British public willing to decide whether moral principles are to be allowed full play in the mapping out of this vital constitution for my country, or is India to be governed along lines divorced from those principles? It is indeed a serious question.

It is one which each of us must ask ourselves, especially those of you who have the power of the vote—a power which we women in India so much desire in order that we may speak with a voice that stands out for moral percepts. I don't wish to minimise the complexity of the Indian problem, but I do feel that if we stood united in a desire to work on moral principle, those problems would unfold themselves and simplify themselves in the most remarkable manner, and the moment we resort to the expedients which are so often divorced from those principles, we have found ourselves without a solution. And I do want to put before you all, in great humility, an earnest plea that each one of you will do your little bit towards helping to foster that spirit of sympathetic understanding and comradeship between the people of India and England, without which nothing can be achieved for either side.

I cannot believe that England—a people born and bred in the traditions of public schools and universities and loving, as they do, the spirit of teamwork—will fail her at this fateful hour. I pray that this wonderful opportunity will be placed in the hands of India again, and I pray that she may not lose it. She stands in great danger of losing it. There is nobody—not one of us in India today, no thinking person—who wants to sever connection with Great Britain. All we want is our rightful place within the Commonwealth of nations as a member of that Commonwealth.

The capacity to place oneself in another's shoes. I always think, is one of the greatest gifts that anyone can have. I would like to ask you to place yourselves in the position of India, struggling for what is her birth-right. We stand in need of your help; there is no danger in giving yourself; believe me, there is none. I always feel that politics without idealism is a dead force; we must have courage, a larger vision and imagination, the qualities born of idealism.

The peace and contentment of India means the peace and contentment not only of England, but it means the peace, prosperity and happiness of the whole world. As a firm believer in the principles enunciated by our great Master in the Sermon on the Mount. I would fain see the living Christ (not the Christ of the Christianity so often represented—especially to us in India—by the narrow creeds of dogma and ritual), the cementing force between your country and mine, and the ties that bind us. He surely, is the embodiment of brotherhood and love amongst the peoples of the world. He is stretching out his hands to the suffering humanity of the world. India is unhappy; India is suffering. May God grant that those who are by precept and example his chosen vessels, may long be spared to influence those in power to come to right decisions in these fateful times.

Rajkumari Amrit Kaur has always been a practising Christian. She has imbibed the Christian ideal from her childhood, and at the feet of Mahatma Gandhi she perfected the art of living it to the full. She articulates here her thoughts on Christians Eve, 1943—thoughts that are singularly free from rancour and recrimination against the 1942 repression by the British. They breathe forgiveness, peace and goodwill towards all men, and women and children and deplore the West's breaking away from the truly Christian ways of life.

CHRISTMAS EVE THOUGHTS

This is the month, and this the happy morn
Wherein the Son of Heaven's Eternal King
Of wedded maid and virgin mother born,
Our great redemption from above did bring;
For so the holy sages once did sing
That He our deadly forfeit should release
And with His Father work as a perpetual peace.

John Milton

It is Christmas eve and my mind travels back to the days of childhood. As soon as I could lisp I remember folding my hands in prayer in mother's lap to the "gentle" Jesus who loved little children. She told us that Christmas was his birthday and that is why every one was happy; for the world would not have been the same had God not sent Jesus into it. Then came many a Chrismastide in England—a season of gaiety and warmth in every heart and a general atmosphere of friendliness and rejoicing, "Peace on earth and goodwill towards men" rang out the glorious message whether in anthems or hymns in churches or in carols in the streets. Strangers smiled at one and wished one well and this in a land where it is considered rude to speak to anyone with whom one is not acquainted.

An now "what a heavy change is there"! Christendom at war for the second time within twentyone years with all the might of armour and science at their back engaged in destroying the greast number in the shortest time. No sorrow but downright exultation at the destruction wrought. Man at war with fellow man, sunk to the uttermost depths, and for what purpose? Whatever ideologies may be placed before the people, however much it may be sought to be proved by either side that they have right on their side, the fact remains that the structure on which their way of life has been built has bred hatered and jealousy and thereby brought the world to a sorry pass. The message of Christ finds no echo in their hearts. Why?

Why has Christianity in the West failed to mould men's lives so as to make them love rather than hate their neighbours? Are the churches guiltless in this respect? Is not their history also replete with lust for temporal power? Have not persecution and intolerance, worse and more horrible perhaps than in the name of any other religion, married their spiritual growth? Has not the fact of the churches, having merged into the hierarchy of the State or being subsidised by it been a definite deterrent to their speaking frankly on live issues? With what conscience have the dignitaries of the Church blessed the arms of their countries that have gone to war to destroy God's creation and acquire material or territorial gain? Battle-torn banners of regiments are hung in churches, church parades for troops are held.

Is all this and more not a glorification of war? Jesus rebuked Peter for using the sword in trying to defend even his Lord. "All they that take the sword shall perish with the sword" but even today Christendom is using it as the final arbiter of men's fates, forgetting that violence can be stable. How can the message of Christ find true root in countries, which continue to hold that might is right?

If, then, we are of opinion that institutional Christianity has not able to instil deeply enough in men's minds the principles for which Christ lived and died, does it not become our duty to raise our voices in no uncertain terms against a way of life which is leading mankind to destruction? And should we not try to probe afresh the way Jesus showed us?

When a lawyer asked Jesus "Master which is the great commandment in the law" the reply was "Thou shalt love the Lord thy God with all thy heart and with all thy soul and with all thy mind. This is the great and first commandment. And a second like into it is this; thou shalt love thy neighbour as thyself. On these two commandments hangeth the whole law and the prophets." And again "All things therefore whatsoever ye would that men should do unto you, even so do ye also unto them; for this is the law and the prophets".

The second commandment is obviously impossible of fulfilment if we are not in love with God for only from love of God can issue forth love for man. Is not Christendom breaking the golden rule every second of the day? Jesus said "Love your enemies and pray for them that persecute you that ye may be sons of your Father which is in heaven. For if ye love them what reward have ye? Do not even the publicans the same?" And yet we listen in every day on the Radio to the most poisonous propaganda of hate from every country at war. The allies of today are in many instances the enemies of tomorrow. How can there be any true loyalties towards men when there is no loyalty towards God?

"Whatsoever smiteth thee on thy right cheek, turn to him the other also. And if and man would go to law with thee and take away thy coat, let him have thy cloak also. And whosoever shall compel thee to go one mile, go with him twin." But have we not more than gone back to the doctrine of "an eye for an eye and a tooth for a tooth"?

The way of Jesus was through the narrow gate, the uraitened path "that leadeth unto life." It was not the way of material gain and unbridled pleasure. He bade us be in the world but not of it. He told us not to "lay up for ourselves treasures upon the earth where moth and rust doth consume and where thieves break through and steal". He told us that we could not serve God and Mammon.

"The kingdoms of this world and the glory of them" were spurned by Jesus. There was no room in his kingdom for the rich man "clothed in purple and fine linen faring sumptuously every day" but there was ample comfort for the suffering beggar "full of sores and desiring to be fed with crumbs that fell from the rich man's table". "How hardly shall they that have riches enter into the kingdom of God" said Jesus to his disciples when the rich man who had followed the letter of the law "went away sorrowful" because he could not make up his mind to divest himself of his "great possessions" even though he was anxious to "inherit eternal life". Is it not the mad lust for riches and, through riches, for temporal power that has made war a chronic disease of mankind that breaks out form time to time with ever wilder fury?

Jesus made no distinctions between high and low, rich and poor, Jew and Gentile. He is said to have preferred the society of publicans and sinners and he allowed harlots to bathe his feet with their tears without fear of pollution. And yet it those who call themselves Christians who uphold more stunchly than others the barriers of race and colour and deny human rights to their fellowmen.

"The truth shall make you free" said Jesus. He feared no man and never hesitated to condemn the sins of those in power regardless of consequences. How little did his enemies realise when taunting and tempting him that they were being unwilling witnesses to the truth in him. "We know that thou art true and teachest the way of God in truth and carest not for any one, for thou regardest not the person of men." How he despised hypocrisy! No greater indictment of it can be found anywhere than in the 23rd Chapter of St. Mathew. And yet truth is the first casualty in war and men and women who dare to speak the truth are either killed of imprisoned. "Beware of the leaven of the Pharisees".

In no uncertain terms Jesus denounced their outward cleanliness which was the thin veneer covering inward evil and greed. He exposed the cant and outward show of their adherence to ritual and orthodoxy and reproached them for heaping on others burdens which they themselves refused to bear and for misleading men.

He knew that this plain speaking would mean an open rupture with those who were seeking to destroy him but for Jesus there was no way but the way of Truth. By contrast do not power politics often restrain those who should do so from denouncing injustice and do they not hereby lend aid to untruth? "Man shall not live by bread alone" said Jesus "but by every word that proceed the out of the mouth of God". Does not this mean that there are higher principles for him than mere material sustenance, that it is the bread of heaven by which man can drive spiritual sustenance and by which alone he can have eternal life? And is not that eternal life to be found in the deepest and most intimate communion with the life and teaching of Jesus? "What shall it profit a man if he gain the whole world and lose his soul?" But are not still in the world of today inspite of past experience, making the economic needs and ambitions of man the end of all our striving and thereby lowering our stature and bringing into being that rivalry and competition for this world's goods which are the root cause of strife?

What more beautiful or diviner code of life could have been given to man than what Jesus taught in his "Sermon on the Mount"? There was God's blessing in abundance for those who followed these precepts. Dean Farrar in inimitable language thus summarises the essence of what Christ revealed to his followers; "the riches of poverty, the royalty of weakness, the high beatitude of sorrow and persecution."

The command 'thou shalt not murder' was henceforth extended to angry words and feelings of hatred. The germ of adultery was shown to be involved in a lascivious look. The prohibition of perjury was extended to every vain and unnecessary oath. The law of equivalent revenge was superseded by a law of absolute self-abnegation.

The love due to our neighbour was extended also to our enemy. Alms were to be given not with noisy ostentation, but in modest secrecy. Prayers were to be uttered not with hypocritic publicity, but in holy solitude. Fasting was to be exercised not as a belauded virtue but as a private self-denial. And all these acts of devotion were to be offered with sole reference to the love of God, in a simplicity which sought no earthly reward, but which stored up for itself a heavenly and incorruptible treasure. And the service, to be sincere, must be entire and undistracted.

The cares and anxieties of life were not to divert its earnestness or to trouble its repose. And what should be the basis of such service? The self examination which issues in a gentleness which will not condemn, in a charity that cannot believe, in an ignorance that will not know the sins of others; the reserve which will not waste or degrade things holy; the faith which seeks strength from above and knows that, seeking rightly, it shall obtain; the self-denial which, in the desire to increase God's glory and man's happiness, sees the guide of its actions towards all the world.

It was in the fitness of things that Jesus should be born in the house of a poor carpenter. How else could he have glorified in his own life the dignity of manual labour or the riches of poverty? He possessed nothing, he had nowhere to lay his life was a life of incessant service to poor suffering humanity. Never a call from any suffer that did not invoke immediate response whether it was for spiritual or physical need. "For himself he seemed to claim no rest except the quiet hours of night, when he retired often to pray to his heavenly Father amid the mountain solitudes which he loved so well".

It was this communion with God which brought the only solace the "Man of sorrow" know in his life on earth. And when he asked his disciples to pray without ceasing, it was because he knew how true prayer elevates a man far above the toil and misery and cares of life, how it strengthens faith and how it brings man near to the throne of grace.

Christianity, apart from a corner in southernmost India, has been of recent growth in our country. It has been brought in by missionaries of various denominations, from Britain and America and in lesser degree from some of the countries of the continent of Europe. Here too, therefore, we have our people belonging to the Anglican, the Roman Catholic, the Scotch and American

Churches. These denominations have been born and bred out of suffering in the western hemisphere.

They have traditions of their own zealously guarded by their members. But it has always seemed to me that these differences are skin deep, for the greater part, among Indian Christians. I remember many years ago a woman servant of mine belonging to the Roman Catholic faith preferring to go to a Presbyterian church nearby where the service was conducted in Hindustani and could be easily followed by her.

The Roman Catholic priest was very annoyed with her, of course, but I am sure there are many of the same category as this woman to whom simple worship from the heart means far more than forms of church service. Are not such really nearer to the heart of Christ? Does not God dwell in the hearts of men rather than temples built by men's hands? I have long since felt, and during these long months of detention it has been insistently broke in on me, that it is time we Christian Indians turned our thoughts seriously towards evolving an order may shake ourselves into one church—a body of followers of Jesus— of the simplest form.

If Christianity is to live and grow in India—and this growth must be measured not in terms of numbers but in terms of the light of Jesus increasingly lightening our hearts and our lives—its roots must spring from our own soil. Our liturgy must be in our own language as also our hymns. I am aware that there are translations extant but personally I have not been moved to the core by them.

It may be that my ear, having been early attuned to English words and tunes, cannot adjust itself to Indian words sung or chanted, often badly or incorrectly, to western music. Would not Indian tunes be more in keeping with Indian words? Would they not appeal more to the hearts and ear of Indians? May we not arrange a liturgy culled from the gems in the glorious liturgies of existing churches with any original additions that our own ministers may add with the common consent of a number of persons charged with the creation of the same? May we not choose gems form the various hymn books in like manner and have them set to Indian tunes? Gandhiji had a lovely translation of the classic "Lead Kindly Light" done in Gujerati and set to a pleasing Indian tune? Are there not many hymns from among say, a 'Bhajanwali' as used in Gandhiji's prayers which we could also include? Than there is the all important question of the ministry.

May we not evolve something more akin to the Rishis of ancient India who lived far from the madding crowd but who trained disciples for service in their Ashrams and to whom Kings delighted to send their sons to be trained in the art of living and ruling? May we not be simple and self-supporting as the apostles of old? They were to take nothing with them; no scrip for food, no purse for money, no change of raiment, no travelling shoes in place of their ordinary palm-bark sandals, they are not even to procure a staff for their journey if they did not happen already to possess one. Like Jusus' own life, the lives of those called to his ministry must be lives of service, of sacrifice, of healing, of doing good, of standing up for the weak, of raising the fallen. He taught us that pomp and ritual, the observance of the letter of the law, spiritual pride and vainglory could not bring in the Kingdom of God. That Kingdom was within us and its first fruit was the true understanding of the spirit of the law from which alone can spring mercy and justice, humanity and love.

The eternal life he promised us was not the future but the unseen, if we had the faith to perceive its presence and is reality. He was the bread and water of life us here and now. The world was to be our neighbour and love was to transcend faith and hope for love was the fulfilment of the law. I realise that human being have to be organised and need forms or government in every walk of life.

If we have a church and a ministry we must have a form of worship and a form of church government. My plea to the leaders of Christian thought whether in or outside the ministry, is to evolve something extremely simply. I feel that, just in the political sphere, the less government we have in the church the better for our spiritual growth. I do not see why we should follow what our brethren in the West have evolved. It is the misfortune of all religious teachings that its essence is often apt, after a lapse of time, to become clouded with ritual and dogma, with mere outward compliance and superstition. It is, therefore, good to strive to stress the essentials and drive away the clouds.

The first duty of any ministry must naturally be to serve its own members whether in towns or villages. The Christian community is for the greater part, poor and ignorant and we can only hope to raise them through whole-hearted service to them. We need not trouble about churches for them. They can worship God under the roof of heaven.

It is the lessons of the life of Christ that they have to learn and these we can only being home to them through our own lives. It is the light within us, if we have it, that will radiate and show them the way. Missionaries from abroad in the beginning did, however, unwittingly, a tremendous disservice to Christian Indians by trying to wean them from Indian ways of life in the matter of dress, name, languages, etc.

To a large extent this has been responsible for an antagonism felt by Indians in general towards Christians and for a certain amount of fear in the minds of the latter of their non-christian brethren. Owing to a healthy growth of nationalism and pride of country Indian Christians have gone back to Indian names, dress, language and such customs as cremation of example which come natural to them. This is as it should be.

Inasmuch as some of the deepest truths during his short ministry were revealed by Jesus to women, why should not women be eligible for the ministry? I personally used to love worship in my friend Dr. Maude Royaden's Church is London for I found in her a minister of Christ whose whole life was "rooted and grounded" in love. The first recorded public utterance of Jesus was to his mother, torn with anxiety for him, then a mere child. "Wist ye not that I must be in my Father's house?" And again later when she, with her other sons tried to wean him from his mission because she feared its perils for him "Who is my brethren? Whosoever shall do the will of my Father which is in heaven, the same is my brother and sister and mother". There must be a complete giving of oneself of God's service. Humanities are secondary.

One of the most touching scenes in his life is the one with the woman of Samaria Jesus, tried after a long journey on foot weary and thirsty with the heat, sits at the well to rest while his disciples go to look for food in the village. To the well comes the woman of ill repute and he asks her—a Samaritan—to give him—

a Jew—water to drink. She is amazed. He ignores the feud between the sects; he knows who she is but he stoops to conquer and, having won her, gives her "the living water" which gushes from within the heart of the believer and springs to eternal life. Then there is the moving episode of Mary Magdalene, one of his devoted disciples to the end. Jesus had come to sup at the house of a Pharisee where, contrary to custom, none of the courtesies done to honoured guests, such as washing of the feet, had been administered to him because of their hatred. But a fallen creature makes bold to intrude in that company, inspite of being a woman, and falling at Jesus's feet she kisses and bathes them with her tears and wipes them with her hair. Finally she breaks the alabaster urn and pours over them the fragrant ointment.

She, condemned of men, knew however, that Jesus would not feel polluted by her touch that she would have his sympathy and the forgiveness for which she yearned. And seeing the disapproval with which his action in allowing the women to minister to him was being viewed by his host, Jesus speaks to him of the parable of the lender and debtors and through it speaks to us for all time of gentleness, forbearance and divine forgiveness, as also that hypocrisy is more hateful in the eyes of God than the most glaring sin. "As often as I think about this event", said Gregory the Great, "I am more disposed to weep over it than to preach upon it". St. Luke mentions Mary Magdalene as first among the women who accompanied Jesus in his wanderings and whose whole life thereafter, was devoted to her saviour's service.

It was given to the Canaanite woman to display that faith which can "move mountains" and which Jesus would have all of us cultivate. "It is not meet to take the children's bread and to cast it to dogs" said the Master to test this women who was in agony of mind for her suffering child. The faithful soul said she was content to be as the "dogs" and eat of "the crumbs which fell from their master's tables" and triumphed.

And what of the adulteress caught red-handed?

The enemies of Jesus dragged her into the sacred precincts of the Temple, shamed and suffering, in order, that they might have the whereof to accuse Him". But there was no dilemma for one who had already laid down the glorious precept "Judge not that ye be not judged". "He that is without sin among you, let him first cast a stone at her", and at this holy rebuke the accusers slunk away. In the living heart of Jesus there was no condemnation but in His Kingdom there is room for repentance and purification of the worst sinner. "Go they way; from henceforth sin no more".

The woman who appealed to Jesus for healing on the Sabbath day was rebuked by the Ruler of the Synagogue for breaking the Sabbath. Jesus there and then denounced the rigid restrictions of a hide-bound tradition which refused to understand the spirit of the law—the law of love.

It was in the loved home of friends at Bethany that Christ tenderly reproved Martha who, while working hard to fulfil her duties of hostess, complained of no help in her task from her sister. "Martha, Martha, thou art anxious and troubled about many things; but one thing is needful; for Mary hath chosen the good part which shall not be taken away from her."

It was the call to listen to Jesus which should take first place rather than the call of the world. And it was this same faithful and devoted Mary who emptied the precious perfume in the alabaster jar over the head and feet of Jesus and wiped them with her hair as a token of self-sacrifice, not counting the cost. Custom and tradition have dealt harshly with women throughout the ages Doubtless, the times of Jesus were no exception to the rule. But when the disciples of Jesus rebuked mere women for intruding on Him, He is in turn rebuked them with the memorable words. "Suffer the little children to come unto me, and forbid them not; for of such is the kingdom of God". He would have us be humble as little children if we are to be partakers of the kingdom of heaven.

It was in answer to the request of Salome who, with all a mother's earthly devotion, asked for preference for her sons in His kingdom that He uttered a solemn warning against unwarranted ambition. "Whosoever would become great among you shall be your minister; and whosoever would be first among you shall be your servant".

What greater tribute could have been paid to the spirit of self-abnegation than was paid to the widow who cast into God's treasury—into God's service—all that she had? "Verily I say unto you, this poor widow, cast in more than all they which are casting into the treasury, for they all did cast in of their superfluity, but she of her want did cast in all that she had, even all her living". The essence of giving lies in self-denial.

As He would his weary way up the hill to be crucified, when all else were dumb, it was the women who could not restrain their tears and loud lamentations and it was to them that Jesus uttered words warning of the evil days that were to come and must come always on people who turn away from the right path. "Daughters of Jerusalem, weep not for me, but weep for yourselves and for your children." In the her hour of the deepest agony He did not forget His mother. He had early left her side for what was a higher call than filial duty. Nevertheless she had been of the few who were true to Him in His hour of supreme trial. One can imagine the crushing weights of her woe as she saw Him nailed to the cross knowing what trials would await all those who would bear witness to Him when He was gone. He tenderly commended her to care of the disciple whom He loved best.

Jesus uplifted womanhood. He made no differences of race or caste or sex. Christian women have, therefore, to play their part in bringing into being the Kingdom of God on earth.

Apart from service to Christians there is a wide field of service to suffering Indian humanity which calls to each one of us. What response are we making to it? If Jesus is the way, the truth, and the life for us, then we have to gird our loins for service. If poverty more cruel and awful then, perhaps, in any other country is to be banished from our land, we have to join hands with those who are trying to remove the root cause of it viz. exploitation by a foreign power and by our own vested interests.

If a new order based on justice, mercy and love is to be evolved we must stand for giving prominence to moral and human values. If ignorance has to be banished, we have to lend a hand in sweeping away the darkness of illiteracy, evil customs and superstition. We have to try to build up healthy bodies as well as healthy minds. If the barriers between high and low have to be abolished we have to serve all equally.

If bribery and corruption, so rife today, have to be eliminated, we have to held to set and demand standards of morality both in public and private life. We have to non-cooperate with immorality in whatever from it exists. If communal disunity is not to mar our national growth permanently, we have to strive to bring about friendliness between man and man. It is the bond of service alone that can prove that humanity is higher than community or race. And in all such service we must welcome men and women of foreign birth, should they wish to join us whether in the ministry of the church or outside, not as missionaries out to convert in order to swell the numerical strength of Christian Indians, but as servants of humanity and of Jesus in the sense that Charlie Andrews was.

He became one with suffering India because he was imbued with the true spirit of his Lord and Master whom he served faithfully to the end. Because Missionaries were foreigners their service has alas, not always been free from the prejudices, of race and colour. They often came with a sense of superiority and were, therefore, unable, except with brilliant exceptions, to become one with us.

If we hate apostasy for ourselves, why should we want others to go in for it? "Not everyone that saith unto me, Lord, shall enter into the Kingdom of heaven but he that doeth the will of my Father which is in heaven". Have the Christian countries proved that their way of life has been better? Is their record in the East an unsullied one? Are not subjugation by force, exploitation and injustice and cruelty resulting from the erecting of the colour bar writ large therein?

In any event, let Christian Indians not worry so much about representation in constitutional bodies of the new India for it is neither numbers nor political power that count but what a community does and how lives that is vital to its growth as also to the growth of the country to which it belongs. We are seven according to the census, a mere drop in the ocean of India's humanity. But we can count form any times that number if we use our talents right. "My strength is as the strength of ten, because by heart is pure" should be our motto. Let us make our ameliorating influence felt in every region of Indian life through single eyes service and without ambition for earthly reward. Our mansions may not be of this world. Let us wake from slumber at the spirit's voice and dare here to number the unseen as our choice.

Let us gladly barter all on earthly ground and let our one oblation be a life of love. True religion is far more than a code of morals and finds its fulfilment in complete surrender to the highest Christians the world over may have been and may continue to the untrue to Christ; the churches may have fallen from the great ideals for which the apostles and the great saints lived and died. But Jesus lives and the verities he proclaimed are eternal.

I believe that the way Gandhiji is pointing to India is the way of Jesus. It demands the whole-hearted giving of oneself; it lays stress on human rather than on material values; it stands for truth and non-violence in every sphere of life. The schemes he has put forward for the regeneration of India are based on love for man wherein there is no room that for exploitation or the rivalries which breed strife. I know the lure of the West is great for our educated classes.

It is said that Gandhiji is taking us buck to the Middle Ages to ways of life which experience has found wanting and that with his passing India will take to the aims and modes of the West. There is ever so much that we can learn from the West but there is equally as much which, from experience, we shall be most unwise in taking from them.

There must be something radically wrong with a structure which nurses the germs of war. Christian Indians will, I am sure, be well advised to consider deeply which way they should adopt. And I, for one, hope that in choosing the better part we may, perhaps, through service in our homeland be privileged to lead troubled humanity once again into the paths of peace.

3

Status of Women

Experience has taught us that if one visits a mohalla one is greeted in the first instance with curiosity but, if the visit is repeated with practical service, the latter soon paves the way for friendship. For ignorance and suspicion can only be overcome by understanding service and love. Washing the children, sweeping dirty rooms, procuring medical aid for the sick, such acts cannot but touch the hardest hearts. Little by little the response comes in simple but touching ways. The poor are, if anything, generous-hearted and if a small band of workers visits even one mohalla daily for any length of time and serves the women and children there, the neighbouring areas proffer invitations too. Once a beginning is made the field of work enlarges by leaps and bounds.

My plea with my town sisters is to give every moment of their spare time to the poor women and bring to them the message of hope and cheer which they so sorely need. The life of educated women in the cities has become so full with their own social engagements that very little, if any, time is left for the service of the needy. Well-to-do women are seen in their hundreds at parties, in cinemas, in clubs, in shops, on the main roads but never or seldom in the haunts of those who constitute the large majority of our sisters and with whose welfare and redemption from ignorance and superstition lies the only hope of our own salvation. This apathy on the part of most of us must go and here too it is those who have the urge to serve who must break new ground.

Every town should have a committee of women dedicated to social service. This Committee should again be divided into small sub-committees each allotted with a special task. Statistics should be prepared in each mohalla, of the children, of the sick, of the widows, of the labouring women, of the facilities for clean water, medical aid and education, of such homes or hovels which are not fit for human habitation, of the incomes of the families, of their working hours, etc. Not until we become intimately acquainted with the needs of the women will we be able to help them. Once the contacts are made small gatherings can be held to talk to the women on hygiene, the proper care of children, diet, good neighbourliness, prevention of disease, discipline, the evils of untouchability, child marriage, wasteful expenditure on ceremonial occasions etc. etc. Classes for the removal of illiteracy, spinning, weaving, basket-making, toy-making, and any special handicraft of the town should gradually be arranged. Women must be made aware of what a pitiful condition our country is in and what part they have to play in making her free. They must be made aware of their latent strength. It is my firm conviction that unless and until we develop within ourselves the belief that moral stamina is able to withstand all the onslaughts of physical might, we shall not be able to divest ourselves of that inferiority complex which millions of years of man's domination has bred in us and nor will be able to help in bringing in a world where might shall no longer be right.

While it is true that in the larger urban areas hospitals do exist for women, my experience in my own province is that the really poor do not get all the attention they need. They cannot afford either the expense of a conveyance to take them to the hospital nor can they afford the other expenses which have to be incurred when they are admitted as in-patients. They are ignorant themselves of the elementary rules of hygiene or prevention of disease. A fair amount of quackery exists to which they often fall victims. Many will not, even if this were available to them, allow themselves to be examined by men doctors. The indigenous midwife, unaware of the laws of hygiene herself, often works havoc and there is a tale of untold woe and misery which need not be if medical aid were really made available, as it should be under any good government, to every individual. Our Committees could, in any case, arrange for the admission into hospital of all such cases as need the immediate attention of doctors. We must organize funds to pay for medicines and nourishment for them while in hospital as well as during their period of convalescence in their homes. Inasmuch as prevention is far better than cure, we must try to instruct the women in our areas in the simple rules of hygiene. Cleanliness is often almost an impossibility for them because of poverty. I have more than once given soap for washing clothes only to find that the soap has been sold in order to provide for the more urgent need of food. Nevertheless, it is the lack of the realization that dirt means disease that is responsible to a large extent for unwashed children, unswept homes, refuse in lanes, a sad imperviousness to smells and insanitary conditions in latrines and drains, allowing children to answer the calls of nature in streets and all the squalor that meets the eye not once but always in the lanes and houses of the really poor in all our towns. This ignorance and apathy it is our duty to fight. It is uphill work. It requires time, patience and funds. But if we undertake it with a will we can achieve a good deal.

Most of the larger towns now have Lady Health Visitors. The scope of service which they can render is immense. Maternity and child welfare centres are a *sine qua non* of the health of the mothers and children of a nation. They are of very recent birth in our towns, and far too few in number. One started by me over 20 years ago has been through many vicissitudes. To get financial aid for it from the Municipality in the first instance was a difficulty. To get people to realize that the Lady Health Visitor is not a practising midwife at the beck and call of those who can pay her or who think they can commandeer her services free has been a problem.

Finally this centre has for some years been run under the aegis of a voluntary Committee of Health of women with the Civil Surgeon and the Medical Officer of Health as Adviser and Secretary respectively and has made good. The Lady Health Visitor attends for confinement only the poor women of the city; she is responsible for both ante and postnatal care; she trains midwives who when they get certificates keep her in touch with the pregnant women in their areas; she holds refresher courses for the midwives continually; they are given small boxes with the necessary equipment; all cases of abnormal labour are made over to the Lady Doctor in the Civil Hospital. She has now two centres in the city, and two in the neighbouring villages; midwives are also trained for work in the villages from which they come, children up to the age of three are brought regularly to the centre to be weighed and examined, local funds are collected for medicines such as cod liver oil for both mothers and children as also for milk and fruit juices; clothes and woollen garments and old linen are also donated. The work could be expanded still further if more were available as also trained help, for one Lady Health Visitor for a town with a population of 1,00,000 is not enough. But I am definitely of opinion, from experience, that the Conference or any Committee of women should take over the supervision of Health Centres from Municipalities, the latter, of course, providing the funds for the proper running of the same.

No untrained dais should be allowed to work. We should encourage our women to go in for becoming trained midwives and lady health visitors. The same applies to lady doctors and nurses. Nursing is a profession which should appeal more to women than any other but alas! it has, owing to the narrow-mindedness of our society, been shunned by girls of the educated classes. It is time we realized the importance and urgent need of this noble profession and encouraged our girls to go in for it. Lessons in first aid, home nursing and invalid cookery should also be arranged for women in our areas. They should be taught what vitamins mean, that hand-ground flour, hand-pounded rice, raw vegetables and greens are necessary items in their dietary. We should try to enforce the free distribution of milk to children and pregnant women by our municipalities. We must insist on medical examination of all school-going children and physical exercises in our schools. There is a wide field for research in medicine which our doctors must take full advantage of and make their contribution.

There is no doubt that the education so far imparted has been neither adequate nor on right lines. The buildings for municipal schools for girls are often if not invariably wholly unsuited. The area is cramped, there is insufficient light and air and no playgrounds. The standard of efficiency of the teacher is pitiably low. Parents have not realised that girls should be educated just as well as boys and there is apathy on their part towards sending girls to schools even if one exists in their neighbourhood. Too often, for the sake of domestic work or marriage, girls are withdrawn from school when they have barely become literate with the result that they lapse back into illiteracy.

Now that Basic Education holds the field we should try to persuade our municipalities to adopt this method of imparting instruction to children from the ages of 6 or 7 to 14 in at least one girls' school in their area to begin with. There should be no delay in beginning. The Hindustani Talimi Sangh should be approached through Shrimati Asha Devi to furnish us with the necessary information. If possible, the Conference should undertake the supervision of the girls' school where the children are to be instructed through a craft, the municipality providing the necessary equipment of the start of the school as also the pay of the trained teacher. If after, say three years' practical experience, the girls in a Basic School prove themselves to be better, mentally, morally and physically, than the children in the other schools, a definite case will have been made out for universal Basic Education.

The lack of nursery schools in our land is a terrible tragedy. Owing to the ignorance and poverty of our women our little ones have literally no proper upbringing. Until such time as the State provides such institutions, it is up to organizations like ours to try to get hold, at any rate, of some of these children and give them the care and attention they need. In all these endeavours, however, we are handicapped by the lack of trained women teachers and voluntary workers. I have often wished that our girls, once they have finished their school or college course, should give at least three years of service in voluntary work of whatever nature appeals to them, before they marry. I know that teaching is a vocation and everyone cannot make an ideal teacher. But the need today is so immense and the means of implementing it so inadquate that I think voluntary workers can render invaluable service. I do also believe that even after marriage, if we were to husband our leisure judiciously, we could give far more of ourselves than we do today to social service. Indeed to husband their leisure is one of the things we also have to teach those whom we wish to serve.

Adult education offers a wide field. Here again much can be done by voluntary endeavour. The abolition of illiteracy is an imperative need but to make persons literate is only one item in the programme of adult education. I have found women, after 25 or 30 years of age, as a rule, quite apathetic to becoming literate. Even if they do become literate they lapse back into illiteracy very soon, partly owing to lack of time to spare from their innumerable household duties and also because of lack of suitable literature for them. The provision of suitable literature is a real need which some of our literary minded sisters might well turn their attention to fulfilling. I am of opinion that we should try our level best to liquidate illiteracy particularly among women under 30 years of age. In my classes I found that reading aloud to the women gave a definite impetus to them to learn how to read themselves. It also gave one opportunities of imparting all kinds of useful knowledge to them, of giving them ethical instruction, teaching them the principles of citizenship, love of country as well as giving them some idea of their present fallen state and how they must better their own lot. It seems to me that this type of all round knowledge is really far more essential for our women than mere literacy and each one of us can impart this provided we have won the confidence of the women in the area concerned.

Handicrafts

The development of these is one certain way to bring some economic relief to women. Spinning, weaving, toy-making, basket-making, needlework, both plain and embroidery, are among some of the main crafts that should be taught. Having taught the women to produce cloth and other articles, it should be our duty to try to dispose of them. The yoarn opun and the cloth woven can be absorbed by the dwellers in the area concerned. It is a thousand pities that we women have not taken a more living interest in the All India Spinners' Association, an organization primarily catering to the economic relief of women. Even if we have not believed in the efficacy of the spinning wheel as a symbol of non-violence and of the moral regeneration of our land, we might have welcomed it as a source of economic betterment of our poor village sisters. But the lure of machine-made cloth and even foreign finery have proved too much for most of us. I have for many years wished the Lady Irwon College, Delhi, to have a handicraft section where we might train girls capable of teaching these to women in need of earning for themselves or supplementing their meagre incomes. Industrial schools for women where they can learn handicrafts are a necessity for every town. Whele taking of education, I shold like to appeal to parents to bring their daughters up to some profession just as well as their sons. Girls must be given every opportunity to rise to their full stature in whatever sphere of activity they may choose. Even if ours is a land of universal marriage we want our girls to have the necessary knowledge wherewith they can earn their own livelihood and whereby they may better serve society.

Views on Harijans

The service of these unfortunate members of our society is a cause that should appeal specially to us. Our sympathies should naturally go out to those who have been oppressed simply by reason of their caste just as we have been by reason of our sex. It is a crying shame that these people who cater for our well being and without whose services we should not be able to exist, are relegated in most towns to live in the most abominable dwellings—if, indeed, we can call their hovels by this name! How very few of us, however, even care to know where and how they live! They are often better off financially than many other poor citizens of our towns but the dirt and squalor in which they live and the ignorance in which they are steeped deserve our immediate attention. The Harijan Sevak Sangh is, in my opinion, the most philanthropic organization in our country today but it too needs workers, especially women workers. I would like to recommend us women to do "dharna" before our municipalities, until such time as they have built decent quarters for the Harijans who serve the town. And, in any case, we can try to get hold of their children, see that they are washed and cleanly clothed and educated. Their proper education is a certain way of making them get rid of that psychology of inferiority from which they, as a class, suffer. I would like to see Harijans girls trained by the score as nurses and midwives and where possible as doctors and teachers. Prejudice against them, as a class, will them *ipso facto* disappear.

Labour

In labouring areas too there is ample scope for us. In the large industrial towns, labour laws have forced the employees to give a certain amount of living, medical and educational facilities for our women and children but we have a long way to go yet. In our non-industrial towns too there is plenty of unregistered woman labour which needs our protection. Even if the output of work is the same, the woman gets paid less. She is often the sport of the men with whom she comes in contact during her hours of work. Their living quarters are often as bad as those of the Harijans and their children are often neglected.

The Simple Life

Inasmuch as example is far better than precept, we must bring about certain changes in our own life before we can ask others to do likewise. There is a terrible amount of wasteful expenditure among our people on the occasions of marriage, birth, death and other ceremonial functions. Whenever I have approached men in this matter the reply has invariably been that it is the women who will not listen to them, however much they would like to curtail expenditure. It is a known fact that many poor families remain indebted for years or even generations because of foolish extravagance on ceremonies and there is also the menace of the dowry system. This must be eliminated. It is a scandalous and degrading custom. We have to set a good example in this domain ourselves. We too have erred grievously in the matter of maintaining a standard of life which many of us cannot really afford. Simplicity in dress, in diet and in life generally will redound to our benefit all round and help us better to influence those whom we wish to serve.

It is a well-known fact that in spite of the Sarda Act child marriage continues. There is no remedy for it except education and more education for the people. Laws help to check an evil up to a point but it is the realization of the evil on the part of every member of society that contributes most towards its abolition. More vigilance on our part and a stricter penalty for the parents will help to some extent.

The same applies to polygamy. Not until woman herself realizes that polygamy is regarding to her status will she be able to make man realise that it is wrong. For the poor man it is sometimes an economic necessity. It is cheaper to have three wives than to have one and pay for two women to work in his fields. Here again if women are educated and self-reliant they will not allow themselves to be exploited. Then too there is the tyranny of custom which makes man, often enough at the instigation of the first wife and nearly always with her consent, take unto himself a second mate for the purpose of begetting a son and heir. Nothing but education can make us refuse to bow to custom and usage which deal harshly with any member of our society. And this ignorance does not by any means apply to women only. Our men need to be educated just as much if not more. The worst opponents of social reform are men who are steeped in ignorance, who have never felt where the shoe pinches and who glibly talk of religion and tradition being in jeopardy whenever any attempt is made to get rid of their domination over women. And what am I to day of some of our educated women who sometimes go in for contracting second marriages or to educated mothers who for material benefit give their daughters to men who are already married? I can only appeal to their better sense and ask them not to go in for hurting a fellow woman. Such acts detract from the dignity of womanhood and lower her moral stature.

Pardah has vanished up to a point and will go absolutely in time. But it is still fairly strict in certain parts and among certain sections. It is inconceivable that any sensible man or woman can still cling, with religious fervour, to a custom which denies to woman all that man himself would not for one moment forego and which has a detrimental effect on her physical, moral and intellectual well-being. It can only be by a full and free contribution on her part to society that woman will be able to set standards of behaviour in all walks of life which shall uplift mankind. If I believe in dictatorship one of the first ugly customs that should be abolished straightaway would be pardah. Men should pause to think before they advocate its continuance while every woman under its sway should rebel against it.

A Universal Code

I have long since been of opinion that we Indian women should frame a new code of laws relating to marriage, inheritance, guardianship, divorce, etc. This code should be optional in the first instance and any one of whatever religion, should be at liberty to be governed by it. If it worked fairly for both men and women, I am sure that as education spread, it would become increasingly popular and would in time supersede all other codes. It would save the trouble of reforming laws which have become complex and even the mildest changes in which seem, at the moment, to arouse an almost fanatical opposition. "Religion in danger" is a very potent caveat which scares even seemingly intelligent persons in the same way as the proverbial ghost does children!

Swadeshi

This is a sphere in which women can and have played an enormous part. To love one's country, to be proud of and cling to its traditions, to glory in art and beauty in all its many forms, to treasure what is produced in one's village or home, town or province comes natural to women. There should be no difficulty then in our taking a vow not to use anything foreign if we can get Indian made goods. Handmade articles have always been valued at a greater price than machine-made. This obtains in all countries. I have mentioned Khadi before. I would appeal again for the realization of its intrinsic merit. With the new orientation that Gandhiji is now giving to Khadi produce, it really rests with townswomen whether they will help to maintain its output so that homespun may still be available to them. Spinning an hour daily—if the ethics of Khadi have been at all understood—should afford a pleasant and uplifting pastime for us. If we could realize that with every thread we draw we are helping to mend the broken warp and woof of the fabric of our national life, we would love the wheel and its music would refresh our souls. In any event home industries should receive our full patronage, if for no other reason than that they bring economic relief to women. Then again we must think out for ourselves whether we are anxious to see our country go the way of heavily industrialized countries or whether we are anxious to save her from the disaster that has overtaken the lands of the Western hemisphere. If we believe that the machine is made for man and its use shall be limited in so far as it helps to lighten man's load and in no case shall it reduce man himself to an automation as happens in large scale machinery, then we shall have no difficulty in doing our best to promote home industries.

Drink, Smoking and Gambling

Alcoholic excess brings almost more suffering on woman than on the victim of drink. Among the labouring classes, among castes such as the washermen and Harijans, in the great Sikh community, alcohol has worked and is working havoc. In labouring areas we can help to wean the victims by opening canteens of non-alcoholic beverages as also by trying to tide them over the drink hour, so to speak, by providing healthful pastimes for them. Women's organisations are working along these lines. More must be done, I have been successful in the case of more than one washerman by providing strong tea for him. It is heartening to learn that the Sikh leaders have quite recently spoken strongly against the drink habit in their community. Let us hope that this effort at reform on their part will spread to the Sikh villages too. Educative propaganda on the destructive effect of alcohol on the moral and physical well-being of all who indulge in it should be an important arm of our work of reform. Smoking too is having its deleterious effect. How often do I remonstrate in Simla with riskshaw pullers, weight carriers and even small boys to give up smoking! I am told that with the rise in wages of the working man he has more to spend on such luxuries as drink, gambling and smoke. Cigarettes have penetrated even to our villages and have displaced the hookah which was, at any rate, less harmful to the smoker. The evil of gambling too is on the increase. We have to set a good example by eschewing these vices ourselves. In the matter of drink, as in many other things, we of the well-to-do classes have followed European custom and it is sad to see many of our young men, in particular, officers in the armed forces today, over-indulging themselves. It is up to us to have the moral courage to refuse to conform to such rules of Western society as are alien to or harmful to ourselves. I know it is a hard task for the wives of officres to stand out against offering alcoholic drinks to their guests. But it is their duty to do so. Co-operative effort in such matters is of great assistance. I know of more than one young officer who has refused to drink and has not lost in popularity but has gained the respect of his brother officers. If one can do it, then all can.

Communal Unity

The lack of this is eating as a cankar into the vitals of our national life. Those who propagate hate and mistrust between man and man are doing a tremendous disservice to humanity itself. No religion but preaches love for fellowman. It is only man's abuse of religion that has led to the present woeful state not only of our country but of the entire world. We may not shut our eyes to the fact that the poison is spreading among our ranks too. If we could have the realization within us of the high calling of womanhood, our finer instincts would rebel against such dissensions and such perversion of religion as stress what is *au fond* immaterial and bring into jeopardy what is definitely vital to the spiritual and moral development of life. Arguments are of no avail under existing conditions. Indeed I often feel that the less said in the press and on public platforms the better it would be. But there are so many common avenues in social service that can and should be explored. I believe it is in the practical fulfilment by common endeavour of all we as women want for ourselves and for our children that an unbreakable bond will eventually be established which will transcend all barriers of caste and creed in our homeland and in the wider world of race also.

For Village Workers

This is a sphere where our organizations have not penetrated. And yet India is a land of villages. If she is to live it must be through the resuscitation of village life in all its phases, moral, cultural and economic. Many years ago I suggested that if our Conference Branches could adopt even one village each, they would be making a vital contribution to nation building. I make the appeal again. But I feel that very few of us, perhaps, of the town and of the older generation will be able actually to adjust ourselves to village life and not until we go and live in the villages will we be able to render any real service. Conference Branches can, all the same, do a good deal by frequently visiting the village they adopt and by keeping a paid worker or workers there to carry out work on lines approved and laid down by our Committee. The appeal to dedicate their lives to service of the villages must be made to the young generation. There are, no doubt, risks involved for women who undertake such work. I feel that young married couples would be most suited to the task provided they were willing to become one with the villagers. But even if there are risks, they must be taken, 'Nothing venture, nothing have' is never more true than today. Our villages are not attractive. The humanity that inhabits them is, apart from its poverty, sunk in the deepest ignorance. They know nothing, they have almost lost the instinct to appreciate anything, they eke out a mere existence. Virgin soil should yield results more quickly than any other and it may be, that if me have the faith, the will and the energy and enough workers, we could, sooner than we imagine, at any rate educate the villager and wipe out the dirt and squalor that reign in village lanes and village home and bring done the incidence of disease. But it is an uphill task and needs real missionary zeal and spirit. The work, however, must be undertaken whatever the hardships and difficulties involved. Here again, apart from teaching the simple laws of personal and social hygiene to the women and children, apart from making them literate and imparting general knowledge to them, apart from a cleaning campaign of the entire village, we have to teach them, above all, the inestimable benefits of co-operation. The village is for all and therefore if trench latrines have to be made to improve the sanitary conditions of the place, all must join hands; if pits have to be filled up and roads or paths made, it must be done by concerned labour; if there is to be a school, all children must go to it; if any cottage industry is to be revived, its produce must be for the whole village. They must feed and clothe themselves first and the surplus only may go to neighbours. If the Panchayat system is to be revived, as I feel it should, the members must be elected by the women, no less than by the men. The villagers must be made to feel proud of their village. Occasional competitions may be held between villages so that an impetus may be given to them to cooperate with our workers in making their surroundings and themselves prizeworthy. Co-operative labour for the common weal must be our motto so that our villages may learn to stand on their own legs and wasteful expenditure on litigation may cease. I am quite sure that if the lesson of co-operation were learnt and practised in our villages which will be the basic units of administration in our country that all the disunity which today exists among our towns folk would, *ipso facto*, disappear. Our workers must keep their own houses and the area round them spotlessly clean, they must eat bread made from hand-ground or bullock-ground wheat, hand-pounded rice, vegetables and fruit such as can be grown in the village, they must not be above putting their hands to some manual work during the course of the day. They must, in short, practise what they preach and there is no one so steeped in ignorance as will not, after some time, being to emulate their good example. The problems of a clean water supply, of sanitation and hygiene, of illness and disease, of illiteracy and ignorance, of untouchability, of child marriage, of widow re-marriage, all exist in villages as well as in towns. There will, in some places, be the evils of drink, gambling and smoking also to be tackled. And everywhere, apart from the reforms already alluded to there is the question of the revival of such handicrafts as will occupy the leisure hours of the villagers and bring them some economic relief. Spinning and weaving have vindicated their right to be fostered. Workers will revive those particularly native to any area. Then there is the most crying need of educating the children. Basic education whatever the craft employed, must be resorted to. Here too those young women who are burning with an urge to serve should get into touch forthwith with Shrimati Asha Devi and get a training in basic education. Students can devote some of their leisure hours to serving neighbouring villages during term and they could give more time during their vocations. I have said that married couples will probably be able to sérve best. But there is no reason why a brother and sister or two sisters or two friends should not do equally well. It is difficult for lone young women to go and settle in a village. Apart from risk, there is lack of intellectual companionship which does, after a time, have a depressing effect. The work to be done too is so vast that even two persons will be hard put to cope with it. But inasmuch as all life is adventure and it is the adventurous always who make history, we must hope for courage from those in whose hands lies the power to make or mar the future of this great land.

Professions and Public Life

I have said elsewhere that every girls should be brought up to a profession. Whether she has need to earn her own livelihood or not is immaterial. Basically it is right that every human being should have the opportunity of developing to his or her full stature in whatever sphere the individual bent may lie. "Learning by doing" is the educationists' motto today. "Living by doing" should be every person's motto and each one of us should be fitted for that "doing". It is an empty life that contributes nothing to its environment by "doing". The need for doctors, nurses, midwives, teachers, artists and experts in handiworks is very great. If all the girl students in India today went in for these professions it would be a mere drop in the ocean of our want. The appeal for implementing this vital lack must needs, therefore, take first place, for health and education are the *sine qua non* of the well-being of a nation. There cannot be any unhealthy rivalry between men and women in the matter of such professions at the moment. Nor, in my opinion, need there ever be such problems in this regard as the countries of the Western hemisphere have had to face and will have to face in increasing measure when the war is over and the spectre of unemployment once again raises its head, provided we plan wisely and refuse to become the slaves of large scale machinery.

There are other professions such as journalism, dairy and poultry farming, agriculture, gardening and architecture in which I should like to see women playing their part. But as, at the moment, I feel the social services need them more than anything else I would like them to give their all to health and education. There is plenty of scope for service for women is municipalities and local boards. They could bring into these bodies a sense of civic responsibility and duty which is sadly lacking there. I know that where women have served on local bodies they have kept themselves above communal strife and personal rivalries and I would like to see more and more of them come forward for such work. At the moment I feel they can be of more practical use here than in our assemblies. But they must take their share in public life. They have acquitted themselves well in the political struggle for freedom. The names of many of them will be honoured when the full history of the courage and sacrifice of the Indian National Congress is written without prejudice in letters of gold. It is women who will perhaps be able to rise above party and communal strife for the common weal and raise the standard of politics. Why should politics be a dirty game? I know how after it is said Gandhiji has mixed up ethics and politics and hence his failure in the realm of politics. When an impartial judgment can be formed of him I am sure it will be recognized that one of the greatest of the many great contributions he has made to humanity is his insistence on Truth in politics. He alone has kept his lamp burning brightly in a world steeped in darkness because of his undying faith in the spiritual values of life. I hope Indian women at any rate will be true to him. For it is he who has raised our stature by showing us a way of life in which woman can play even a nobler part than man if she becomes conscious of her innate strength. It is often said against us—and I think there is a large element of truth in his accusation for the average run—that we do not study deeply enough. If we are to take a creditable share in public life, we must be keen students of and intimately acquainted with the burning problems of the day. Facts and figures must be at our finger tips and ways and means of redress of any grievances and inequalities or of reform must be carefully thought out so that we may not be worsted in argument.

I personally would like to see a State Social Service under a Free India in which women can take their full share. It is a tragedy that we have no social service training centres even now. Camps are good exercise and may serve as refresher courses but we need proper schools where the right training may be imparted.

I have mentioned dairy and poultry farming, agriculture, gardening, architecture, among subjects for women to study. The care of the cow should really come instinctively to us by tradition almost, as it were. Is her well-being not a symbol of health and happiness for us and our children? Then, if we are to serve the villagers, why should we leave knowledge of agriculture to men only? Growing of fruit and vegetables, so necessary for our proper diet, must be our special care. Ours is a land of hovels at the moment. One of the first things a national Government must do will be to provide proper living accommodation for every family. Women architects will have ample opportunity and scope for planning cottages suited to our requirements, bringing all the knowledge of housecraft and artistry into the building of our houses. In short, there is no sphere of national life where we cannot contribute provided we have the will to serve and are industrious enough to acquire the requisite knowledge.

The States

Coming as I do from a State, having opened my eyes in a palace, and having spent the early years of my childhood in all the pomp and paraphernalia of princely India, I cannot but be deeply interested in their welfare. It is a tragedy too deep for tears that our ruling Princes have not come up to standard and that what is called Indian India is no better off and in many instances much worse off than British India. There has been too much stress on the non-essentials of pomp and ceremony and a poor imitation of the system of government in vogue in British

India. The Princes have not had the training or education necessary to fit them to rule and hence the natural feeling in the minds of national India that there is no room for them in the future polity of our Republic. I say Republic, advisedly, for I am sure India will evolve a socialized State when she has won her freedom. But since this is a booklet for women I am here concerned only with what my sisters in States can do. All that has been said in the preceding pages about service in towns and villages is equally applicable to the States. I do think, however, that Indian Princesses can and should take the lead in social service in their domains. Just as we educated well-to-do women are out of touch with the vast majority of our women, so are they out of touch with their poor subjects. This gulf must be bridged. A much more simple form of life, less luxury, less extravagance on what are non-essentials should be adopted, a good example in the matter of education on right lines of their daughters must be set, a refusal to give their girls in marriage to Princes who are already married should come natural to those who are often relegated to a back seat themselves, rebellion against the dreadful custom of pardah should be resorted to. No social reform in a State can be of any value if the rulers themselves do not conform to standards essential for civilized society. I know how helpless Indian Princesses are against the tyranny of age-worn and evil customs and my heart has bled for many a one. But on the analogy that God helps those who help themselves it is time that they ceased to suffer in silence. They have many sympathizers who would, at any rate, harness public opinion against the wrong doer.

It should not, in any event, be beyond the reach of Indian Princesses to bring light and life to their women subjects. They could draw up and carry out plans for housing, for a proper water supply, for sanitation, for prevention of disease, for medical relief, for equal wages for women, for maternity and child welfare clinics, for basic education, for creches, for nursery schools, for schools, for cottage industries, for the removal of untouchability, for rural uplift and all other social reform. They would not or should not meet with the opposition which we have to come up against in British India owing to official prejudice. I know how much has been done in certain States in the matter of housing, rural uplift and even for the removal of untouchability and the development of handicrafts. But it is a drop in the ocean. The gulf between the rulers and the ruled is too wide. It is up to the Princesses to try to bridge it. If they took the lead they would find many women in the States to work with them. That only socialized States will be able to exist in the future is a lesson that our Princes would be well advised to learn from now. How marvellous it would be for them if by reason of their service to their subjects they could unanimously be elected to remain at ·the heads of their State governments!

Internationalism

It is but natural while we are struggling for our own freedom that the manifold problems of our own country should absorb all our energy and thought. But we cannot afford not to look beyond our borders. The world has been narrowed down by means of scientific discoveries which have willynilly drawn us nearer to each other. Two successive world wars have also shown that the actions of one nation have repercussions far beyond its neigbours. More over humanity is one inspite of its varying nationalities and if there is to be peace we must strive to bring into being a world where there shall be goodwill. The colour bar, the mad lust for domination can only disappear if human values are appraised higher than material gain. There is something radically wrong with the entire structure of human relationship that makes man delight in killing man whether it be in the name of civilisation or religion or anything else. Two wrongs do not make a right, hatred must beget hatred and what is brought into being by violence can and will always be destroyed by greater violence. It is this fundamental truth that women have got to bring home to the people in their respective countries. No peace treaties can avail that have revenge as their basis and a self-righteous arrogance and hypocrisy in the so-called victors. Women are the natural preserves of life. Life grows from within them. They could make their influence felt if they would be big enough to rise above the walls of narrow nationalism that confine us today. Just as communism calls to the workers of the world to unite, let us women of the world unite and stake our all for a life worth living. Love conquers all things. We have it in us to give if we could only realize our moral strength and non-co-operative with violence in whatsoever form it raises its head.

I do not suppose that I have said anything new for any one of my co-workers but inasmuch as few of us are giving ourselves as whole-heartedly to service as we should, I hope my words may have some effect and give some help to those who have felt frustrated or who do not know where and how to commence. Above all I trust my appeal to the young to gird themselves for service will not go in vain. I know that placed as we are under a foreign rule which has sapped our mentality and done inestimable harm to us if not ruined us morally, materially and culturally we can do little until we are free from the chains of slavery. But freedom will come to us as surely as the darkness of the darkest night vanishes at dawn and it is for preparing ourselves for that great day that I appeal for giving and more giving of ourselves. The future can only be ours if we work for it here and now without a moment's delay. The past has its lessons for us, the future its hopes, but the hopes can never fructify if we let slip the shining hours of the present. When the great day dawns and our own government looks for servants ready to go forth at its bidding to banish all that is bad and usher in all that will conduce to the greatest good of the greatest number, let it not be said of us, women, that when we should have been working hard to uproot the weeds that were choking our growth we stood by idle. Ours is a rich inheritance. Let us prove ourselves worthy of it.

> In the Gandhian concept of society women had a definite and important role. As a close associate and devoted follower of Gandhiji and as a woman with a fine blend of Indian and Western culture, Rajkumari Amrit Kaur is one of the very few who are well qualified to speak on this subject, to which she does full justice in her broadcast talk on the All India Radio network on Gandhi Jayanti day, October 2, 1953.

WOMEN IN A GANDHIAN SOCIETY

It may be said without fear of contradiction that no leader in history commanded during his lift-time whether at home or abroad, the immense following that Gandhiji did. And certainly no man evoked such whole-hearted devotion from women. The reason is not far to seek. A passionate lover of humanity, an implacable foe of injustice in whatsoever form or sphere, it is small wonder that he early espoused the woman's cause for, in spite of the unrivalled culture and high ideals of society ancient India placed before us, we had unfortunately fallen far from fact that happy estate and one of our big tragedies was the fact that women instead of being man's equal and co-sharer and helpmeet, became his subordinate. Throughout his long life of service Gandhiji never hesitated, whenever opportunity offered, to preach against the wrongs done to women in the name of law, tradition and even religion. He spoke strongly against enforced widowhood, against purdah, against the dedication of girls to temples, against prostitution, against early marriage, against the dowry system, against the economic and marital bondage of women.

"Man and woman are equal in status". "I am uncompromising in the matter of woman's rights. In my opinion she should labour under no legal disability and suffered by man. I should treat daughters and sons on a footing of perfect equality". "It is sad to think that the Smritis contain texts which can command no respect from men who cherish the liberty of woman as their own and who regard her as the mother of the race". "The saying attributed to Manu that 'for woman there can be no freedom' is not to me sacrosant"—these are but a few lines from the many Bapu wrote on behalf of suppressed womankind and are witness of his burning desire to see woman restored to her natural and rightful place in society.

In the freedom struggle, in his own institutions and programmes of work, her invariably gave equal place to women and nothing delighted him more than the success of women in any sphere.

Those of us who had the rare privilege of coming close to him and of learning from him found in him not only a wise father but what was far more precious a mother before whose all-embracing and understanding love all fear and restraint always vanished.

"Woman is the embodiment of sacrifice and suffering" was the immensely high tribute he paid to our sex. But with all his championship of the woman's cause, all his generous appraisement of the virtues of their sex and appreciation of their difficulties, he was equally uncompromising in what he expected from them and he was a severe critic of the weaknesses that had crept into the mind of woman whereby she had willingly subordinated herself to man.

He held that the laws of nature were wise and fair and that while woman was made frail as compared physically with man, she had been endowed with a moral strength which was at once her crowning glory and her fortress against all attack and temptations.

He was old-fashioned enough to believe that woman's greatest service to society lay in her as mother of the race. Woman's place was primarily in the home where she was charged with the heavy responsibility of keeping the home pure, a place radiating love and happiness and of bringing up offspring in the proper way. At the same time he was modern enough to believe that woman was eligible in every way to work in all spheres other than in the fighting forces and more than that he was of opinion that they should be given the chance of shouldering responsibility in all constructive activity. And if, as he held, the Government itself was the main vehicle of constructive activity in a Welfare State, there was no reason at all why the highest office in the land should not be held by a woman.

There was, therefore, no difference, in Gandhiji's opinion between the place of man and woman in society. The one was complementary to the other. Neither could do without the other and there were certain spheres which were specially woman's and in which she should be proud to excel.

That women in general and Indian women, in particular, have to remember today when we celebrate the birthday of the Father of the Nation is not so much about our so-called rights but our duties. He told me once that there was no item on his constructive programme in which women could not play a leading part—indeed he expected them to do so and just as they came forward in their thousands in response to his call to take part in the freedom struggle and just as their contribution during this glorious page of Indian history has won for them equal political rights with man, I believe Gandhiji calls today to every daughter of the poor, the down-trodden and the oppressed and thereby fulfil her real destiny as the embodiment of sacrifice and suffering.

4

Ideal Education for Women and Their Development

I

Happy he
With such a mother! faith in women kind
Beats with his blood, and trust in all things high
Comes easy to him; and tho' he trip and fall,
He shall not blind his soul with clay.
Alfred, Lord Tennyson
in Ode on the Death of the Duke of Wellington.

I speak from a country whose women today are steeped in ignorance. Poverty and ignorance are a natural corollary to foreign domination and these facts are grim realities in India today. Inasmuch as the standard of life and thought of a country depends on the standard of understanding attained by the mothers of the race, woman's education is of vital importance.

Education, if it be real, is one of the greatest gifts of life. It should teach us how to live completely, how to use all our faculties to the greatest advantage of ourselves and others. The goodness of a society ultimately depends on the nature of its citizens and since woman has a special role to play in the rearing of the race it follows that she should first and last be educated to realise the high calling of womankind. If we admit that it is not possible to be a good citizen of the world unless one is a good citizen of one's own country it follows that in the first instance one has to drink deep at the fountain of what is best in the land of one's birth and thereby derive inspiration. Indian traditions of womanhood have from time immemorial taught adherence to duty no matter what the cost and our heroines have been embodiments of that spirit of service and self-sacrifice which springs from unbounded faith. It is for the true development of this spirit that education must strive.

For the child it must begin from even when it is in its mother womb. The way she lives, the thoughts she thinks help or hinder the growth of her offspring to be—for child is made out of the very essence of her body. Marriage is much more than a biological function. It can be successful only if it is entered upon as a sacrament, as a union not of bodies but of souls, and it is the offspring of such marriages that will be the best progeny that good parents can offer to the State. A child can only prosper if the soil in which it is nurtured is properly cultivated and tended and this early training can best be performed by the mother. The domestic sphere is woman's special, domain where she can find ample scope for fullest development. Indeed motherhood is in itself a vocation, and training for it must be given first place in the education of our girls. Women the world over have to ask themselves as to how far they are to blame for that prostitution of marriage which, by lowering the moral standards or society, has in reality injured most their own sex. There is no gainsaying the fact that usage and custom has dealt harshly with women. They have had to submit to man-made laws. But inasmuch as submission to superior physical force invariably means the lack of inner strength in him who submits, women must turn the searchlight inwards and strive to develop that latent force within, which can at once give the lie to the doctrine that might is right. The proper training of the young is, therefore, a heavy responsibility which woman may not shirk. Rather it should be a proud privilege for which we must train girls so that they may be able in turn to impart to their children that training in goodness which produces "in the youth a passionate love and desire of becoming a perfect citizen, knowing how to be just whether as ruler or as ruled". No education gives a proper education for citizenship which does not strike the inner chords of nature. It is the heart that chooses for the mind and it is the moral feelings of an individual and therefore, of society or a people that should be their main safeguard. Moral quality should take precedence over mental and there can be little doubt that a good character is the result or both heredity and early environment. The family being the social unit of mankind it is the woman who has to create the home atmosphere which provides the necessary discipline. She must foster virtue, the spirit of service and sacrifice, charity, industry and love that loves for love's sake and knows no distinction of caste, creed or race.

Since no person may be a burden on society, girls must be brought up to realise the dignity of labour. Basic education in India as propounded by Mahatma Gandhi has gone a step farther than learning by doing. It means learning through a craft and has been accepted by our government as the basis of all future education here. The experiment is in its infancy but such results as have been achieved up to date augur well for its success. Self-help is not an expedient. It is a principle and if India is able, as I hope she will be, to evolve a social structure based on non-violent village economy which will enable her to be self-sufficient in regard to her primary needs, basic education will not have played a small part in achieving this consummation. The dignity of labour does not depend on the nature of the work done nor on the remuneration it carries but on the motive power behind that work.

Women have been the best custodians of culture in all countries. Culture in the highest sense connotes that which has been acquired by man in the moral and spiritual domain. It connotes beauty and is not beauty truth and goodness? Girls must be well-versed in the history, literature and art of their countries. They must be educated to be wise enough to conserve what is good and strong enough to uproot what is bad.

Discipline and co-operation are lessons that must be learnt early in life.

Inasmuch as the State is a political association good government is a factor of the highest importance. Girls must be educated to make their contribution to good government. They have to be intimately acquainted with prevailing conditions. They must stand fearlessly for the righting of wrongs. Loyalty to the general good or, in other words, to truth must transcends loyalty to party. By means of their loyalty to the higher values women must contribute towards the creation of a healthy public opinion. For them at any rate, politics may not be a dirty game. True citizenship is always inconsistent with personal or party selfishness. There is no room in it for narrow racialism which breed mistrust and hatred between man and man, and no sacrifice should be deemed too great for a citizen to make for the honour and freedom of mankind.

If girls are educated in the lore of good citizenship of their own land they will instinctively become good world citizens. Two world wars in the life of one single generation have left the world prostrate. Pious platitudes of making a better world by world leaders without a strong condemnation of the way of life which has made the holocausts possible are not going to lead humanity anywhere. Punishment of so-called war criminals, humbling to the dust of the defeated nations, drawing up on paper of charters of freedom are not the remedy. Women have a glorious opportunity today to join hands on a common platform and say that they, at any rate, do not believe in and will not co-operate in that which goes to make war. Wars are the outcome of national greed, of narrow nationalism which seeks its own, regardless of human values. Experience of war shows that women indulge in race hatred and prejudices just as much as men and thereby dishonour the best in them. They who should by very reason of their sex be gentle and merciful throw these qualities to the winds and subscribe to the doctrine that war is the final arbiter of man's fate. Is the root cause of this the fact that they have for centuries allowed themselves to submit to physical force? Let us pause and think. No amount of charters of freedom or political and civic rights are going to bring women into their own. Only the realisation of the latent power within will uplift and strengthen them. No mere intellectual preparation, however all embracing, will suffice. Something much deeper is needed, something that inspires, something that stirs the noblest sentiments. The rejection of religion has been the root cause of all the world's ills. But it may not be the religion of ritual and dogma which has succeeded in dividing man from man. It must be the religion which teaches us to look upon humanity as one. If women make the contribution that they should towards making their own State a great moral agency they will see to it that no injustices exists in any sphere of life. If selfless devotion and the spirit of sacrifice are their badge they must cling to the only anchor that holds, the anchor of non-violence. That alone can bring about that spiritual comradeship among women united for the world's good. The world would not then witness the tragedy of the Jews nor the iniquitous treatment of Indians in South Africa and the colour prejudices everywhere that would relegate whole sections to perpetual domination by the so-called powerful nations. Arming for further warfare by the nations would cease. Science would be turned to constructive instead of destructive use. But all this requires that woman should first find herself. It is this faith in the ideals of womankind that must be unculcated in girls from their infant years so that they may be fitted to turn ideals into realities.

"The soul's armour is never well set to the heart unless a woman's hand has braced it! and it is only when she braces it loosely, that the honour of manhood fails!"

II

Rajkumari Amrit Kaur's Convocation Address to the Government College for women, Amritsar, delivered on March 8, 1952, brings out her clear-cut views on the part that educated women have to play in India life—a life of dedicated service in the fields of health, medicine, hygiene, education and the like. It is for them, she says, to give a lead to their untutored sisters to take their proper place in shaping the destinies of the nation.

EDUCATED WOMAN

It is always a pleasure to me to come in contact with youth and particularly the student world. As a social worker and a champion of many years standing of the women's cause, I am naturally more than keen on proper and increased facilities for the education of our girls. No country can really progress in the real sense of the term if the calibre of the mothers of the race is not up to the mark and we have to admit that Indian women by reason of the harsh treatment meted out to them over centuries by custom, law and usage have literally become victims of ignorance and superstition. From this well of darkness we have to rescue them and bring them into the light which is the birth-right of every citizen of a free country. Perhaps no country has given to the world such high ideals of womanhood as India. If you turn to the pages of our ancient scriptures, epics and mythology, you will find the story of heroines and goddesses, perhaps more beautiful ideologically and more worthy of worship and adoration than those in any other country. Further I believe that today too, as was shown by the fine part played by women in the freedom struggle they are filled with an incomparable spirit of devotion to duty and self-sacrifice. The recent elections and the number of women that exercised the vote surpassed all expectations. This too shows that women even in the rural areas are awake and alive, anxious to shoulder responsibility, desirous of education for themselves and their children and keen to improve their living conditions.

With the field as ready as it is for cultivation, it is but meet and right that the handful of Indian women who are educated should pause and think how they can contribute the maximum effort towards the work which is only waiting for labourers. I am, therefore young friends, going to put before you today some of the thoughts that arise in me. First of all what is the primary aim of education? I believe it is to achieve what Plato called the "good", what Jesus Christ described as the Kingdom of Heaven and in our own times what Mahatma Gandhi has named Ram Rajya. If we have this ideal of education in our minds then surely the knowledge we are out to achieve will be the key to the secret of a life worthwhile. Life is a challenge at all times and therefore a quest for the knowledge which can strengthen man to put himself in tune with the world around, with its laws and the Creator. In this quest, which certainly does not end with education in either school or college but continues throughout life, man has to find himself in order to be able rightly to appraise life's values. In any event if true education is the expounding of the art of living, I have a feeling that our educational institutions do not give to this facet the emphasis is deserves. It was for this reason that Gandhiji broke away from the stereo-typed system of education and presented 'basic education' to us, which was not for children only but was meant by him to extend to the entire gamut of learning. And he placed this emphasis on his idealogy because basic education glorifies human labour and bears witness to culture and to religion by inculcating in the student from his earliest years the basis of well doing or creative living.

It has seemed to me that our schools and colleges prepare our youth for professions perhaps, or for passing examinations or various subjects without always creating within their hearts and minds that motivation or that urge to contribute an essential service to the community. In other words, whatever, profession one may or may not adopt, it will be worth nothing if all the knowledge we have gained is not looked upon as a vocation and vocations can never be divided into classes. The humblest manual worker is contributing just as much if not more than the most learned scholar towards the general good. Indeed one has to pause and think whether the most fundamental or the deepest truths of life are not found more often through hard manual labour than through book-learning alone.

Some one has rightly asked the question whether in the stress and strain of modern life which scarcely gives one time to pause, in a world where we are becoming more and more mechanised, we have not lost the art, as it were, or how to blend doing, knowing and being in order not only to have a balanced life and personality for the individual but also to create that spirit of integration in the community, in the nation and indeed in the world, which alone can bring into being an atmosphere of peace. I would like you young people in any event to look upon all that you imbibe here in the way of knowledge as a trust for use for the betterment of life not only for yourself but for your fellow human beings. We live in a complex world. Our own country too is full of problems. Wherever or whenever life is extra difficult it should not make us down-hearted. Rather should is spur us to greater effort, greater united effort to surmount the difficulties and hardships which face us.

Our Constitution has given women the right to take our place shoulder to shoulder with men. But in order to do so we have to have not only the same standards of education but that education must give our girls more self-confidence and more independence of mind. I believe that if women will bring into public life, in fact into "the daily round, the common task" those virtues which are particularly theirs, the virtues of humility, self-control, reverence and above all love, they will certainly contribute greatly towards the remoulding or salvaging of civilisation which stands in danger of complete annihilation if we have another war.

There are so many avenues of service open to us. If every one of the girls who are studying today in all the colleges of India were to become teachers, nurses or doctors they could all serve the country in these vital spheres and we should still not be able to fulfil our needs. Therefore I would like to appeal to the girls of this College and through them to their sisters in other similar institutions that if every educated girl would pledge herself to give at least three years of service to the country before marriage in any of the professions I have mentioned, it would give to us an unceasing flow of workers who are today of vital importance to progress. Ours is a land of universal marriage but inasmuch as marriage is not an end in itself there is no reason at all why even after marriage our women should not take up part time work whether on a voluntary or a paid basis.

I often wonder whether educated girls brought up in cities realise even the fringe of the needs of our country—that is to say of rural India. If they could see the distress, the want, and the ignorance and superstition which aggravate that distress and want, perhaps they would be inspired to make some sacrifice for those who have not had a chance in life. The cry for schools and hospitals from the men, women and children in Himachal Pradesh haunts me. We have almost got into the habit of putting the blame for all our woes on the lack of money. My experience tells me that it is not so much money that is needed for reform and progress as the will to do and workers.

So, young friends, let us turn the searchlight inward and ask ourselves what we are doing and what we are going to do to better our condition. Where reform is concerned cannot you and our brothers determine not to marry until the girl is at least eighteen and the boy earning his livelihood; cannot you both refuse to marry where dowries are demanded? You would, even with these two reforms, contribute enormously to the problem of population control and to the amelioration of the unhappy state of mind of parents who are often brow-beaten into producing large dowries. Cannot you banish untouchability in practice by serving Harijans? Cannot you help with manual labour in the growing of food, making of roads, sinking of wells, removal of illiteracy, domiciliary service as doctors, nurses and teachers to the poor areas of cities and villages? I could go on for hours telling you of the hundreds of ways in which you can serve India today. Governments can accommodate only a certain number in their accredited services but the service of the masses can embrace every one of you. What does India need today? She needs the love, the burning passionate love of her youth, the hard work, the enthusiasm, the zeal born of true patriotism. And who possesses all these in greater measure than youth? As Health Minister I want nurses, doctors, health visitors, masseurs, medico-social workers who will relieve the monotony of the life of patients, village health workers, experts in nutrition, research workers. There is as much demand in the field of education as there is in health. Further we want architects, builders and technicians. Why may not the immense needs of building appeal to women just as much to men? Indeed I always feel that women should by instinct design better dwellings than men and what about the contribution women can make to the fine arts? Opportunities for every bent of mind are there waiting to be seized. I wish you well and I pray that each one of you may be enabled to fit herself for being a true soldier in India's battle against poverty, disease and ignorance. "The undertaking of creative work in a spirit of service is an essential condition for a good life" and never before is the call to "love one's neighbour as oneself" more urgently needed than today. "With bowed heads and open hearts may we offer ourselves. We can do no more and we dare do no less".

III

Rajkumari Amrit Kaur has decided views on the role of women in life. Here she discusses military training for women.

I confess to a sense of sorrow at the increasing desire in women to go in for military training. In one sense this cannot be wondered at because the recent tragic happenings have shown that anger arouses the lowest passions in man and when he is thus roused his first victims are women. The abducting of women and children constitute a grave stigma on our society and think that we have to resort to police and military aid to relieve these human beings is truly humiliating. When anger and passions have cooled down it should surely be possible for the guilty to atone for the errors of their ways by voluntary return of their erstwhile prey. In any event women are scared and they want to be able to protect themselves and with the majority of mankind they imagine they will be safer and stronger if they know how to use firearms.

Military training which disciplines them, which teaches them cooperative endeavour, which gives them lessons in First Aid and Ambulance work in the field, which will make them self-reliant and fearless, is all to the good. But for women to want to learn the use of firearms goes against the best traditions of all that the ancient culture and civilization of the womankind of every land have stood for. I would like to draw the attention of my sisters to the lesson Gandhiji taught us during his long ministry on earth. Sita, as he often used to say, withstood the might of Ravana not through any earthly weapons but because of her unassailable purity. Women will, I hope, always rely on their strength of character and soul force and not give up the way of non-violence, not only for the sake of their own sex but for the sake of the country and the world.

5

Social Service : Her Main Inspiration of Life

I

An All-India body of Social Workers was established in 1947 and an All-India Conference of Social Work was held in December of 1948. Rajkumari Amrit Kaur in her address from the President's Chair stressed the importance of social and sociological problems that face the country which would be difficult to tackle of only voluntary effort were to be relied upon. She, therefore, advocated the employment of paid workers who could work with missionary zeal and supplement the work of voluntary workers.

"As soon as public service ceases to be the chief business of the citizens, and they would rather serve with their money than with their persons, the State is not far from its fall."

Jean Jacques Rousseau

Men and women inspired with the zeal for reform have both individually and collectively, for many years past devoted their lives to this great cause. In an ancient country such as ours and which has gone through so many vicissitudes it is no matter for surprise that evil customs should have crept in and that growing poverty, ignorance and disease should have submerged the general mass of the population to such an extent as to render them unable to think for themselves or extricate themselves from the darkness which has enveloped them. The coming into being of this Conference of social workers, as I see it, is with a view to coordinate, intensify, expand and give guidance to all existing endeavour in this most important domain rather than become another one in the long list of existing organisations. The need for an agency of this nature is, in my opinion, very vital if we are to harness to the best advantage our limited resources and put an end to the overlapping of work.

Political independence has come to us and brought in its wake immense problems which need courage, faith and joint endeavour on our part if they are to be solved in due course and in the proper way. You held your first meeting when the influx of refugees into India was at its peak. To meet the immediate needs of these poor human beings was a stupendous task in itself but to rehabilitate them permanently is an even bigger problem requiring all our energy and resourcefulness, both mental and material as also moral. It is a rare opportunity for social services.

Social service is an all-inclusive term and cannotes a very wide variety of work to all who care to devote themselves to it. In our country in particular there is an infinite range and so staggering is the immensity of the task that one does not know whether to begin. For, if we are honest with ourselves, we will have to admit that all our best endeavour so far has merely touched the fringe of our requirements. It was only natural that social workers should, in the main, have been drawn from among the small educated minority of men and women living in the cities and that their endeavours should have been limited to their immediate vicinity. To find both means and leisure for volunteer work is not always an easy task for those who have their own occupations and yet India can proudly count many of her sons and daughters as reformers and social workers of first rank, second to none in the world, who have lit the torch of social reform, broken through out-moded custom and tradition, and ploughed their way across other insuperable difficulties simply by means of their vision, courage and faith. It is in the wake of these honoured ones, the giant among them being our beloved Gandhiji of ever blessed memory, that we have to try to follow.

It will be my humble endeavour today not to dilate on the need for social service which is an accepted axiom but to place before you my views as to how this Conference can best tackle the gigantic tasks which confront it. The field is immense but the labourers are few. Therefore, the first problem that arises is from where and how to get the workers. Up till now our work has been more or less confined to cities and the workers have been honorary. Voluntary endeavour must by its very nature very according to the time the honorary worker can give. I have long been of opinion that if we are to make rapid headway in organised social service, we must have paid workers. This does not mean that there is no to room for the honorary worker. Social service will always need honorary workers for inspiration and guidance will naturally come from them. To obtain the right type of paid workers we must recruit from among those who are willing to accept only a living wage and are prepared to undergo hardship and inconvenience—in other words, the paid service must also be composed of men and women who are fired with missionary zeal for a cause, in dedication to which they believe they are rendering the truest service to the country. For such workers we need to have training schools. It will perhaps not to difficult for such centres to be established in our cities or even in our factory areas. Much work can be done here but if we admit, as we must, that India is primarily an agricultural country and a land of villages we must concentrate more and more on training centres in village areas in order to draw workers from the villages themselves. If our national edifice is to be built on sound foundations we have to start all our work from the primary unit of our social structure which is the village.

I have said that social service is an all-inclusive term. Truth to tell, if we have rightly understood the meaning of our political independence every adult is, or should be, a social servant inasmuch as he should endeavour to live well and do his duty in whatsoever sphere of life he is placed by Fate. Good citizenship connotes social service. The government itself, it is of the people, is the biggest agency for social service in any State for it takes upon itself the duty of catering to the needs of the people committed to its charge. In the past, dictated as the policies of Government primarily were by foreign interests, social service was looked upon as something wholly distinct from what the Government was doing for the people. Indeed reformers and Congress workers, in particular, were often in conflict with authority where really these should have been no conflict. But now the picture has completely changed. The Government is ours and it is for social workers to help it in the carrying out of welfare plans and for the Government to make the fullest use of those who are capable of rendering intelligent and useful service. The question of a conflict of interests cannot now arise and the social worker can therefore go forward with confidence, believing that he is required and valued both by the Government and the people. Friends, our responsibilities are very great. We have literally to begin from scratch, as it were, in every sphere. To combat ignorance, poverty and disease is no easy task when these are spectres stalking the entire land. Our national Government at the Centre has been faced with calamity after calamity ever since it came into being. Other difficulties apart, the economic crisis is by no means over for we have to meet inordinate expenditure on refugees and defence which leaves next to nothing for our programmes of development, to the putting into action of which we had all been ardently looking forward from the moment we gained our political independence. In all our work, therefore, we are, for some time to come, going to be handicapped by very limited resources, both financial and human.

I have been among those who have always wished that there might be departments for social service both at the Centre and in the Provinces. I am still of that opinion. But these departments may not think in terms of holding office in the secretariats of our capital cities. It is not paper work that is needed for social service but men and women who will gain their experience in the vast field of endeavour and thereby be in a position to give guidance and inspiration to others. I have spoken of training centres in villages. One medical man, one public health man, one woman doctor, one health visitor, one nurse, one male teacher, one woman teacher, one veterinary doctor, one agriculturist, one spinner, one weaver, all expert at their professions and filled with the spirit of service would be enough to reform an entire village or a group of neighbouring villages. If this Conference of Social Work could, in this second year of its life, get together a band of workers such as I have mentioned above I am sure it will be generally admitted, even after a year's labours, that the attempt has been worthwhile. Is see no reason whatsoever why, in whichever area the Conference is able to choose to begin their work, the Government of the Province concerned should not only give them the land required for putting up village huts for these poineers but put up the requisite dwellings for them and give them a living wage. Once they have won the confidence of the villager—which they will surely do if they serve them in the true spirit—the opportunities for service will widen and the good seed sown is bound to take root and grow into something big. In course of time it should not be beyond the bounds of possibility to envisage a group of such workers being supported to a large if not to full extent by the villages themselves. Love and service are ever the best magnets. They connote the true missionary zeal which does not recognise defeat, which is capable of infinite sacrifice and which is therefore ensured of success in the long run.

Our people are ignorant of the laws of life and fall an easy prey to disease. I am quite certain that if in both city and village they were made aware of how essential it is to good health to live cleanly, if they were taught the A.B.C. of hygiene and sanitation, if they knew how to extract the best food values even from their meagre dietary, if mothers were educated in the proper care of themselves and their children and taught all the other lessons, so simple to those of us who have known them from childhood but which are unknown to the general mass, we should be combating illness and epidemics in a practical manner. It is a tragedy that in an age when such means as the radio and the cinema and travelling dispensary have made aural and visual education so easy to impart, our country is sadly lacking in health education, indeed in all education and general knowledge.

It is neither right nor possible to give priority to any one nation-building activity over the other for all are vital and indissolubly linked one with the other. There can be no health without food, without education and without proper housing and sanitation and no equitable distribution without proper communications and so on. But I do wish to emphasise with all the earnestness at my command that if the health of the nation continues to remain at the present-day low level, and indeed continues to deteriorate, there can be no hope of progress. The sick and the hungry child cannot learn, the sick and hungry adult cannot produce. Diseases consequent on malnutrition and under-nutrition, bad housing, lack of sanitation and sewerage are spreading rapidly. The general social worker can do yeoman service on this preventive side which is equally if not more important than the curative and if medical personnel put their shoulders to the wheel and were content to use their talents as best as circumstances permit in the remotest corners of the land we should certainly be making progress in a living way. I often wonder when I receive requests for scholarships to study overseas whether the best post-graduate courses for the majority of our young doctors and teachers also are not in our villages, whether the man who performs an operation in a village hut without much except his own resourcefulness and spirit of service to sustain him or the man who teaches without books or blackboard is not performing a bigger deed than he who has all the advantages of modern science and equipment at his side in a city hospital or school. We could banish leprosy from our country if we could have enough colonies for sufferers from this disease and segregate the children. This calls for workers with the lamp of compassion and love burning brightly in their hearts. Colonies for convalescents from tuberculosis are an urgent need too for this disease is a growing menace and without such colonies there is little chance of full recovery for T.B. patients. Neither of these need much money but they do need workers and skilled farmers and handicraftmen. And what of homes for destitutes for delinquents, for defective children and for the blind? All these need the care and attention which have not been theirs up till now. The beggar problem not only persists but seems to be growing. The animal in man has not yet been exorcised and social diseases have infected as many as 37 per cent, of the population. The vast mass of our people still lives in hovels and there is no city that is without slums.

It is doubtless the duty of the State to begin in right earnest to tackle all these questions and no government today but would like to do all in their power for social progress. Many Provinces have with faith and courage embarked on Prohibition inspite of loss of revenues thus showing their desire for the moral well-being of the populace. But their financial resources are limited and I have no doubt that Conferences such as this one have to be content to make a beginning such as I have suggested. Self-help is ever the best help. An all inclusive group of social workers can do a tremendous lot without much expense to the State; they can banish ignorance and disease to a larger extent in their area and they will themselves constitute the best training centre for the village worker for they will inspire in him the spirit of self help.

You must all have read of the appeal which I have recently had the privilege of putting out on behalf of India's children. In the Western hemisphere children are given first priority. If there is danger in times of war, it is they who are removed at once from the danger zone; if there is lack of food and milk they are the only ones who, as far as possible, are not allowed to suffer; their education and their health are never neglected. But even while everyone recognises that children constitute the wealth and hope of a nation there is little that we are able to do for our offspring. I do hope this appeal will find a warm response in the heart of every adult in the land. There is no reason why every man and every woman should not willingly give one or two rupees a month for the welfare of their children. If they are given practical proof that this donation will mean a daily free meal including milk to every poor child to begin with in our schools, recreation parks for women and children and creches for babies while their mothers are working, they will, I am sure, willingly subscribe. Children are a woman's special heritage and I rely on them to make the children's fund not only a resounding success as far as this first appeal is concerned, but a permanent feature of social service, an all-India structure in the highest and truest sense of the term.

I have mentioned many fields of work. As a matter of fact, Gandhiji's pamphlet on the Constructive Programme is a classic for social work and the organizations which he founded are there to be helped by all who believe that in service of that nature and through those agencies lies our salvation. I would commend to this Conference with all possible emphasis that if we wish to build a worthy memorial to this great son of India to whom we owe an irrepayable debt we can best do so by keeping alive his activities and building on the foundations so well and truly laid by him.

Then there is the question of high prices. These in their turn lead to an endless demand on the part of labour for increased wages. Cannot social workers offer their services and run Government food, cloth and other essential commodity depots where the populace can get the necessities of life at controlled rates? It seems to me to be one definite way of getting rid of blackmarketing and the ugly profiteering that goes on unabashed today. Government must procure the commodities and this work could begin straightaway in the cities. As regards rural India, if we follow Gandhiji's village economy the villager need never be in want.

I would also like to draw the attention of this Conference to the urgent necessity of bringing into being both village and city co-operatives. These will not only make life easier for the people but also create that spirit of co-operation so essential for the general well-being.

I may not detain you any longer. It is for the workers assembled to draw up a programme of work for the ensuing year on which they can embark at once. An annual conference is good only in so far as it enables us to exchange ideas and learn from each other's experiences. It is practical work in the field that is needed and I hope that it will be possible for us during this year to lay the foundations of a Sevagram in every Province and State.

In conclusion may I refer to the crying need for the raising of standards of integrity. They have fallen as they always do during any upheaval. It is up to the social worker to set and demand standards of truth and love in all our dealings with each other. Political independence means and must always mean added responsibilities. No right but involves a corresponding duty. Independence was won for us under the banner of Truth and Non-violence. If we fall away from those eternal verities we do so at our peril. The need for adherence to these today not only in our own country but in the entire world is of paramount importance. Our State is a newborn infant. To make its environment such as will help it to grow strong and healthy, is the duty of every loyal citizen. There is much within the body politic today that is hampering this growth. Bribery and corruption, nepotism, narrow provincialism, indiscipline, ever-increasing demands on the financial resources of the State without any constructive effort to strengthen the same, love of power and office rather than of service, selfish exploitation of the ignorant, all such need to be uprooted. Joint endeavour, harnessing of all our limited resources for the general good are absolutely essential if we want a stable and efficient government.

A vast field of adult education lies open to the social worker today. Our constitution is on the anvil. Soon electoral rolls will be prepared and those on it called to vote. If every social worker devoted himself to nothing but the task of educating the voter from today onwards he would be rendering an immeasurable service to the State.

The lot of the social worker is a hard but nevertheless a glorious one. His road winds uphill all the way. There is no promotion for him in his service in the accredited sense of the term. He works in unknown haunts; his is often a lone endeavour and it may be that he will never see its fruit. But India calls and calls in special measure to her youth to enter into the arena and fight against all that darkens, all that cramps, all that retards, all that divides. "The race is not to the swift, nor the battle to the strong." The victory is to those who with aching hands and bleeding feet dig and heap and lay stone on stone, and who cheerfully bear the burden and the heat of the long long day. The challenge is there. We dare not refuse to take it up. May God give every son and daughter of India the courage, the strength, and the faith to find their freedom in selfless service of this dear land and through her of the world.

"Thou hast not failed! Where holy love and truth
Contend with Evil, failure cannot be!
Their sorest scars claim reverence, not ruth.—
Their worst repulse is still a victory!"

II

In her Convocation address to the Tata Institute of Social Sciences, delivered on December 3, 1950, Rajkumari Amrit Kaur appeals to the youth of India to make the social service ideal their goal in life. She appeals to the trained workers to help the untrained volunteer to give of his best.

The Tata Institute was founded from the benefactions of the Tata family which, in the words of Rajkumari "has been one of those families who have made themselves known all over India, indeed all over the world, for their contribution not only in the field of industry but also in wider field of humanitarian endeavour. Among the many institutions for human welfare that have been founded by them, the Tata Institute of Social Sciences must take a very high place. It was apparent to all that India needed social service but it was indeed a clear vision that foresaw the need for organising social work in a scientific manner."

IDEALS OF SOCIAL SERVICE

"Religion was nearly dead because there was no longer real belief in future life; but something was struggling to take its place—service—social service—the ant's creed, the bees' creed.

John Galsworthy
in Over the River

In a country where there had been an awakening after an age-long sleep, it was perhaps only natural that social reformers should spring up and inspire others to work for that reform which a cramped and custom-ridden society had to undertake, if the country were to progress. Philanthropy came into the picture as it always should and does, and many voluntary societies undertook work with incomparable zeal and devotion. But as so often happens with voluntary endeavour, especially when it is pioneer, work is often organised in a haphazard and unscientific manner and this has happened and continues to happen even today in our country.

India, as I have often said before, is a dry and thirsty land panting for the cooling and refreshing waters of devoted service. For this service we need qualified personnel. As in all progress in every sphere in the past few centuries it has been the West that has pioneered so also it is they who have stressed the necessity for the introduction of high standards of training for social workers. Indeed, in a scientific age, social service has been recognised as a science. Applied Sociology, Psychiatry, Applied Economics, Applied Psychology, Case Work, Group Work, Public Welfare Administration, Criminology, Correctional Administration are terms familiar to all students of social science. Study and practical research in these subjects have developed in an amazing manner and are daily adding to the knowledge of techniques and specialisation which help to create new fields of human learning. It is a recognised fact that in no field of work can there be progress without due attention being paid to the human entity. It is obvious, therefore, that in a country which is preeminently in need of social service, every endeavour must be made to find the personnel that will fulfil that need. We must accept the scientific approach which is at all times the practical and creative approach and which will enable us to serve in a special manner our special needs. It is for this reason that all lovers of Indian well-being must rejoice that we have an Institution of high standing in this great city of ours and that both Baroda and Delhi Universities have recently sponsored similar institutions within their jurisdiction.

We have had the good fortune to have produced during the last century social reformers of a high order and there have been, still are, in our country many men and women, both known and unknown, who have sacrificed their all in the cause of social service. But ours is an immense task and workers are few. There is therefore at all times a need to coordinate all our resources both financial and administrative as also of leadership, so that none may be wasted. It is immensely important for us to raise the social and economic status of the social worker. This is particularly necessary in the difficult situation in which we today find ourselves. Time was when volunteer effort was forthcoming without much difficulty. Volunteers were drawn from the ranks of the well-to-do educated classes. But now those who were well-to-do are no longer affluent enough to provide for themselves the necessary resources. Again those who are willing to serve often do not know how or where to find an outlet for the satisfaction of their urge. Time and again too the capacity to serve adequately is absent because of the lack of training. Owing to financial stringency, Governments too are, in the unhappy position of being unable to absorb all the material at their disposal.

Nevertheless whatever difficulties there are have to be surmounted. If we acknowledge the need for social workers, we acknowledge also the need for training them. The workers trained in this and similar institutions are, it must be remembered, persons of post-graduate qualifications. They are builders of society, men and women well equipped to weave a new pattern of society. As such, they are not one whit less important than the teacher, the doctor, the nurse, the administrator or those who go into the Police or the Armed Forces. Their field of work, though specialised, is extremely varied. They work in labour areas, they work for family and child welfare, in schools, in hospitals, in camps, in fact they are there to lend a helping hand in times of distress and to show people how to live in normal times. They fulfil a definite need even in the most socially advanced countries in the world, as such, they should be given the economic security and status that is their due. I have seen for myself during the three years that I have had the privilege of serving the country in the cause of health what a very important part the social worker can play in the hospital, in the sanatorium, in colonies and in health propaganda in the village. Their help is invaluable both on the preventive and curative side. And I know that this will apply equally in the cause of education, of labour welfare, of maintaining discipline and high standards of public and private morality if the right type of workers are available. I feel, therefore, that there is need for a change of outlook on the part of the State towards the social worker. Social work must be a recognised profession and the welfare and employment of social workers should become increasingly a national responsibility. Facilities should be forthcoming in independent India for the growth of this vital profession. Those who are trained should be registered and I believe that an army of good social workers will stand the country in good stead at all times and be the finest weapon of defence against all outside attack as well as internal disorder. There should be ample room within the aegis of the Ministries of Education and Health for the development of social service through persons trained in the social sciences. The governing bodies of social service agencies should also offer the fullest co-operation and freedom for action to trained social workers. Indeed they must employ them in order to place their work on an orderly basis. In often feel that the money at the disposal of voluntary social service agencies would be far better spent on work in however small an area than on Conference and Committee and office work. Most of us know that what should be done. To find personnel to do it is the problem—a problem which must be tackled forthwith.

Fifteen years is but a brief moment in the life of a country and yet in these few years this Institute has sent out nine batches of graduates, many of whom are now holding responsible posts in their specialised fields. The batch that is going out into service this year will add a few more drops to the stream that will, I sincerely hope, continue to flow unceasingly from here. Yours, young friends, will not be an easy task. Indeed, owing to circumstances beyond our control, life for us all has not been easy ever since we gained our political independence. Our plans for the expansion of our nation-building activities, which would undoubtedly have absorbed men and women of your equipment, have had to be put almost in cold storage, as it were, and I can enter heart and soul into the frustration caused in the minds of our youth who are willing to serve and yet are unable to find employment. But you and I and all of us have to keep burning brightly within us this urge to serve and to believe that it is a long lane that has no turning. In the meantime we must turn our hand to whatever task lies nearest at hand. Political independence means nothing if it does not bring to each one of us the realisation that we have now to shoulder added responsibilities. To make our mar the future lies in our hands and particularly in the hands of youth. The sands in the hour glass of time are running out for many of us who worked for India's independence. We had the priceless privilege of being led by a man of outstanding genius and dynamic goodness. You are the proud possessors of a rich heritage to which this great son of India added unparalleled lustre. He was the ideal social worker. However immersed in political work he never forgot the cry of the hungry, the sick, the downtrodden or the oppressed. Indeed the independence he craved for India was in order to bring relief to suffering humanity and not only the suffering humanity of this land of ours but of the world—for the world is very sick today. For him the constructive programme—and I would like you to make that constructive programme of Gandhiji, (written I so well remember in about six hours on a train journey) your charter. It was the life blood of the Congress. He believed, and he was right, that those who rendered devoted service to the rural population in particular were the real builders of India, far more important from the point of view of bringing in the Kingdom of God on earth than those who were in seats of power or authority. When we cast our eye towards the vast needs of our country, the task of the social worker is indeed an unexplored area. What can we do to protect our masses from exploitation, from disease, from internal feuds, from harmful customs? What can we do for the delinquent and the defective child or for children as a whole, for are not our children our greatest wealth if properly nurtured? What can we do for the beggar, the crippled, the maimed, the aged and the blind? What can we do for the leper or for those who suffer from T.B. who cannot return to full time work? What can we do to rescue the criminal from his crime, the drunkard from the evils of intoxication, and what solace can we give to those in mental distress? What can we do to instil a sense of true citizenship in our people? What can we do to encourage the spirit of co-operative endeavour? What can we do to set and demand high standards of integrity in both private and public life? All this has got to be done and done efficiently. Laws can only take us up to a point. It is the realisation within us of what is good that alone can save us.

I have said that a scientific approach to problem is a correct and practical approach. Nevertheless no amount of scientific knowledge will be of avail to the social worker who does not have in him an unbounded love for humanity and faith in it. Whether you teach people how to live, whether you minister to their needs in any sphere, you will always have to lay yourselves out to understand their difficulties, their limitations. Only by putting yourselves in their position, only by living with them will you be able to give them the right lead and draw them to you. India calls and it is in village India that social workers must find their true calling. On you, who have had the advantage of a post-graduate training, will rest the responsibility of training others and training them in the practical field. There are few graduates but there are countless young men and women willing to graduate in the school of service if only they can receive help and guidance. It is for Institutes like this and those of you who have graduated here to draw up courses of training for the less highly educated but nevertheless eager young souls whose energies may not be allowed to run waste but must be harnessed for the good of humanity.

I wish this Institute many years of expanded and increasingly useful activity and all the new graduates have my special prayers that you may find the richness and beauty of life in your labour of love, that yours may be a vocation and not a profession and that you may be enabled to carry the torch to the people of our land who are in darkness and in suffering. God bless you. Jai Hind.

III

Rajkumari Amrit Kaur's interest in moral and social hygiene and her constructive approach to its manifold problems is well known. Her Presidential Address to the All-India Conference on Moral and Social Hygiene delivered on October 19, 1950 clarifies many of the issues.

THE SOCIAL CANKER

"Not till the sun excludes you, do I exclude you."

Walt Whitman
in "To a Common Prostitute."

However great the emphasis that governments and the press in every country may lay on the pressing nature of economic and political problems, there is no gainsaying the fact that social problems cannot be left to take care of themselves. Their urgency is of equal if not really of greater import, for man cannot live by bread alone. Hence it is that the League of Nations and its successor the United Nations have both decided in their wisdom to finance and maintain the Specialised Agencies which stand for humanitarian endeavour in all spheres of life.

For centuries prostitution was regarded as a necessary evil in Europe. This assumption was based on a false belief that continence was harmful to the average man both physically and psychologically. But with a rapid advance in the science of medicine, psychology and psychiatry, there has been a marked change in the attitude of the West to this major social evil. The theory that prostitution was a necessary evil began to be questioned and was finally openly refuted. As far back as 1905, the German authority on the subject M. Von Gruber wrote :

"There is not a shadow of proof to show that continence is damaging to health." To the continent, continence becomes progressively easier. It is what the sages in every country from time immemorial have advocated. Self restraint in any sphere has never hurt. On the contrary it invariably uplifts."

Medical opinion too is clear that the damages done by self-indulgence "far overshoot in number and gravity any harm attributable to continence."

Another eminent authority on the subject A. Moll write : "I am convinced that the overwhelming majority of persons are not in the least injured by continuous continence whether during youth or afterwards. The longer one is continent, the more readily is continence borne."

The British Social Hygiene Council is of opinion that in the interests of the race and of the individual it is essential that the stability of the family in marriage should be preserved and social habits and customs should be adjusted to this end. No one will deny if marriage is, as it is certainly looked upon by all religious, something very much more than a physical contract between man and woman, that it is in fact a moral partnership undertaken for the upliftment of both and for the future of the race, there is every reason to agree with the findings of the British Council in this respect.

Prostitution must therefore be looked upon as objectionable not only because it leads to the personal demoralization of the prostitute herself and the man who indulges in prostitution but of countless others as well. It is the chief factor in the spread of venereal diseases and this in spite of the modern rapid cures which only serve to lull people into a false sense of security for a cure is not guarantee against future infection.

Prostitution being a potent factor in moral degradation must naturally be associated with other forms of immorality. Hence areas where brothels exist, whether that area is officially segregated or its existence merely ignored, are nearly always scenes of violent crime and disorder.

The theory that by having segregated areas the evil of prostitution is minimized, is quite unfounded. Indeed the opposite has been proved. The League of Nations instituted enquiries concerning international traffic in women and children both in the West and in the East. These enquires were conducted by a special body of experts. It was their task to ascertain the extent to which the system of licensing or recognizing houses of prostitution existed in different countries and whether the so-called "safety measures" attached to the system were fruitful in protecting public health and other against the dangers arising from prostitution. Further the League conducted investigations in an attempt to find out whether in those countries where no such system existed, or where it had been abolished, there had been any unfavourable results.

The first report published in 1927 stated categorically that "the existence of licensed houses is undoubtedly an incentive to immoral traffic, both national and international."

The second report published in 1932 said : "The principal factor in the East is the brothel and in the chain of brothels which are at the disposal of the traffickers, particularly the brothel in the place of destination of the victim. The most effectively remedy against the evil therefore is, in the Commission's opinion, the abolition of licensed or recognised brothels in the countries concerned."

As for the fear that unfavourable result might follow the abolition of licensed brothels, experience has proved that there are no adverse effects. As a matter of fact in most towns the situation in regard to prostitution and its consequences improved with the change, and there has been no desire to return to the previous system.

With regard to the effect on the incidence of venereal disease, the evidence furnished to the Committee showed either that the position has improved or that no change for the worse had been experienced. The report on the effect on public order was equally satisfactory. Little difficulty was experienced in maintaining order in the streets and was no evidence that the number of sexual offences had increased. It may be said that the chief cause for Prostitution is Demand. Prostitution is a trade like any other in the sense that it is governed by the law of Demand and Supply. Unlike most other trades, the party that benefits most by it is not the prostitute but—a third party. It is the pimp and the brothel keepers that thrive on the sordid gains of prostitution. It is naturally in their interests to stimulate an ever increasing demand. And those who encourage young men to think and believe that continence is impossible and harmful are unconsciously playing into the hands of these social parasites. What we need for our young people is, in the words of Sir Arthur Newsholme "that training of character which cultivates right habits in life, on which can be based satisfactory control over illicitones."

Besides the main cause Demand, to feed which may an

innocent girl is trapped with false promises, there are other causes that lead women to the degradation of commercialised vice. It is usual to ascribe all the blame that is attached to prostitution to economic causes. But poverty, even abject poverty is only one cause. Thank God there are many more women who, in spite of dire poverty, cling tenaciously to their honour than those who take to prostitution to still the pangs of hunger. Nevertheless poverty in the shape of sordid surroundings, unhappy homes, lack of education, lack of any resources in the community that could act as a stabilising force, do deprive the young girl of a healthy physical and mental environment.

According to the Copec Reports there are several factors which drive women into prostitution. Unhappy and ugly homes, unprotected youth, a desire for money, for better clothes as means of inspiring greater notice or respect, for change or excitement, a spirit of indolence and dislike for work, the sense of disgrace and complete catastrophe which a girls is often made to feel keenly if she has been seduced or has had or is going to have an illegitimate child, the fear of consequent loss of employment and of character induce general despair, the type of weak character which always tends to take the line of least resistance the desire for sexual indulgence in those who cannot properly be called defectives.

Whatever be the causes, however, human nature is the same everywhere and India no less than other countries in the world has to face up to the problem and strive to cleanse society of an evil which has been allowed to corrode it for too long and on which people are almost afraid to speak from a false sense of propriety. It may not also be forgotten that while society has always been quick to outcast the woman, the man who indulges in the vice is not shunned. There cannot be two moral laws and social justice demands equal condemnation of both sexes.

The aim of this Conference is to presumably to study the problem objectively and with sympathy and understanding. Where the measures already taken have proved successful they should be strengthened. Where they have not been successful every attempt should be made to discover the cause as to why they have failed and other methods tried to root out the evil. It is very necessary for this Conference also to formulate a plan of action which will not only been lightened and thorough but also practical and which will make due allowance for the financial stringency and other great difficulties with which India is faced today. It is not enough for a small band of workers to attempt to save this problem. We want hundreds of Josephine Butlers who will stretch out the hand of fellowship towards those sisters whom circumstances have compelled to follow a wrong path. We want hundreds of men with the spirit and understanding of Gladstone to fearlessly condemn the wrong doers among their own sex. Better housing, the raising of the standard of life, education and propaganda will all help to combat this great evil. For the work that this Conference has taken up, for the initiative which they have shown in calling together of this kind I congratulate the member of the A.M.S.H. and I wish them every success in their deliberations.

IV

In a broadcast speech delivered on December 24, 1950 on the Indian Broadcasting network, Rajkumari Amrit Kaur pleads for a new approach the question of the prevention of crime and discusses the relative efficacy of the new and old methods.

CRIME AND PUNISHMENT

"It is acknowledged that neither convict prisons, not the hulks nor any system of hard labour ever cured a criminal."

Fyodor Dostoyevsky

"If you give to a chief, he cannot steal from you, and he is no longer to theif".

William Saroyan
in the "Human Comedy"

There is no gainsaying the fact that while man is born with the divine spark within him, he is also subject to all the frailties of human nature. To create a society where all shall be good, happy and contented has been the aim of human endeavour from time immemorial but it has not been an easy task and if one were to judge human progress by the sorry state of affairs that exists in the world of today one might even be tempted to ask whether the human race had really progressed at all. For surely war against one's fellow man is the greatest crime imaginable. But there may never be lack of faith in humanity in any of us.

Now crime is a word which can be used to convey more meanings than one. It may be a violation of the law in any sphere;

the offence may be small or it may be heinous. That is the common interpretation and such crimes are committed by individuals of very race, in every country and in every clime.

But there are also crimes committed by society as a whole, by groups, by tyrannical governments, by fanatics which are no less dangerous and which are not so much a violation of the law, and by law I mean man-made law, as a gross violation of the laws of life.

We live in a scientific age and we often blame science for many of our woes. We live in a machine age and we often blame the modern system of life for an increase in crime. But are we as human beings right in attributing blame to circumstances rather than to our own weakness? I have a feeling that man has always been liable to fall a victim to evil deeds and invariably the motive for such has been the selfish motive, whether it be for self-aggrandisement, self-enrichment or for love of power and domination and such passions have impelled equally individuals, communities, races and nations.

I do not, therefore, feel that we should allow ourselves to be unduly depressed and say that crime is on the increase or that man is more criminally minded today than in days gone by. Might it not be that with our increased contacts with and therefore more detailed knowledge of conditions in the world we are more aware of our shortcomings. Further, I like to believe that in spite of the sorry state of affairs that exists in the world today and to which I have referred, there is progress going on all the time.

The mere fact that there is enlightened interest on such a subject as we are discussing today and that there is an increasing urge within man to strive for the greatest good for the greatest number are heartening signs and should give us hope.

From time immemorial in the sphere of crime those in authority have dealt our punishment to the wrong-doer. These methods were barbaric to begin with. With the advance of civilised society much healthy change has taken place. Reformatories have come into being for the young, jails are more places of detention then of penance, capital and corporal punishment have been abolished in many countries, special attention is being paid to juvenile deliquency and, generally speaking, in dealings with the wrong-doer a far more humane outlook has been and is being brought to hear on the whole question of crime and punishment.

Now what impels a human being to commit a crime? Strain and stress of life which include hunger and want, passions to which man is heir and ambition by which sin fell the angels may be said to be the main factors. If we can eliminate hunger and want we can also eliminate a great deal of crime. To conquer the frailties to which human nature is prone is a more difficult task. Nevertheless nothing is too difficult to attain. If the will to attain it is there. Early and proper education of the child is very important.

The child who is weak-minded or delinquent or prone to more mischief than the normal child needs extra care. Women with the natural instinct of mother love in them are the proper persons to be trained and put in charge of such children and this should be the burden of the State. Moreover ethical training for the young is a *sine qua non* of building up a moral society.

While such training is probably imparted up to a point in all schools, educational authority should have social workers whose duty is must be to make the necessary contacts with the home life of the children. Environment plays an immense part in the building of character and may not be ignored. And what applies to the child applies also to the adult.

The Welfare State is undoubtedly the ideal state and in any event Plato's axiom that the state comes into being to make life good cannot be disputed. Every state brings on to its Statute Book such laws as will help to maintain a stable society but something more is needed to sustain the human being in his hour of weakness. It is therefore good that all the advanced countries of the world are recognising civics as a social science and relying more and more on trained social servants and above all on the psychiarist.

There is something wrong in the mental make-up of the human being or the society or race that resorts to crime or violence in order to set right a grievance either real or imaginary. He or they have therefore, to be treated. Where bad conditions of life drive to despair, they must be eliminated, where rivalries and jealousies supervene there is always room for mediation.

It seems to me therefore that man's tendency to crime can be checked if he is brought up well from his infant years, if the State can make him contented and happy as far as his physical, material and mental requirements are concerned and if the services of the turned social worker and the psychiaitrist can be full utilised.

The days of condign punishment without any human sympathy and understanding are gone. We have to have some correctives because man, by the very nature of his make-up, needs to be deterred from wrong doing but no punishment may ever drive him to anger or despair. Rather it should uplift him and he should have the consolation that there is room for him in a well-ordered society if he turns from his evil doing.

The crime of war too can be eliminated if we cease to imagine that war is a solution of any of our problems. In fact no problem is impossible of solution if the will to solve it peacefully is there. The root causes of murder and loot—and war is a glorified form of murder and loot however much we may camouflage it by calling it a war of ideologies—are material greed and the lust for power. The hope of the world lies in cooperation and the working for a world government.

We live in a beautiful world, made fearsome and ugly only by our own shortcomings. Crime and its natural corollary—punishment—will decrease in such measure as we are able to bring to the general run of the people those conditions of life which will make them happy and contented and educate them to a true appreciation of life itself and what are its real values. As a great poet has said—

"Let us no more contend, nor blame
Each other, but strive
In offices of love how we may lighten
Each other's burden in our share of woe."
And again it is our duty to strive to be noble—
"And the Nobleness that lies
In other men, sleeping but never dead—
Will rise in majesty to meet our own."

6

As Health Minister in Central Government

I

For ten years Rajkumari Amrit Kaur was the Minister of Health in the Union Government. Elected on the Indian National Congress Party ticket, party discipline prevented her from voicing her feelings and opinions on subjects with which she was not dealing. Freed from this restraint, she has been talk freely in advocacy of a rational approach to India's problems. The article below was published in the "Onlooker" Independence Day issue of 1957.

TAKING STOCK

In many respects 1957 is a memorable year. Not only will we have concluded a decade of political independence but we have taken some vital decisions in regard to many things, including the re-organisation of the States, and how to arm ourselves for the fulfilment of our second Five-Year Plan.

Everyone is, or should be, well aware of what we have been able to achieve during our First-Five-Year Plan. There is no doubt that, comparatively speaking, there has been wonderful progress in every sphere. Availability of food and all kinds of agricultural production have increased; some of the big river valley projects are functioning while others are in process of completion, communication facilities whether by air, road or rail, as well as postal and telegraphic services, have shown quite a remarkable upward trend.

Industry, both private and public, is making commendable strides; industrial and other housing is apparent everywhere even though, as in all countries of the world, it just cannot keep pace with the demand; oil and mineral prospecting show encouraging results; plans for the production of atomic energy are afoot; education and health have not lagged in spite of the fact that social services get the least share of the country's revenue. Above all, the per capita income has increased and those who, previous to independence, had next to nothing do certainly have something now. In other words, there are palpable advances in every sector and an impartial observer can sense that the country is alive and humming with activity. What is more, people everywhere are demanding better living conditions. All this is enough to hearten the most pessimistic, and not depress the most over-expectant among us.

Since all our efforts have been directed with a view to the betterment of our rural population, credit must be given to Central Government for having laid enormous emphasis on helping the villages. Roughly speaking, seven out of every ten persons in our country have to turn to the land for their living. Gandhiji when in 1932 he founded the All-India Village Industries Association, drew our attention to the fact that India lived in her villages and it was our duty and to our advantage to work for their all-round upliftment because, in the ultimate analysis, it was to them that we would have to look for the welfare of our country. And how right he was! Therefore, it is indeed good to feel that Community Projects and National Extension blocks have been and will continue to be given top priority in our plans. *Pari-passu* with the all round betterment of the peasant, the keynote of his progress, of course, depends on agricultural production for which he is being given every encouragement.

The encouragement to small-scale industry is proof positive that the Government has not forgotten artisans either. Artistry in hand-made articles is part and parcel of the tradition and culture of country and needs every art, however, unless we treasure it as something worthwhile. I was saddened when in China to see that what used to be the most exquisitely handwoven pictures, which when framed look for all the world like hand paintings, being turned out by machines. When I asked why a lovely art was being allowed to die, I was told that hand-work was too costly a thing to maintain in the modern world. The wages of the artisan had quite rightly to be brought on a par with the factory or other worker. The price of his output naturally went up. Who was going to buy costly objects d' art now?

India, has therefore, to choose between following the pattern of the western world which is dominated by the machine age or carve out a via media of her own.

Looking back as I do over the past ten years, I am naturally more competent to speak of detailed progress in the field of health for which cause I laboured heart and soul for a decade. I would like to say, with all humility, that we can look back with pride on a good record of advancement in what is a vital but at the same time a very difficult field to cultivate. Not only did we have to begin from scratch, because the majority in this vast land were without medical aid and relief of any kind, but there was also the problem of producing more trained personnel and the vexed problem of over-riding poverty, ignorance and prejudice.

That the Government of India was quick to decide that prevention is better than cure, was indeed wise. The priority given to the care of the mother and child has yielded dividends. To rid the country of the pests of malaria and other insect-borne diseases, to try to give a protected water-supply to the villagers in order to stem the onslaught of water-borne maladies, to strooo the importance environmental hygiene and educate the ignorant masses to understand the simple laws of health, to stimulate research in both modern and in the ancient systems of medicine, to train auxiliary health personnel to work in the villages, to encourage the noble profession of nursing, a calling which had been so sadly neglected, to combat on all fronts the menace of tuberculosis, to study the problem of nutrition, to bring to the fore the urgent necessity strengthening local self-government institutions, and last, but not least, to maintain as high a standard as possible of modern medical education and given facilities for post-graduate education in our own country—these have been highlights of our endeavours during the first decade of our independence.

That the foundations have been well and truly laid has been graciously acknowledged by our Prime Minister in his foreword to the book published by the Ministry of Health in which the story of ten years has been narrated in a very readable manner. But, of course, no one knows better than I how little has really been done compared with the vast needs of this great land of ours. Much criticism is levelled at the Centre and State Government in regard to their shortcomings. Stress is always laid on the needs that still remain to be fulfilled and what has been accomplished in the face of heavy odds is often if not altogether forgotten. This is human nature and doubtless all Governments have to realise that what they do for the people is always taken for granted and only those on whose shoulders lies the heavy responsibility of planning and carrying out the plan can really know what difficulties beset their path and how great are the limitations which hamper speedy progress. It is difficult enough for an individual to realise his own limitations. How much harder must it be for us to appreciate the limitations of others.

Ours is a federal structure of government. Much as sometimes I would have liked the Centre in the early years of our independence to have had more power—in other words, to have a unitary form of government—I realise that in a big country like ours, with its States varying in every way as they do, the surest way of developing and of training our people in the art of governance and thereby growing to our full stature is the democratic way. One of the highlights of my work in the development of health services for the people was the close cooperation and understanding and loyalty which the Health Ministers of the States gave to the Union Ministry. Indeed, no progress would have been formulated had it not been for the close liaison maintained throughout between the Centre and the States.

Another source of great joy was the help received from abroad. The great Foundations of the U.S.A., the specialised agencies of the United Nations, the Colombo, Plan, the T.C.M. and UNICEF with their liberal help and guidance in ever so many ways made the task of the ministry much lighter and it gave us all opportunities of forming real friendships and of making our contribution towards the building of international goodwill and understanding on which alone can the foundations of peace be built.

Another great step forward which has been taken by our people have been the salutary measures on social reform. There was no difficulty in women getting their political rights and being put absolutely on a par with men in the Constitution. But custom and usage had dealt harshly with Indian women and nothing dies so hard as custom. India's women must be eternally grateful to Gandhiji in the first instance and to our Prime Minister in the second for having given their unstinted support to the advancement of the fair sex. Women have had endless opportunities given to them of making their contribution to public life and by and large, they have not failed. This is indeed, a good augury for the future.

Internationally India's voice has come to be recognised as something that counts. How much of this we owe to our Prime Minister, his personality, his integrity of purpose and his devotion to the cause of world peace will probably be far better appreciated when the history of this period comes to be written in later years. The duty of each one of us now is to strengthen his hands in every way so that the tensions that alienate man from man and the war clouds that darken our horizon may be dispelled.

It is good at all times when we look in retrospect, as we must on every Independence Day, to turn the searchlight inwards in order to see and acknowledge where we have failed to achieve what we set before ourselves and rededicate ourselves anew to further service to the country.

In spite of all that we have been able to achieve, there are some happenings which must give us pause and there are definite questions which we must ask ourselves. By and large it is the ruling party that is mainly responsible; for after all it had had the power concentrated in its hands and it has been its prerogative to give a lead to the country.

Has power corrupted? Have the loaves and fishes of office taken priority over service for the general good? How far have nepotism and favouritism superseded merit which should be the only criterion for appointment to any post? How heavy has overhead expenditure become? Are the number of Ministers and Deputy Ministers always appointed because they are needed or in order to placate whether individual or party interests? Is there honest supervision over the vast field of plan expenditure?

There are universal complaints about the lack of integrity. What is being done to combat dishonesty both material and intellectual in every sphere?

The Unity of India is vital to progress and yet narrow provincialism seems to have raised its ugly head throughout. Even the language question seems to disintegrate rather than units. Any suggestion, however laudable, which is intended to make us think and act on an All-India basis is turned down. I myself feel very strongly that All-India Services should be revived and English should be given its due place. Both are factors which help to create an All-India outlook.

Has local self-Government, which is fundamental to good government, not been neglected vis-a-vis the more glamorous government by cabinets and legislatures?

Communalism and casteism, both enemies of nationhood, have not been eliminated. The minorities and scheduled castes still suffer from a fear complex and often from a sense of injustice at the hands of the majority party. As we embark on the Second Five Year Plan we must ponder deeply over shortcomings, and exercise all the non-progressive forces which work as a canker in our society. If they continue to exist, success will be chimerical. Our Vice-President recently emphasised the fact that the greatest need of the hour was character. I wholly endorse his views. We have to return to the ideals which Gandhiji placed before us when he took charge of the freedom movement, but we have to return to them not only in word but in action—in truth and in spirit.

The Princeton University conferred the Doctorate of Laws on Rajkumari Amrit Kaur, *honoris causa*. The citation read out by the University Orator at the 209th Commencement at Nassau Hall on June 12th, 1956 runs as follows :

"Minister for Health of India since 1947, she had rendered distinguished service in the social development of her nation's service, she has gone amongst the poor and the weak, the mothers and children, the sick and the starving, not only with messages of hope and faith but also with substantial and highly affective programmes of action. For eighteen years disciple and secretary to Mahatma Gandhi, she shared the work of making India politically free. Now she carries on the immense task of raising the standards of health and well being of the people of her native land. She stands thus as a living image of faith, hope and love—believing like St. Paul that the greatest of these is love."

The second oldest alumnus referred to in the citation is Mr. H. Golaknath of the class of '82 who after graduation, joined the Presbytery of New Brunswick and was ordained as Minister in Princeton.

Rajkumari's speech at Princeton deals with the historical aspect of India's civilisation, with the development of social economy and with the growth of political consciousness in India. It also deals with India's present day problems and the efforts being made to solve them.

ON INDIA'S HERITAGE, PROBLEMS AND PROGRESS

Righteousness exalteth a nation.
The Old Testament
Proverbs XIV : 34.

Methinks I see in my mind a noble and puissant nation rousing herself like a strong man after sleep, and shaking her invincible locks; methinks I see her as an eagle mewing her mighty youth, and kindling her undazzled eyes at the full midday beam.

John Milton
in Areopagitica

It was about nine years ago that the guiding hand of Great Britain was withdrawn from the administration of India and the people and their leaders were given full freedom to shape the future of the country, on lines they considered best for their material, moral and spiritual advancement. The national struggle, which preceded this great event, had been carried out under the guidance of one of the greatest men the world has ever produced—Mahatma Gandhi; and the spiritualisation of the campaign for freedom, advocated by him and enforced as far as was humanly possible, has an abiding effect on those who were closely associated with him and, to a varying extent, on a much wider circle of the men and women of India. Gandhiji's main strength was that he refused to accept the position that permanent values could, at any time, be sacrificed for the sake of immediate advantage and that, even in the midst of strong provocation, fundamental principles should never be given up to meet the needs of the hour.

It was thus that, although he and the unarmed masses he led were made the victims of an Imperial Power determined to use all he resources at its command to break down opposition, he held aloft the banner of non-violence in thought, word and deed under which his followers were to pursue their campaign for the liberation of the country. Absolute dedication to truth and the cleansing of one's heart from hatred towards one's opponents through the purifying influence of love were to him the guiding principles of his life. Thus, politics was not a field in which a battle of wits was to be played out with all the ingenuity at one's command. It was only a part of that larger sphere of human life and activity in which he believed that man's conduct should be guided by sound ethical principles and not by considerations of expediency.

On me, who had the rare privilege of being very closely associated with Gandhiji for over eighteen years during the period of this historic struggle, the conviction continues to grow, that the spiritual he handed down to us is by far the richest we have and that the guiding light of Gandhian ideas and ideals will, in spite of many lapses, help to lead the nation though the encircling gloom of all its trails.

Before I begin to tell you about what we in India have been attempting to do during the past eight or nine years and about our hopes and aspirations for the future, I feel it would be appropriate to say a few words regarding India's spiritual and cultural past. Our progress, if it is to be guided no proper lines, should take note of the background of experience through which the country has passed. I believe that, while we should take full advantage of the contributions that scientific progress and development of technology can and must make towards a steady improvement of our national life, our programme of social advancement may not create a break with the past. The lives of individuals and of nations can grow into fruition only when the channels of communication with the roots of their existence are kept intact, because the rising sap of social and spiritual advancement, which promotes progress, can continue to fulfil its function only when such contact is maintained.

India has been, throughout the ages, deeply influenced by religion. Hinduism, Buddhism, Islam and Christianity have all helped to enrich her cultural heritage. Hindu Philosophy, with the highest conception of the Godhead on the one hand and the most crude froms of animistic worship on the other, represents a range of catholicity of religious beliefs and practices, perhaps unparallelled in the history of the world. There is, at the same time, in the simple faith and homely life of the large mass of the rural population, something of that kindliness which makes them hospitable to the stranger, in spite of their own meagre resources, and that element of other-worldliness which while it may tend to reduce ambition and the zest for advancement in life, nevertheless invests their outlook on life with the radiance of a simple joy in the common things of everyday existence. Buddhism, while it was uprooted from the land of its birth by resurgent and militant Hinduism under the leadership of Shri Shankaracharya and his followers, has still remained a live force by the contribution in made towards the permeation of the spirit of "ahimsa" or non-violence. Islam was inconoclastic in that it sought to destroy existing patterns of religious thought and experience but it brought, at the same time, a spirit of brotherhood and of social justice within its own fold and these influences have no doubt exerted beneficient effect on Indian life.

As regards Christianity the south-western strip of territory on the Malabar Coast was one of the earliest regions in which the teachings of Jesus found fertile soil for their propagation. Christian thought has had a profound effect on India and I can say with pride that in no non-Christian country are the life and person of the Lord Jesus held in higher esteem and reverence than in India. Ours is, indeed, a land in which a confluence of various types of religious thought and practice has helped to develop the growth of a culture which, in spite of a wide diversity of existing forms of expression, has yet promoted the emergence of a broad unity characterising the life and thought of the nation. In Gandhiji, this cultural heritage of India found its fullest expression. It was because the people instinctively recognised the fact that millions were content to sacrifice their all under his leadership and that the hard path of self-discipline, which the practice of non-violence requires, was readily acceptable to them.

In attempting to describe briefly India's spiritual and cultural heritage I cannot do better than quote certain extracts from the writings of India's greatest poet of modern times, Gurudev Rabindranath Tagore. They are gleaned from his book.

"Sadhana" which consists of a series of discourses on the fundamental principles of Hinduism. "When the first Aryan invaders appeared in India it was a vast land of forests, and the new comers rapidly took advantage of them. These forests afforded them shelter from the fierce heat of the sun and the ravages of tropical fire, and materials for building cottages. And the different Aryan clans with their patriarchal heads settled in the different forest tracts which had some special advantage of natural protection, and food and water in plenty.

"Thus in India it was in the forests that our civilisation had its birth, and it took a distinct character from this origin and environment. It was surrounded by the vast life of nature, was fed and clothed by her, and had the closest and most constant intercourse with her varying aspects.

"Such a life, it may be thought, tends to have the effect of dulling human intelligence and dwarfing the incentives to progress by lowering the standards of existence. But in ancient India we find that the circumstances of forest life did not overcome man's mind, and did not enfeeble the current of his energies, but only gave to it a particular direction. Having been in constant contact with the living growth of nature, his mind was free from the desire to extend his dominion by erecting boundary walls around his acquisitions. His aim was not to acquire but to realise, to enlarge his consciousness by growing with and growing into his surroundings. He felt that truth is all comprehensive, that there is no such thing as absolute isolation in existence, and the only way of attaining truth is through the interpenetration of our being into all objects. To realise this great harmony between man's spirit and the spirit of the world was the endeavour of the forest-dwelling sages of ancient India.

"In later days there came a time when these primeval forests gave way to cultivated fields, and wealthy cities sprang up on all sides. Mighty kingdoms were established, which had communication with all the great powers of the world. But even in the heyday of its material prosperity the heart of India ever looked back with adoration upon the early ideal of strenuous self-realisation, and the dignity of the simple life of the forest hermitage, and drew its best inspiration from the wisdom stored there.

"The first invasion of India has its exact parallel in the invasion of America by the European settlers. They also were confronted with primeval forests and a fierce struggle with the aboriginal races. But this struggle between man and man, and man and nature lasted till the very end; they never came to any terms. In India the forests which were the habitation of barbarians became the sanctuary of sages; but in America these great living cathedrals of nature had no deeper significance to man. They brought wealth and power to him, and perhaps at times they ministered to his enjoyment of beauty and inspired a solitary poet. They never acquired sacred association in the hearts of man as the site of some great spiritual reconcilement where Man's soul had its meeting-place with the soul of the world.

"I do not for a moment wish to suggest that things should have been otherwise. It would be an utter waste of opportunities if history were to repeat itself exactly in the same manner in every place. It is best for the commerce of the spirit that people differently situated should being their different products into the market of humanity, each of which is complementary and necessary to the others. All that I wish to say is that India at the outset of her career met with a special combination of circumstances which was not lost upon her. She had, according to her opportunities, thought and pondered, striven and suffered, dived into the depths of existence, and achieved something which surely cannot be without its value to people whose evolution in history took a different way altogether. Man for his perfect growth requires all the living elements that constitute his complex life.

"Civilisation is a kind of mould that each nation is busy making for itself to shape its men and women according to its best ideal. All its institutions, its legislatures, its standards of approbation and condemnation, its conscious teachings tend toward that object. The modern civilisation of the West, by all its organised efforts, is trying to turn out men perfect in physical, intellectual and moral efficiency. There the vast energies of the nations are employed in extending man's power over his surroundings, and people are combining and straining every faculty to possess and to turn to account all that they can lay their hands upon, to overcome every obstacle on their path of conquest. They are ever disciplining themselves to fight nature and other races; their armaments are getting more and more stupendous every day; their machines, their appliances, organisations go on multiplying at an amazing rate."

"The ancient civilisation of India had its own ideal of perfection towards which its efforts were directed. Its aim was not attaining power, and it neglected to cultivate to the utmost its capacities and to organise men for defensive and offensive purposes, for cooperation in the acquisition of wealth and for military and political ascendancy. The ideal that India tried to realise led her best men to the isolation of a contemplative life, and the treasures that she gained for mankind by penetrating into the mysteries of reality cost her dear in the sphere of worldly success. Yet, this also was a sublime achievement—it was a supreme manifestation of that human aspiration which knows no limit, and which has for its object nothing less than the realisation of the infinite".

I have quoted these extracts from Tagore's writings but not for the purpose of conveying the impression that the aspirations of modern India are towards a return to the pristine simplicity of forest dwellings and a life of contemplation. The conditions that exist today are widely different from those in which our forefathers lived. We have to grapple with the enormous problems of sickness and suffering, of poverty and misery, of social injustice resulting from large inequalities of income and of lack of opportunities to earn and live under proper living conditions. In attempting to solve these problems India does desire to utilise to the full the resources of science and of modern technology but her heart harks back to the need for that wider appreciation of human values without which the power that man has accumulated through the advance of scientific knowledge may turn out to be an instrument of self-destruction. Control of one's environment has littles meaning without man being able to exercise adequate control over his own self. While India sees much to admire and to adopt in the vigorous civilisation of the West, she feels that if her future is to be developed on proper lines add her contribution to the sum of human welfare is to be of value, the advance she make must be a growth originally related to the fundamental ethical ideas and ideals which are enshrined in her own well-established traditions of the past.

I now turn to some of the major events that followed the tragie partition of India and the grant of independence to the two separated countries. Almost immediately, there started an exodus of enormous numbers of people from their well-established homes through hundreds of miles of territory—the inhabitants of which often proved hostile—and their settlement under difficult conditions in unfamiliar surroundings. This exodus caused untold suffering, and for the first two or three years our energies had perforce to be diverted solely towards the rehabilitation of these unfortunate millions. Much has been done for them but much still remains to be done and, indeed, even today West Bengal is face to face with a problem of great magnitude if the exodus of Hindus from East Pakistan continues as at present.

We are proud to feel, however, that the cause of the minorities has not been allowed to suffer in spite of the partition of India and today millions of Muslims live in peace and amity within our borders. India's Constitution guarantees full protection, irrespective of religion, colour or caste and ensures equal treatment to every citizen. The highest offices in the land are open to all and there is full freedom of worship. There can be no clearer or more convincing testimony of the soundness of this policy than the handsome tribute which the King of Saudi Arbia paid to Government and people of India, after a recent tour of three weeks in the country, by stating that the 45 million Muslims of India enjoyed full rights as citizens and that their future was secure in the hands of the Government of India.

Great social changes have come in the wake of our attainment of independence. There were over six hundred States of varying sizes administered by Indian Princes. The efficiency of administration in these states varied considerably and was, on the whole, below the level which the Provinces in the territories under the British had attained. Some of them had, in the past, been so badly administered that social justice demanded that the people of these States should be liberated from such misrule and given the opportunity to have a voice in public administration. Moreover, from the national point of view, an integration of these several hundreds of Princely dominions scattered indiscriminately over the country into large well-knit territories with a considerable measure of autonomy to develop for themselves was absolutely essential. The transformation of over six hundred States into large territories was carried out within a period of less than two years. Looking back on this marvellous achievements one is struck with the fact that it was a bloodless revolution in which hundreds of Princes, who had for centuries exercised sovereign rights over their territories, willingly gave up power and prestige and descended to the level of the common man in India.

An equally bloodless revolution was the taking over by the State of large tracts of land in the lands of Zemindars or land owners who, although they received compensation for this transfer of territory, naturally lost the position and power which ownership of land confers on its possessors. Is it not amazing that such uprooting of vested interests and rights was carried out without a hitch over the country as a whole and that men of wealth and social standing who were adversely affected by the change, reconciled themselves to it without protest? I cannot help feeling that the deep-rooted tradition of India with its emphasis on sacrifice on the part of the individual for the common good, must have played its unconscious role on the minds of the Princes and landowners who were called upon to make the sacrifice. The grandeur of the achievement is seen to be all the grater when it is remembered that these phenomenal changes were brought about within the first few years of the new Government of India taking over the administration of the country.

It seems to me that these events demonstrate beyond any shadow of doubt that great social changes can be brought about in any country by throwing responsibility for public administration on the leaders of the people. Those who formed the governments at the Centre and in the States and the large majority of legislators were for the greater part those who had thrown in their lot with Gandhiji in the country's march towards freedom. They had spent long years in working with him to learn about the needs of the people and to attempt to minister to those needs as best they could. As administrators they may have possessed little or no experience, but even so they could approach the problems of the country with intimate knowledge of the people, with a freshness of mind and with the determination to solve them in spite of all difficulties. Therefore they could dare to undertake and accomplish tasks of great complexity which no foreign Government could possibly have taken upon itself to solve.

The foreign policy that India has adopted has unfortunately been a matter of bewilderment and of misunderstanding and mistrust on the part of certain nations. But this foreign policy, which can be briefly described as friendliness to all countries and enmity towards none, is again based on India's cultural heritage and the spirit of tolerance, which is an important part to that heritage. India refuses to believe that any question, however important and complicated it may be, is incapable of solution, if the difficulties that exist are sought to overcome in a spirit of mutual adjustment and no understanding of each other's point of view. She believes, at the same time, that certain evils like colonialism must be eliminated at all cost.

Their continued existence harms not only the subject country but also the ruling power by blunting its sense of justice and fairness through the dominating influence of self-interest. Above all, India considers that this way is no method of solving any problem, howsoever pressing its demand may be on the country that seeks such a solution. Under modern conditions war can inflict untold sufferings on the belligerent nations and even cause damage to neutral countries because, from the point of view of the economic life of the people, the world is increasingly becoming a single unit and the disruptive forces that act on any part of the world will extend their disastrous effects to other parts as well. Moreover war, with its latest engines of mass slaughter and widespread devastation only helps to create other and more acute problems than the ones it set out to solve. In these beliefs we know we have stout allies in the United States, perhaps more than in any other country, because the democratic way of life which your great country has from the beginning made its own. It is nevertheless difficult to adopt and maintain an attitude of strict adherence to the principle of friendliness to an enmity to none because such an attitude is likely to be misunderstood by both parties when the world stands broadly divided into two opposing groups.

Even so, both in the interests of India and of a large number of Asian and African countries whose major preoccupation must today be the maintenance of peace and concentration of effort for national reconstruction and improving the standard of life of the people, our Prime Minister has duringly the past several years, rightly stood out as an ardent advocate of self-government for colonial peoples; of the acceptance of the principle of co-existence of nations even though they may differ in their ideological approach to the solution of national and international problems; and of a broad programme of cultural and economic co-operation to promote human welfare, particularly in the under-developed regions of the world. Such a programme, apart from the material advantages it may bring into being, will undoubtedly help to make the nations come closer together and to promote a better understanding among. After all the solution to all the major problems lies in the hearts and minds of men and the ultimate motive force for social amelioration springs from a mutual understanding of the people of the world. Indian has reasons to hope that even now the clouds of suspicion are lifting and that time may help, eventually, to assure the world that India's attitude to the different changing international problems is motivated solely by a spirit of goodwill and toleration towards all countries.

The extracts I read from Tagore stressed some significant differences between Indian and Western cultures. As the great poet has himself pointed out there is no intention to imply, by this comparison, any superiority of one type of culture over the other. In fact they should be considered as being complementary to each other. The West has promoted an unprecedented advance in material welfare. It has, at the same time, demonstrated the evolution of a political system which seeks to confer no the citizens a wide measure of freedom. But this political freedom remains largely illusory unless it is accompanied by economic freedom, the right of every one to be trained for gainful employment, to secure that employment after training and to obtain adequate wages to meet the requirements of healthful living. The trend towards socialism, which is present to varying extent in all these countries, is the symbol of the onward march of Western nationals towards the fulfilment of this economic freedom.

What is the position in India? We have, indeed to go a long way towards the development of that material which can provide to all our people those minima that are necessary for a healthy life. In attempting to do so we are drawing heavily on Western experience and Western technology and we are deeply grateful for the help we have received and are continuing to receive from many international agencies and from this country and the great Foundations of the U.S.A. in particular. Even so it should be possible for India to evolve patterns of development which, while promoting the full use of the knowledge of the West, help to integrate with such development some of the essential features of India's cultural past. For instance, can our industrial progress be promoted with an adequate emphasis on the welfare and value of the human beings who form part of the process of development?

Can industry be decentralised and made to develop in surroundings which admit of man's close contact with Nature instead of crowding the workers into urban centres with their degrading conditions? Can the relationship between the employer and the employee be developed on the basis of better understanding and mutual co-operation instead of the present state of militant trade unionism and of the settlement of disputes through the medium of mutual struggle, which is detrimental to the interests of both the employer and the employee as well as of the industry? Can a fuller infusion of India's cultural traditions into the thoughts, aspirations and actions of our people help to create the proper atmosphere for a sane and human approach towards the solution of such problems? I believe these are thought-provoking matters worthy of consideration.

(Rajkumari here gave a detailed analysis of the progress made in India since Independence and the effect of various measures taken on the socio-economic life of the country. She also stressed the magnitude of India's problems.)

We are determinated that poverty, hunger, disease and ignorance shall be banished in due course from our land and that shall be able to offer to our people what your great President Abraham Lincoln was pleased to say was the right of every human being to have.

Our problems are of a magnitude which it is impossible to imagine until one comes face to face with them. I have tried to give you an idea of how we are trying to solve them. In a country where we have to battle at every turn against ignorance, againt disease, against hunger, against want in every sphere, the road to prosperity is long and arduous. Indeed it winds uphill all the way. But withal, there is ever the beacon light of faith in a great endeavour which will surely sleam for us if we owe allegiance to the watchwords of Truth and Love to those of us who are engaged in the task of building a new India is may not be given to see much if any of the result of our labours, but we pray that we may be enabled to lay a right the foundations of the structure on which succeeding generations will be privileged to build. But however "travel-sore and weak" we may be, when we reach our journey's end, there will always be the consolation of having had the privilege of working for the uplift of a part of humanity which stands sorely in need of that upliftment.

Before I sit down, may I, Mr. President, extend to you and to all the members of the Faculty and students of this centre of learning and other friends present here today, and through you to a wider world, a message of greetings and goodwill from my country? We have so much in common on which we agree. We stand, as you have stood through the ages, for the freedom of the human spirit. I trust we may be privileged to work hand in hand for the cause for which every human being today yearns, the cause of world peace.

Rajkumari Amrit Kaur, Minister of Health in the Government of India since 1947, contributed this talk to the General Overseas Service Survey of some basic problems of Western civilisation today.

IN THE LIGHT OF ASIA

> Freedom is an indivisible word. If we
> want to enjoy it, and fight for it,we
> must be prepared to extend it to every
> one, whether they are rich or poor,
> whether they agree with us or not, no
> matter what their race or the colour
> of their skin.
>
> Wendell Louis Willkie
> in "One World"

Knowing my limitations I have accepted with diffidence what I consider is a privilege to participate in the General Overseas Service series 'What Price Freedom? because I realise that persons of eminence and of wide experience are speak-n on topics of vital importance at this stage of human history, a stage which may well prove to be the turning point towards a glorious future of peace, prosperity, and plenty for all or towards an era of unprecedented suffering and distress. If, which God forbid, the latter eventuality should envelop the earth it will surely be due to man's inability to replace hate by love, greed by generosity, racial animosity by fellow feeling, understanding and sympathy and national pride and arrogance by a just and large-hearted appreciation of the claims of other nations.

With such immense issues facing us we are indeed at an important crossroad on the broad highway of human destiny. Science has placed at our disposal enormous power to reshape our environment to our heart's desire and to create conditions which will make life worth for all. Our hearts and minds have not, however, expanded simultaneously to take advantage of these new powers and to use them for constructive work on the basis of promoting prosperity for all mankind. Cleavages between nation and nation continue, the spirit of colonial exploitation has not ceased, the colour question with all the indignity it heaps on certain sections of humanity remains in prominence in some countries and, in addition to all these disruptive forces, ideologies based on differing systems of social organisation and on the attitude towards religion, such as Communism and democracy, tend to divide the world sharply into opposing camps with a grim determination to ensure survival for themselves even at the risk of provoking a war to the finish.

In the midst of all these forces which help to create conflict can common ground be found on which the nations of the world may attempt to build the future of the human race with the purpose of progressively weakening destructive forces and of strengthening those which make for the emergence of active participation by all countries in the pursuit of common interests? Constructive thought and action towards this end can alone constitute a positive approach towards the removal of the basis causes which tend to produce world-wide disaster. On the other hand, all forms of negative approach such as negotiation from positions of strength or the threat of massive retaliation and to arouse fear and hatred and cannot, in my humble opinion, lead to mutual understanding or lasting peace.

The East, comprising countries with as their western boundary a line from the Urals to Suez and with their onward spread into the Pacific, contains perhaps more than half the population of the world. In the past the West dominated the East and for ages carried out intensive colonial exploitation. Such exploitation has not completely disappeared. Because of the fact that some governments and the peoples of that area are weak and disunited, the grip of the West on the economic life and indirectly on their internal administration continues to varying extents. All these have to change and change completely if a new outlook is to be promoted whereby co-operative effort by all countries on the basis of equality can be established for the furtherance of the common good.

It should be remembered that hundreds of millions in the countries of Asia and the great continent of Africa and suffering from poverty, hunger and disease on a scale unknown to the people of the West. To these millions it is the fulfilment of man's primary needs of food, clothing, shelter, and relief from sickness which are more important than all the benefits that ideological democracy promises to the individual through the freedom which it seeks to foster. As Stephen Spender has aptly put it : 'The interests of the very few people in the world who care for the values of freedom must be identified with those of the many who need bread, or else freedom will be lost'.

Both the West and the East are talking today of the welfare state as an ideal to be achieved. My own conception of the welfare state includes not only economic betterment so as to provide for the people certain minimum standards of living essential for a healthy life but also those wider opportunities for social, cultural and recrational pursuits without which the promotion of a fuller and happier enjoyment of life is not possible. The West, with its past rooted in the fundamental principles of Christianity, and the East, with its religions stressing—as, for example, in Hinduism and Buddhism—the essential unity of man with creation as a whole and renunciation or non-possession as the supreme vehicle through which alone he can travel towards the attainment of this ideal, have much in common to motivate co-operative effort for the establishment of the welfare state.

Are the people of the West, who enjoy a role of predominance today prepare to come down from their privileged positions to the dusty soil of common endeavour, to work with the toiling races of Asia and Africa and share with them a part of their sweat and tears in the glorious task of building a future of promise for all mankind? A change of heart on a scale unpredecented in history will be necessary as a prerequisite to such an ordering of a new state of affairs in the world. I should like to refer to a few fundamental departures from existing patterns of personal conduct and of public administration which all nations must accept before we can be certain of such a change of heart.

All traces of colonialism and racial antagonism must disappear from the face of the earth. Government by an alien power, however benevolent is may be, can be no real substitute for government of the people by the people for the people. If an illustration of the extent to which the withdrawal of foreign rule can help to create a true national resuagence were needed we have only to turn to my own country, India. The magnanimous act of liberation to which the United Kingdom agreed in 1947 has worked a peaceful revolution in human thought and action which, I hope and believe, will have a tremendous effect on the future of the world. It has helped to bring the two countries closer together than ever before. It has enabled our National Government to tackle a number of important domestic problems with vigour, with a clear understanding of local needs and conditions, and with growing success in the harnessing of the support of the people towards the carrying out of social and economic changes on an amazing scale. We are only at the beginning of the glorious path of adventure on which India has started. But those who are privileged to participate in it are heartened by what is being achieved even though they feel that, in relation to the magnitude of the task to be accomplished, what has been done may appear to be wholly insignificant.

The establishment of a welfare state in any country requires extensive social and economic changes, the cumulative effect of which would be to promote the production and distribution of goods necessary for the life of the community on the basis of maximum benefit to the people as a whole, and to bring about a redistribution of income so as to reduce considerably the existing range of disparity between the highest and the lowest. Further, in regard to the available resources for exploitation and the size of the population to be supported by such resources even when they are fully developed, there are great variations between countries.

Development Resources for All the World

It is for earnest deliberation, therefore, whether the welfare state can become a practical proposition without the different countries agreeing to part with their sovereign rights and to accept a single world government which is able to develop the resources of the earth for mankind as a whole.

As a first step towards the consummation of this ultimate ideal, will the nations, particularly the favoured ones, agree to a joint exploitation of at least a part of their resources under the auspices of an international agency like the Untied Nations so that these resources may be applied to areas where the needs of men for immediate relief are most acute?

There are undoubtedly many difficulties to be overcome before even this partial solution can be achieved. The first and foremost essential is a change of heart or a moral and spiritual revolution in the minds of men whereby the sufferings of their neighbours and even those of peoples far distant from their homes will become an intense concern to themselves and act as a compelling force to turn apathy and indifference into a strong urge of human sympathy, which makes such sacrifices as may be necessary turn into willing acts of love.

Democracy is today called upon to meet the greatest challenge it has had to face throughout the ages. Its concern for the preservation of the right of the individual to act according to the dictates of his conscience and for the maintenance of those cherished ideals which religion and social ethics have handed down through the centuries will prove to be of no avail before the mounting wrath of millions, to whom starvation and suffering and the picture of growing prosperity under a materialistic philosophy may make an irresistible appeal to turn away from the slow and uncertain progress which democracy holds forth for them.

The critical times in which we are placed emphasise more than ever before the truth of the ancient saying that those who are without vision will perish. With vision, courage and undying faith in the magic power of love and charity democracy can make of the future of mankind a glorious adventure with opportunities for all for adequate self-expression and for unhampered accession to moral and spiritual strength. The extent to which this great vision of the future will be realised depends on each one of us and on the way in which we influence our own thoughts and actions to strive continuously towards the desired goal. In so doing there can never be any fundamental clash between the ethical aims of people from whatsoever part of the world they hail or to whatever religion they belong.

In her inaugural address at the opening of the United Nations Branch in Delhi on the 26th of June, 1956, Rajkumari Amrit Kaur appeals for a spirit of tolerance, understanding and goodwill. "Amor Omnia Vincit" Says Rajkumari and to this flame alone we must turn for guidance in our efforts to dispel and break through the veil of fear and mistrust.

NO PEACEFUL COEXISTENCE

Grant us brotherhood, not only for the day, but for all our years—a brotherhood not of words but of acts and deeds. We are all of us children of the earth—grant us that simple knowledge. If our brothers are oppressed, then we are oppressed. If they hunger, then we hunger. If their freedom is taken away, our freedom is not secure.

Stephen Vincent Benet, in a prayer written for and read out by President Franklin D. Roosevelt to the United Naitons on Flag Day, June 14, 1942.

Four years ago today, when the world had just emerged from the experience of a terrible tragedy, the people of different countries took a pledge to save succeeding generations from the scourge of war. They reaffirmed their faith in the principle of human rights, they agreed to try to establish equality among men and women and nations, large and small, to bring about conditions under which justice and respect for obligations arising from treaties and sources of international law could be maintained, and to promote social progress and better standards of living. To achieve these ends they pledged themselves to practise tolerance, to live in peace as good neighbours, to maintain international peace and acceptance of these principles, that armed forces shall not be used again.

It is as well as for us to remind ourselves of this pledge. When this pledge was taken the world had gone through all the horrors and suffering of a second world war. No one but hoped that such a tragedy would not occur again. But today, alas! we still live under the shadow of another crisis. Indeed only last night has come the sad news of the breaking out of hostilities between North and South Korea. As we all know a spark anywhere today may start a world wide conflagration.

Shall we allow millions to suffer again, millions to die, millions to be rendered homeless, millions to be maimed and driven to poverty and hunger? Surely not. It must be the duty of every one not only to alleviate the continuing suffering of the aftermath of the last war but also to prevent another conflagration. The nervous strain and anxiety of the possibility of another war which is consuming the world today must be brought to an end if the world is to live. At a time such as this, we should support and strengthen the hands of Mr. Trygve Lie, the Secretary General of the United Nations, who is striving hard and devoting all his energies to find a solution to this problem. We need to dispel and break through the existing veil of fear and mistrust and to replace it by confidence, tolerance, understanding and goodwill. Love alone conquers all things. It is to that sacred flame that we must turn for guidance.

No atmosphere of mistrust but can be dissipated by employing all the resources of conciliation and constructive peace-building at our command. Goodwill can be secured if we accept, believe and act upon the possibility of a peaceful coexistence among all the nations of the earth in spite of their differing economic and political systems. Negotiations can succeed if they are undertaken with a will to peace, not in a spirit of appeasement, but with a genuine desire for the general good.

Measures for collective self-defence and regional remedies of other kinds are at best interim measures and cannot alone bring and reliable security from the prospect of war. The one common undertaking and universal instrument of the great majority of the human race is the United Nations. In adhering to the principles laid in their Charter lies the hope of the world. We must cease to think in terms of narrow national interests.

Peace is indivisible and the security and welfare of each country exist only in terms of world security and welfare. Co-operation must be universal or it is not co-operation.

The United Nations Organisation stands as a symbol of this high endeavour. It beckons to all to follow the right way. In the history of mankind there comes a time when nations determine their own destiny and are called upon to make a choice. May this choice be for everyone, without exception, an expression of the international conscience and solidarity without which peace is not possible.

I would have us all remember that the strength of the United Nations is not really vested in the strength of the Governments but of the people. It is therefore up to people like you and me, each in our own sphere, to work for tolerance, understanding and goodwill and thus generate the forces for peace. We are of a world fire brigade which alone can extinguish the fire.

You will notice from the flags around this lawn that we are flying the flags of some countries who are not yet members of the United Nations. We are not confining ourselves to countries represented at the United Nations. We are part of a non-Governmental Federation whose work extends far beyond blocs, curtains, political regions and geographical demarcations. It is a federation which has branches in all countries.

The very existence of these associations is proof enough that there are people in every country who want peace and are moreover working for it. It is for associations such as this to devote time and effort and utilities all the energy at their command to influence and help all governments to work for peace. In as much as thought is more potent even than action, let us think aright. If we do so we shall also act aright.

In Rajkumari Amrit Kaur's view "Wars are immoral and are not only incapable of solving any problems but actually create worse ones". In the paper on "Disarmament and the Ban on nuclear Weapons" that Rajkumari read for the Bureau of Parliamentary Studies on December 8, 1957, she deals with the spiritual aids to eradicating from the minds of men the "fear complex" which is the root cause of all armed conflict.

BLUEPRINT FOR SURVIVAL

After having been persuaded to read a paper on "Disarmament and Banning of Nuclear Weapons", I have often wondered why I allowed myself to be inveigled it doing so. I am singularly ignorant about arms of any sort or kind and I know nothing technically or scientifically about nuclear bombs and radio active fall-out.

Those who will be kind enough to listen to me today will, I plead, listen to me as one among the many humble millions of citizens of all the countries of the world who dread the possibility of another war, having had the misfortune of witnessing two holocausts in their lives and, perhaps, even more so as a woman, for women are the worst sufferers in war. They are meant by nature to conserve life. As mothers of the race, as protectors of culture and of good traditions eminently concerned with the happiness of the home which connotes human happiness, as radiators of love, I believe their voice is far too little heard in the world of politicians in whose hands lies the destiny or fate of this planet of ours. You will, therefore, bear with me and forgive me if what I say is perhaps not what you had expected.

It is just over twelve years since the last war ended on a note of pessimistic realisation that it had solved nothing and achieve even less except for a wholesale destruction of men, material and morale. The last was the greatest and the saddest casualty. It brought in its wake the germs of a fear complex which in its turn has sown the seeds of future wars. While the defeated nations lost much, the victors gained nothing. The great disaster which we euphemistically called war to end all a wars has, as we realise today, created fresh tensions which may well make us rename the last armageddon as a prelude to other and more terrible conflicts.

Be it, however, said to the credit of the then leaders of the different nations that having suffered greatly they, at least in the period immediately following the termination of hostilities, were led in all honesty to create the body known to us as the United Nations Organisation, to be followed by the creation of what are called the U.N. Specialised Agencies, such as UNESCO, WHO, FAO and others. These latter have done and continue to do some fine work and in the UNO itself, with all its shortcomings, none of us must lose faith. Indeed to strengthen is must be our endeavour. It is today the only light on a dark horizon for it does beckon mankind to her things. The theory of "One World" had been advanced even earlier. In the prayer read by him to the United Nations on Flag Day, June the 14th, 1942, President Roosevelt said "One world is but a small star in the great Universe. Yet of it we can make if we choose, a planet unvexed by war, untroubled by hunger or fear, undivided by senseless distinctions of race, colour or theory". These sentiments were echoed and re-echoed all the world over and were epitomised in the clause in the Constitution of UNESCO which embodies Lord Attlee's now famous word, "Since wars begins in the minds of men, it is in the minds of men that the defences of peace must be constructed."

As I said a few moments ago, it is just twelve years since the horrors of the last war which culminated in Hiroshima, evoked such excellent sentiments. But in spite of the *bonafides* of the builders of U.N.O., it is now patent to all that unless something tangible is done to avoid conflict, we might even head towards another war, more perilous and devastating than all the in any part of the world since history began. Since such conflicts have their beginnings in the minds of men and have their roots in the tensions created by a fear complex, we must first of all eliminate viewing always with suspicion and mistrust the motives and intentions of others. It appears to me that it is not merely the problems of disarmamont or the banning of nuclear weapons and tests that have to be solved. Rather the solution lies in the removal of the root cause itself. Disarmament cannot banish fear and nor can the ban on nuclear weapons and tests because, by themselves, they mean only a certain curbing of the weapons of war and methods of warfare and not the elimination of the basic causes that govern their construction and utilisation. What the world wants today is an agreement to "ban all wars" because wars are immoral in every sense of the term and are not only incapable of solving problems but actually create worse one.

Saints, sages and philosophers of all ages have ever decried war. Their dicta hold as true today as when they were given to the world centuries ago. It was Seneca who posed the question of the morality of war. "We are mad" he said, "not only individually but nationally. We check manlaughter and isolated murders; but what of the war and the much vaunted crime of slaughtering whole peoples?" We talk glibly today of the immorality of genocide. But do we ever pause to think of war as genocide in excelsis? We do not, simply because we are still drugged with the opiate of all the outworn shibboleths that glorify anything and everything that pertains to warfare. The man who saves a drowning person at the cost of his own life or renders any other outstanding humanitarian service does not get the recognition for his valiant deed that it assuredly his due, but the man who leads in mass murder in battle is sure to be decorated for valour and to be reckoned for ever as a hero.

It is not his innate heroism that is valued so much as his heroism in battle. Therefore, the first and foremost thing to do, if we are to make this earth of ours a safe place to live in, is to bring up future generations in the realisation not only of the fallacy but also of the criminality of war, and one way of doing so can be by effecting a complete reorientation in the methods of teaching history and general knowledge. There are many more things of importance in the history of the growth of civilisation than battles and wars. The change from the theocratic domination of the first Christian millennium to a plutocratic or bureaucratic domination of society today, evolutionary processes like the industrial revolution of nineteenth century and the dynamic advances in science have done very much more to shape history than wars. Since this it so, is it not our bounden duty to present to the impressionable young mind history and the world in their true perspective? I place the proper education of the citizens of tomorrow on a very high pedestal for the future is theirs. Children know no barriers of race, caste or creed. These must not be instilled into them. There must be more and more interchange of youth in our educational and social institutions so that race prejudices may die a natural death and international goodwill and understanding grow in our hearts as naturally as a flower grows to its full beauty in a good soil.

There are those who will say that this is but a long term solution and will naturally ask what about the present? How do we set out in our quest of the 'Golden Fleece' of peace in our own time?

Before we launch into consideration of this, let us pause for one moment to consider what wars of the future mean. Mankind today sands on the brink of disaster, even of annihilation and total extinction. Every day we get news of the explosion of a new kind of atomic or hydrogen bomb, each more deadly than the earlier one. Scientists now talk of a cobalt bomb which will eclipse both in its devastating effects on whole tracts. Only the other day we were thinking in terms of the strato and the ionospheres. Today the conquest of outer space is a reality as are the chances of showering destruction without meeting with opposition. The intercontinental ballistic missile bodes no good to civilian and non-combatant populations far removed from the theatres of war. In fact the conquest of space will mean that war can never be confined to a particular area or nation or even to a group of nations but will be a global war in the absolute sense of the term, bringing death and destruction to even peaceable people who are not involved in any way in the ideological or any other differences of the main parties contesting for supremacy.

I am no scientist, as I have said before, and I cannot speak with any authority on fusion and fission bombs, radioactive fall-out, thermonuclear dynamics, strontium—90, and the dangerously high increase in radioactivity both in the vicinity of the site of explosion and in the world's atmosphere. But I do know, as millions of people know, that the latest nuclear intercontinental, ballistic and space missiles are capable of causing death and destruction on a scale unprecedented in human history. And that is not all. The horror of the sufferings of the victims of the Hiroshima bombing is too vivid in our minds to be ignored. Not only did this single bomb turn the city into a shambles, but it left its radioactive mark on the city's unfortunate inhabitants. It has had even more serious consequences on the entire surrounding region—sterility of human beings, animal life and vegetation, deformities and inheritable degenerative diseases. In fact it has proved to the world that the ultimate result of atomic blasts will be the creation of newer and bigger deserts which, in a total war, will embrace the entire surface of the globe and threaten the human race and all other life with .... Towards that appalling end I fear, wittingly ....unwittingly, the world is steadily and inexorably moving unless .... and there certainly is an unless about it—we remove the root causes of conflict in human minds. We must need draw up a blue print for survival if we desire that the human race shall survive. And since all physical efforts like the race for armaments, the increase in the use of scientific discovery and invention for the forging of bigger and bigger weapons of destruction, the keeping of an uneasy peace by a show of strength, have signally failed, it must become increasingly obvious to all of us that any new approach to the solution of the problem of world survival must of necessity be based on the spiritual rather than on the material values of life.

The first essential consideration for a spiritual approach is that our minds and hearts must be tuned into the message of the Divine Being. All the Prosphets and Sages have preached it and the followers of different faiths can find it, if they only search for it, in their own religious precepts. Coming as I do from the land of Buddha and Gandhi and brought up in the Christian faith, I see it everywhere in the teachings of all. In about three weeks' time, we shall be celebrating the nativity of the Prince of peace. He gave to the peoples of the world, torn by mutual hatered and dissensions, the divine message of love. But it is as likely as not that even during Christmastide, a season of "peace on earth and goodwill towards men", we shall read of a new nuclear weapon or a new ballistic missile being tested of tried out. It hurts to feel that the Christian nations only pay lip service to the immoral message of Jesus Christ, summed up in the two words "universal love."

It was also the principle tenet of the religion which Gautama Buddha, the enlightened, preached to a tension-ridden India. Horrified by the carnage and destruction caused by his successive wars, the Great Emperor Asoka turned to the Buddha's path of peace, ahimsa and love. We in India try, however, humbly and falteringly, to follow these tenets. To remind us of them we have given pride of place to the "Asoka Chakra" in our national flag. There has been yet another who, in our own times, has preached the same gospel and given us the same message. I had the priceless and rare privilege for many years of being close to Gandhiji when he gave to us—and through us he hoped to the world—a panacea for its many ills—the path of non-violence and truth. Force, he held, can never be conquered by force. "*Amor omnia vincit*" runs the old adage which states a timeless truth for it is only love that can conquer where force fails. The conquest of the fear in the minds of men today can be conquered by Non-violence and Truth. In the words of the Mahatma, "Non-violence is an active force, it is a "weapon of the strong".

It is the law of love and therefore there in no fear, for love and fear are contradictory terms. The law of love will work as the law of gravitation works, whether we accept it or not. And just as a scientist works wonders out of various applications of the laws of nature, even so can a man who applies the law of love with scientific precision. For the force of non-violence is infinitely more wonderful and subtle than the forces of nature. The man who discovered for us the law of love was a far greater scientist than any of our modern scientists. The more I work at this law, the more I feel the delight in life, the delight in the scheme of this universe. It gives me a peace and a meaning of the mysteries of nature that I have no power to describe. There is no gainsaying the fact that if man could be impregnated with this force, he would be able to withstand all violence.

Gandhiji always maintained that non-violence was a mighty force which could be used by individuals as well as communities. It was the one answer to domestic as well as political disputes. He claimed that its universal applicability was proof, if proof were needed, of its permanence and invincibility. He once wrote that this force of non-violence was to violence, and therefore to all tyranny, all injustice, what light is to darkness.

It is, therefore, in the fitness of things that we, all of us, really effect what we, in the days of our struggle for political freedom, used to ask for from the British, namely a change of heart. Unless we try to understand our neighbours, trust the *bonafides* and thereby make them trust us, we cannot really conquer either our own or their fear. When we have conquered fear there will be no need to carry on an armaments race; no need to utilise scientific advances for forging new weapons of war. I hold that even in the context of the present stalemate in the United Nations, the Gandhian method, if tried out faithfully, would pay dividents. The West's desire to limit the size of the Disarmament Commission, their reluctance to dissolve the Sub-committee, the Russian instance on the abolition of the Sub-committee and the enlargement of the Commission to include all member nations of the U.N., the many other resolutions calculated to patch up differences, these are all palliatives.

They provide no real remedy, because the canker has now invaded even humanitarian organisations which follow no political ideology and hence have no political bias. Power politics are vitiating the atmosphere for they too are born of a 'Fear Complex'. All of us want to avoid conflict, We Indians are wedded to the concept of what has now come to be known as 'dynamic neutralism'. Our attitude is often misunderstood but it is the legitimates offshoot of the Gandhian concept of truth and non-violence. We have given it the shape of non-alignment with any power blocks in the hope of trying to understand each other and in our humble way helping to case tensions. Non-alignment is certainly not isolationism. The world is far too small and too dynamic an entity for any country to imagine that it can live to itself. But since fear is man's worst enemy, no headway can be made unless it is eliminated? How can it be eliminated? Certainly not by worshipping at the shrine of the monster itself. Many statesmen have said in an unabashed manner that we can only avoid war by showing the "enemy" that we are stronger than he. I would like this fallacy to be given the lie because if we play perpetually with fire, we shall certainly and however inadvertently, cause an irrevocable explosion.

I venture, in deep humility, to place before this gathering a few suggestion which I believe may help to allay the fear that grips the world :

1. Since no problem is incapable of solution, if the will to solve it is there, there must be continuous meetings of those mostly concerned and those who can help to ease existing tensions, regardless of how long or how difficult the discussions on the practical but at the same time rapid phasing of disarmament may be. The urgency and essentiality of a solution cannot brook delay and no country may leave these discussions until agreement has been reached.

2. To this end all nations, big and small, must pledge themselves never to resort to war for the settlement of any dispute.

3. No nation must refuse to cooperate in this endeavour.

4. The creation of world police force must be taken up for serious consideration at once. I realise that we have not

progressed enough on the moral spiritual plane to do without something of this nature as a deterrent to crime.

5. Nations that break agreements must be made to feel that they are outcasts of society. Non-violent non-cooperation with an evil doer is ever the best remedy for reforming him.
6. No scientific discoveries should be kept secret and since all knowledge is meant to enhance the welfare of humanity, these discoveries should be the property of the world. Such an agreement between the nations would certainly mitigate fear.
7. The less money spent on armaments the more will be available for the all-round development of the economically backward countries and for the relief of human suffering.
8. More and more emphasis should be laid on and more funds should be allotted to the specialised agencies of the United Nations for the excellent work they are doing in the field of international cooperation and helping where help is most needed, regardless of race or area.
9. If we demand standard of behaviour from others, it follows that we must turn the searchlight inwards and see that there is integrity of purpose and good neighbourliness and space within our own borders and that we are willing to subserve our personal interests for the greater good. The way of non-violence is the hard way—demanding even the supreme sacrifice but therein lies salvation.
10. Finally at all times must human beings be protected from the hazards of nuclear fall-out. The of repeated and all-inclusive appeal from the Red Cross International Conference must be honoured by every nation.

I have spoken with a full heart. For many years with Gandhiji and for ten years as a Minister of Health with the Union Government of India I have come face to face with poverty and human suffering. I have no doubt that it can be mitigated if the where withal to mitigate it were there. It can be there if we build up our defences other than any armaments. The world is very beautiful, the heart of humanity, and I have had the rare privilege of meeting the humanity of many lands, is sound, the language of the heart of humanity is also one, even though it expressees itself in varying sounds and scripts. There is a universal and a burning desire for peace and friendship. I do not therefore despair that, however, vexed the problems may be, they will be solved and humanity will be saved to serve humanity.

In India, Local Self Government is a subject dealt with by the State Governments and the Central Health Ministry exercises coordinative and advisory functions. To Rajkumari Amrit Kaur, who was incharge of the Health Portfolio at the Centre, it became increasingly obvious that the grass-roots of the health problem lay in concerted action by the local self government bodies and health administrations at the district level. To that end an exchange of views between the State and the Central Governments and different State Government interests became necessary and Rajkumari called a meeting of the Ministers and officers of the local governments to provide a forum for such discussions. In her Inaugural Address delivered on August 6, 1948, she poses the different problems that face the country in this field of governmental activity.

ON LOCAL SELF GOVERNMENT

No conference of those responsible for local self government has been called so far because the subject falls entirely within the provincial sphere. At the same time amongst us must have at least two living rooms, a kitchen and a bath room, a verandah and a little courtyard, where they can sleep in the hot weather. The solution of these problems of housing, slum clearance, pure water supply and improvement of sanitation will, no doubt, require time and money, but I am sure all of us will agree that it is high time they were tackled in right earnest by the authorities responsible for local administration.

Maternity and child welfare centres provided by local authorities in most parts of the country are inadequate and often badly run and it is also common knowledge that hospitals when they have been run by local bodies have generally been so neglected that those in charge of them have bagged for them to be provincialised. This is only another instance where the lack of a proper sense of citizenship has resulted in bad and inefficient administration. It is as a consequence of the same lack of a proper civic sense that bribery and corruption are rampant during elections, and afterwards too, because self-interest comes before the general good. These and other defects of which you, who are in charge of local administration must be far more aware than I am, have to be remedied if the community is to progress and if the people are to be given the rights of citizenship. It is for us assembled here to discuss ways and means of bringing about the necessary improvements. People should be educated to conform to certain standards of behaviour as citizens. Only if we set them ourselves can we demand standards of integrity from others. Co-operative association in the matter of health, education, agriculture, and building will help, I feel sure, to inculcate in us a better sense of citizenship. It is largely because we have been used to think in terms of caste and community that we have been unable to work as a team, in such a manner as to ensure good and efficient administration, while giving full scope for the expression of the popular will. I would like here to mention a few points which deserve close attention from authorities responsible for local administration whoever those authorities may be or whatever forms they may take.

In most of our cities, and here we must not think so much in terms of a few capital cities but in terms of the mofussil areas, schools are neglected, their buildings are poor, the teachers are badly paid and hence their quality is poor. This applies particularly to girl schools. There is no provision of milk or free meals for children such as exist in even the poorest towns of a country like Britain. There are generally speaking, no proper playgrounds for them, no nursery schools, no creches and no medical examination for children.

Another social need which has been sadly neglected by our local authorities and needs urgent attention is the provision of proper housing for the people, especially for the poor. Harijan quarters of labouring people everywhere that I have seen are deplorable. There seems to be little or no proper planning in the matter of housing and in crowded areas occupied by the poor, sanitation and hygiene are hopelessly neglected and the drainage is often poor or non-existent. Adequate attention is not always paid to a proper water supply. It must be the aim of local bodies to see that all slum areas are cleared and the provision of proper housing for the Harijan and other workers must be their primary concern. In this matter I have always felt that a single room tenement to accommodate a family must be absolutely banned. It is unnecessary to dilate on the grave evils, both physical and moral, that must inevitably result from such over-crowding. The poorest the subejct of local self government is of such vital importance to the general well being of the people, that I feel it would be definitely beneficial if a forum could be provided where those responsible for this important arm of the administration all over India could meet together periodically, exchange ideas and discuss problems of common interest. It is with this idea therefore that I have convened this conference.

I have always felt that very much more attention should be paid to evolving first class local administration which would really be the basis of universal good government in the country. I think if we are true to ourselves, we shall have to admit—however reluctantly—that our local bodies, generally speaking, have not yet attained that standard of administration which it must be the goal of every one to attain if the independence that has just come to us is going to be made worthwhile. There are, of course, various factors which, each in its own measure, have contributed to this unfortunate result, but I have no doubt in my mind that the low standards of administration in our local bodies, which have made provincial governments in the past curtail the powers of municipalities and local boards, is due in large measure to a lack of sense of citizenship amongst us are people. And here we may not blame the general mass of people whose ignorance and poverty make them easy victims exploitation. We, of the educated class, must turn the searchlight inwards and see where we are to blame. While for its proper functioning the whole structure of local self Government, as all forms of democratic government, must rest on the strong foundations of an enlightened public opinion and a keen civic sense amongst the citizens, it is at he same time necessary to ensure that the machinery of local government is framed.

It is almost always explained that local bodies have not been able to discharge properly the numerous and important functions devolving on them because their financial resources are slender. While this is no doubt largely true. I am not sure whether it can be claimed that local bodies everywhere have been careful to mobilise all their resources carefully and to use them in the best manner possible for the good of the community. You must all be aware of the criticism that in many local bodies under-assessment of taxation is a serious evil and in many places the authorities fail even to collect in full the taxes actually assessed, leaving large arrears-uncollected. As no organisation can function properly without adequate finances, it is obviously essential for local authorities to see that their taxes are properly assessed and collected. It is equally essential to see that the monies so collected from the taxpayers are properly and usefully spent to the best advantage of the areas concerned. This can be ensured only by a properly organised machinery for local administration which should be both honest and efficient. There should be strict supervision in the matter of contracts and the selection of the executive personnel of local bodies should be entrusted to some authority which will not be subject to pressure of undesirable influences to any land.

I have long been in favour of a department of social service in all branches of administration. This would mean training-centres for would be municipal and district board employees. There should also be committees of voluntary workers who would keep in touch with local needs, help in organising cooperation and keeping the peace, impart civic and health instruction to adults, supervise the distribution of, for example, milk to children, run community kitchen, assist the local bodies in every way, keep abreast of local opinion and maintain a high standard of integrity as well as of efficiency. I found in my own home town where I served for three years a member of the municipality that my health centre worked exceedingly well when it was run by a committee of voluntary women workers. The Health Visitor in charge was then freed from rendering special service to the members of the municipality or district board. The same applied to the inspectress of municipal girls schools. Women teachers often have a hard time when their appointments or dismissals are in the hands of men. That is one of the reason why I have always been most anxious for women to serve on local bodies. Their presence on municipal and district committees should raise the tone and standards of deliberation and work, as they should be expected to bring in a finer spirit service.

There are many other things which local authorities will have to do to provide amenities for living in both rural and urban areas. Children's play grounds and parks for the public are essential in any plan for building model townships and it is high time that the authorities responsible took up the remodelling of our villages. No longer can villages be neglected. It should be possible to solve the problem of remodelling villages effectively if the problem is tackled in a systematic manner. Surely, remodelling of one or two villages a years should not be beyond the bounds of possibility for every local board? As every one is aware, food and milk adulteration is widely prevalent in this country constituting a very grave threat to national health and in the matter of suppression of this evil the local authorities have to play a very considerable part. They could also play a most useful part in organising dairies to ensure a proper supply of milk to the cities.

Most of our cities are infested with beggars many of whom are children or sick persons. It is essential to see that these unfortunate children are reclaimed and given opportunities to develop into useful members of the community and that the sick destitutes are properly cared for. It is the duty of local authorities to deal with this problem in an effective manner. Every city must have a poor-house and an alms-house for the aged.

There are no doubt many other points concerning local self government. But whatever may be the needs to be met, ultimate success will depend on the existence of a proper organisation with adequate means, which will be honest, efficient and vigilant.

It was Mahatma Gandhi that set into motion forces which have spelled the resurgence of Asian and African nations. It is no wonder that Rajkumari, one of his most earnest disciples, should in the course of her address to the Sixth Session of the African Students Association (India) delivered on December 26, 1957 present a new and glorious vision—the formation of a "United States of Africa". Rajkumari has been a patron of the African Students' Association since 1953 and has been in close touch with social and political developments in that great continent.

THE NEW AFRICA

I was very happy when my young friend, Mr. Mbujiana asked me to join in this afternoon's ceremony.

I love youth and I am a great believer in youth. In the world of today where suspicion and mistrust of each other are causing tension between nation and nation, one of the best ways of bettering these unfortunate conditions is for youth to come more and more together. Just as children instinctively know no barriers of caste, creed, colour or race, so youth too, by and large, have no such prejudices. It is their privilege to plan their own future, to dream dreams, to live together in hostels, to indulge, in other words, all the time, while they are students, in cooperative endeavour. I myself had the privilege of being educated in a foreign land but I was never made to feel that I was a stranger or a foreigner and my loyalty to my alma matter, both school and college, remains the same today as in those far-off days. It is a tie that binds.

I am therefore very happy that our Universities are giving opportunities to youth from Africa to come and study in our institutions.

Africa used often to be called by some writers as "the dark continent", presumably because very little was known about it. In any event many foreigners who went to that continent to shed light on the darkness ended up mostly by acquiring portions of the country for their own benefit. Nevertheless, Africa has emerged from its darkness and is very much in the limelight today. It is good to feel that more and more education is spreading and surely, even though perhaps slowly to the way of thinking of Africans and their friends, colonial domination is being lifted and the sons of the soil are becoming masters in their homeland.

You, young friends, who have come to our ancient land to learn in our universities will have great responsibilities to shoulder when you return to your country. We can only hope that you will have found your stay with us not only beneficial from the point of view of acquiring knowledge but that you will have formed friendships with our youth which will be helpful in strengthening the bands of friendship between our ancient country and your comparatively new continent. Africa has a glorious future before it. I cannot possibly hope to see the fulfilment of what must be your dream as well as the dream of all freedom loving peoples—a United States of Africa. But you young people will have the great privilege of working for it. And if the education of some of your youth in our institutions of learning will have helped each one of you to fit yourself to shoulder the heavy burdens which you will have to shoulder in order to make your country, with all the natural resources available to it for exploitation, take its rightful place in the family of nations, it will be a source of great satisfaction to your friends in India.

Many Indians have gone to Africa in a spirit of adventure and have found themselves there. Gandhiji constitutes a special link between our countries, a link that can never be broken. I do sincerely hope that friendly interchange of youth and of trade and the strengthening of cultural ties will continue to grow as the years go by to the mutual benefit of both our countries.

We live in a world in which the shadow of conflict makes us sad and fills us with fear. At the same time there is much to make us rejoice too. Science has conquered geographical barriers and brought us all very near each other. You young people have to see to it that the mental barriers which often divide man from man are also conquered and that we resolve always and in any circumstances to settle our disputes in a friendly way and agree to live and work together for the welfare of humanity as a whole. The mind of man may not be bounded by narrow prejudices. Rather must it be our constant endeavour to rise above them.

We are meeting here during what is known is a season of 'Peace on earth and goodwill to men' and it is on that happy note on which I would like to inaugurate your gathering today and wish you every success in your meetings as well as every happiness and prosperity in the New Year about to dawn.

As Independent India's first Health Minister, Rajkumari Amrit Kaur was the directive force behind the dynamic effort that was being made to build up the nation's health. Today, freed from the many preoccupations and responsibilities of a Cabinet Minister's life, she views current trends in politics with the detachment of a statesman. If she appears to spare no words, it is only because she feels strongly that some of the happenings in India today are detrimental to the interests of her beloved country.

QUO VADAMUS?

Whatsoever things are true, whatsoever things are honest, whatsoever things are just, whatsoever things are pure, whatsoever things are lovely, whatsoever things are of good report; if there be any virtue, and if there be any praise, think on these things.

The New Testament,
Phillippians, IV : 8.

Though little dangers they fear,
When greater dangers men environ
Then women show a front of iron;
And gentle in their manner, they
Do bold things in a quiet way,

Thomas Dunn English,
in Bettty Zone Stanza.

I am glad that those in charge of Gandhi Marg have undertaken to awaken thought into happening in our country today because these are certainly disturbing Gandhiji always stood for turning the searchlight inwards whenever he was faced with the solution of a difficult problem. If he was unable to bring conviction to the heart of his opponent, if anything went wrong within his own circle or the party, he even went to the length of undertaking a fast simply in order to purify himself and get the guidance from above that he invariably sought at all times.

There is no gainsaying the fact that all is not well with us. Wherever one goes, whomever one meets, one senses a universal feeling of depression and frustration. The depression is due in some measure to the high cost of living, the inability to meet one's daily wants, the feeling that there is an absence of getting a sympathetic hearing or justice anywhere, and there is frustration because of the growing unemployment among educated youth, a sense of insecurity among those who would like to serve and yet have no channels of work open to them and above all because of the widespread and ever increasing evils of corruption and nepotism.

Gandhiji was ever so right when he said that political independence was only the first small step towards the attainment of the Ram Rajya of his dreams. Political power, he always held, could corrupt and would corrupt rapidly those who wielded it if they did not at all times place a greater emphasis on the moral and spiritual values of life. Therefore it was that during his incomparable leadership of the freedom movement, he laid equal if not greater emphasis on the constructive programme and after we had gained our political independence he advised that the Congress which throughout the years he had endeavoured to strengthen through service to the people should devote itself wholly of the uplift of Indian humanity through social work. His advice in this as in so much else has gone completely unheeded and what is the result? If we are honest with ourselves we will have to admit that power has corrupted the party and there can be no improvement unless someone is strong enough to sweep the augean stables with a very heavy broom.

The natural result of the corruption wrought by power whether of an individual or of a party is internal and unhealthy rivalry. Wherever the lust for power exists, human welfare becomes at once subservient to political expediency and it is this sad state of affairs in the Congress Party that is gradually making the people lose heart. Our past history should have taught us many a lesson but if the rot that has set in is not stopped, who knows but that we may become the victims once again of outside agency? It is therefore high time that the leaders of the rulling party turned the searchlight inwards and asked themselves why there is such a falling off in standards of both thought and behaviour, why there is not that enthusiasm today to build up our country that there was under Gandhiji's leadership to win our political freedom through sacrifice and service. Again if we are honest, we will ask ourselves whether there is not something wrong with our leadership. Every day the people are "called upon" Ministers, whether State or Central, to tighten their belts, to work hard, to think only in terms of India and not of their State, to eschew caste and communalism, to worship at the shrines of big, enterprises which are the keys to economic progress, at look upon the building up of the country as a big adventure and to be disciplined. And certainly these are desiderata to be adopted by the minds and hearts of and acted upon by every patriotic Indian.

But what is happening in Congress itself? It is indeed a sorry spectacle to see internal strife raging in almost every State with the result that good government just cannot be. The dawn of independence raised bright hopes in the hearts of every Indian but only the other day a poor man said to me, and it made my heart ache to hear him, "No one today has any hope left that life is going to become better for us". In the same way people from more than one former "princely state" have said that the rule of the Rajas and Maharajas was better than Congress rule. Brahmins seem to be unable to live in peace and amity with non-Brahmins, Andhra had to be separated from Madras, Gujerat from Maharashtra, Assam cannot tolerate Bengalis, Hindus have not retained the confidence of the Sikhs, all the minority communities are unhappy because of the lack of generosity towards them on the part of the majority community. The division of India on a linguistic basis is working havoc with our unity. Where indeed are we going? And with what face can the Congress party ask people to do things which they themselves are not doing.

What can we all do to try to remedy what is undoubtedly a sad state of affairs? Never having been a politician in the accredited sense of the term, I daresay any suggestions that come from me will not find favour with those whose only object in life is to keep their party in power. But since it is wrong to criticise and not offer any constructive solutions, I venture to put on paper what has been on my mind for some time past.

1. The time is ripe for having the best men and women in the country appointed as Ministers, regardless of their party affiliations, in other words, we should have a non-party Government. There is a great deal to be said in favour of what Vinobaji has recently advocated, viz., that politicians should also put an age limit on themselves as they do on all servants of governments. The Prime Minister of the U.K.'s recent list of Ministers showed that no one of those recently chosen was more than 52 years old and the majority were in their forties. I will not believe that there isn't enough talent in India but we have to look for it also outside the Congress party.

2. The greatest lack in the country today is the lack of integrity. Economic distress may be responsible for it to some extent but dishonesty has come into being everywhere. It would be a good plan if the highest in the land were to wander incognito round the lower courts, for example, or indeed anywhere in the mofussil areas and even in some of their own concerns, and see with their own eyes what is happening. Not only is corruption rampant but efficiency is at a low ebb. And it is not only material dishonesty but intellectual dishonesty too that has to be combated. Further, the falling in moral standards is greatly to be deplored. Parents do not dare to allow their daughters to walk alone after sunset in Delhi—the capital city of India—lest they be molested. This certainly was not so under the British or even during the first five years of independence. Here again example is far better than precept and it is of no consolution to anyone to

be told that there is more dishonesty in India than in any other country or that the private life of an individual is his own affair. Caesar's wife must be above reproach if we are to command universal respect, Gandhiji always laid the greatest stress on moral character and no one in his encourage was allowed to hold office in any of his organisations who was not of good character. Moral lapses were dealt with an iron hand by him and he commanded respect and obedience because of his own high moral calibre and the rigorous discipline which he exercised over himself. He never asked anyone to do what he was not doing or had not done himself.

We talk of student indiscipline but forget that the behaviour of youth everywhere is a reflection of their up-bringing at home and in educational institutions and therefore a reflection of the conduct of their elders, alasi every often not their betters. Teaching is a vocation for more than it is a profession but it no longer attracts the best minds among us. Why? Teachers must be better paid and so must administrators so that they may have enough to live on and, above all, no political pressures should be brought to bear on them. Moreover the ratio of teacher to pupil whether in our schools or in our colleges is lamentable. No good influence can be exercised over the students when the teachers are not men of the highest calibre and when, even if they are, they cannot possibly reach out to the pupils committed to their charge. There should be much more screening where admittance to universities is concerned and those not fitted for college education should be diverted to polytechnics.

We should avoid having one new university campuses in our capital cities. Another question that must arise in the minds of many of us is whether we are wise in not giving any religious instructions to our children. Speaking for myself I value more then I can say the religious instruction which I received from my mother in my early childhood, and in letter years in school in England. It has become almost the fashion, as it were, for college youth to say that in this age of scientific wonder it is impossible to believe in God. I was deeply struck with a poor villager's words not so long ago. He had lost his only son and later his only grandson and when I expressed my sympathy with him, he said "God blessed me when he gave them to me. He has now taken them. They were never mine and I must accept their loss too as

His blessing". How I wish all of us could be as rich in faith as this poor so-called uneducated villager!

3. But then are we not losing contact with the massess? Our elected representatives sit for practically 8 months in the year in Delhi and likewise in the capital cities of their State. I am more and more being forced to the conclusion that parliamentary democracy as adopted by us is really unsuited to our genious and not in keeping with our traditions and level of education. It is the lure of power in the State and Central Governments and legislatures that is the root cause of our intrenecine strife, the insistence on linguistic divisions and the relegation of the constructive programme to a very very subsidiary place. The adoption of the slogan of a Welfare State might even gradually kill voluntary endeavour because it is wrong for the State to imagine that it can do everything and it is bad for the people also to feel that they need do nothing because government will do everything for them. To kill private initiative has everywhere led to fascism and a totalitarian state is undesirable in every way.

4. We resort to legislation for the righting of all our wrongs. Since 1947 there are so many laws that lawyers and judges have both told me that it is difficult to keep pace with them. If we were to abide by the wisdom of those who have said quite rightly that "that country is best governed which is least governed" I believe we would achieve the same results by education and persuasion as we want the law to achieve if only we could have bands of devoted workers in the all our district headquarters and villages. To pass laws which can be easily evaded is in reality to bring the law into contempt.

5. Food production is our main headache. Can this not all be brought under one ministry, the Ministry of Food and Agriculture? Why should the Community Development Ministry be attempting the same thing? This is only one instance of the extremely cumbersome administrative machinery that has never ceased to grow since we attained our independence. It would be interesting to know how much per capita the cost of our administration today works out at State trading has not been a success and I sincerely hope we shall abandon this slogan. And

state trading in foodgrains will be a perfect disaster. Nor con cooperative endeavour be forced from above in any sphere, least of all on our formers who have throughout the ages completely identified themselves with the land they hold. And I also wonder whether we are not concentrating far more on large or even gigantic public undertaking in the industrial field to the detriment of the small scale and village industries, the development of which was the central theme of Gandhiji's scheme of Indian uplift. Even where our big river valley projects have started functioning, farmers are often not taking the water because of its high cost! .

6. Local Self-Government is a *sine qua non* for good government and an excellent training ground for developing a sense of citizenship. But the history of this sphere since independence makes sad reading. I did, as Minister for Health and L.S.G. for ten years, make many appeals to the State Ministers to persuade their governments not to contest seats to panchyats, municipalities or corporations on a party basis because real servants of India could be trained here and the country needed its best women and men to work cooperatively in this field as social servants. But my plea was not accepted because again it is a question of power and patronage in the hands of the party machine with the long distance view always taken of the quinquennial elections. The Delhi Corporation is a glorious example of party strife coming in the way of work for the betterment of the conditions under which the poor live. And as for the Panchayat raj which is being brought into being now, one can only hope that these bodies too will not go into wrong hands. The danger is great.

7. Linguistic area were retainly constituted by Gandhiji because he believed that this was the only way for Congress to make mass contacts. Ordinarily speaking linguistic areas, created solely for the purpose of a more efficient administration, should not contribute towards the disunity of the country. But this is exactly what has begun to happen and should be a warning to those in authority.

Radical troubles nearly always need radical remedies. It is high time those in power sat round a table and tried to find these remedies. We spend hours discussing foreign policies and happenings abroad but do not seem to find adequate time to give on happenings at home. If any decisions go contrary to our wishes in court, we have no hesitation in changing the constitution. I personally would like to see the present constitution altered since the form of democracy evolved by it has not fitted in with our needs. A unitary form of government which would cost the country much less, with smaller units of administration all over the country might be better and would give every one ample opportunity of working in his own sphere in a constructive manner. The country might be divided into zones rather than States with a few Governors who could have wise advisers at their elbows and could send a certain amount of time at each headquarters. But I daresay it is no good today dreaming of what might have been!

In any event, non-party governments everywhere can be a reality.

No child finds its it difficult to learn four languages but it is criminal to burden him with four scripts. Why cannot we adopt the Roman script and why cannot English be recognised as a language of India considering it is spoken by lakhs and will continue to draw people into its fold? In any event it should continue as the language for administration. It is a goodly heritage and a unifying force which should not be lost.

Parliament should not sit for more than six months in the year. The number of ministers and deputies etc. should be reduced to a minimum. The cost of administration must be brought down. The All-India services—administrative, judicial, medical, police, forest and education, should be revived. Far more should be done for small scale industries and Richard Gregg's advice regarding farming, compost etc. should be followed. Private enterprise and voluntary endeavour should be encouraged everywhere. In other words, we should return with zest to the way of life shown us by Gandhiji. If we don't, the future cannot be bright.

II

The health problems of a nation cannot be solved unilaterally; they also depend to some extent on simultaneous development in other spheres of national economy and the social and material advancement of the people. But though interdependent each of them has its own specific problems calling for both short and long range solutions. This aspect is well brought out in Rajkumari Amrit Kaur's broadcast talk on "Health" in the series. "Towards a Socialist Society." The talk was broadcast on the All India Radio network on August 8, 1955.

HEALTH : TOWARDS A SOCIALISTIC SOCIETY

The health of the people is really the foundation upon which all their happiness and all their powers as a state depend.

Benjamin Disraeli,
Earl of Beaconsfield
in a speech on July 24, 1877

The health of a nation is more important than the wealth of a nation.

Will Durant
in "What is Civilization".

In this series of talks on the theme, "Towards a socialistic society", my predecessors have already dealt with agriculture, industry and labour, all spheres of activity which are of such great national importance that both the government and people of this country are deeply interested in a joint effort to promote development on the soundest possible lines. I claim, and I feel I am right in doing so, that the subject of Health, on which I am privileged to address my listeners today, is of as much importance as any of the others already dealt with. In fact a sound physique and a healthy mind form the foundation on which alone each one of us can build a life of usefulness to others and to ourselves and derive from our day to day existence, that enjoyment of happiness and of successful accomplishment which makes living truly worthwhile. The purpose of my talk is to place before you the picture as I see it, of our national programme of health development which, I believe, is being organised in a manner designed to fulfil the requirements of a society marching onwards towards the realisation of a socialistic pattern. I fully recognise that the attainment of health and its maintenance require a wide variety of services to the community, including adequate provision of food, clothing and shelter as the basic minima for all.. In fact nearly all activities associated with civilized community life have their bearing on heatlh. It is, therefore, far from my thoughts to minimise in any way the solid contributions to the national health campaign which different branches of governmental and public activities, such as agriculture, education, housing and industrial development are making every day. But, speaking as the Union Health Minister, I am naturally led, in this talk, to concentrate on the organisation of health services and on the development of certain associated activities such as the training of health workers.

Let us first ask ourselves what the requirements of a legislation, while the executive authority to carry out the provisions of such legislation is vested in State governments. This concurrent field covers, among other things, regulation of the medical and other professions, control of the spread of disease from one State to another and labour welfare. The problems associated with health functions, which are under our Constitution the responsibility of the State can hardly be solved solely on the basis of action by individual States. These States differ widely among themselves in regard to their available resources in funds and in trained personnel as well as in existing facilities for the training of different types of health workers. To lease them to work out their own solutions to these difficult problems will obviously mean that the existing disparities between States will not only continue but will tend to become increasingly accentuated as the years go by. The more progressive States will make successive advances with lapso of yeaıs, whlle the less favourably situated will recede steadily to the background with their growing inability to keep pace with the successful ones. It is here that the main task of the Centres lies. The need for a coordinated advance on fairly uniform lines throughout the country is so obvious that it requires on special mention. The Constitution provides for the establishment of a Central Health Council with the States as members. This Council was established about four years ago and it has had three annual sessions at which matters of common interest were discussed and lines of policy for the country as a whole were adopted. I am indeed happy that these successive meetings of the Council have demonstrated an increasing measure of understanding between the Centre and the States and a growing desire to deal with the country's health problems on the basis of active cooperation between the Central and State Governments.

I shall now refer to some of the achievements already secured through joint effort between the Government of India and State

Government. A national malaria control campaign intended to cover the entire population of 200 millions affected by the disease has been steadily in progress during the past two years and about 75 millions have already been brought within the scope of the malaria control programme. Similarly campaigns on a national basis are being organised against filariasis and leprosy while an environmental hygiene programme, starting with the provision of protected water supplies, is also making progress.

The training programmes for health workers, including doctors, nurses, midwives and health visitors, have shown marked advances during the past seven or eight years. At the time when our country gained independence the number of medical colleges in the territory comprising the Indian Union was 16, today it is 34. The number of total annual admissions to medical colleges was about 1,800 eight years ago, today it is about 3,000. Many of the new colleges may be expected to increase their admissions steadily when their development becomes complete and the number of persons admitted may then go up by a few more hundreds. The process of establishing new colleges has not stopped. It is expected that the next Five Year Plan will add another ten colleges to the existing ones.

In order to make India largely self-sufficient as regards post-graduate medical education the Central Government has pursued a threefold path, the development of an upgrading programme whereby certain departments such to those relating to Anatomy, Physiology, Obstetrics, Gynaecology and Neuro-Surgery in selected medical institutions in different parts of India are improved, the establishment of an All-India Institute of Medical Sciences in Delhi in which undergraduate and post-graduate training facilities of a high order will be brought together to serve the needs of the country as a whole; and the creation of teaching and research institutes for special diseases or for particular branches of medical care.

The development of post-graduate training facilities is being steadily pursued on these lines.

As regards other health personnel also there have been striking advances in our training programmes, although the needs of the country are so great these increases naturally appear to be insufficient. Between 1948 and 1954 the member of midwives has risen from 760 to 1,750 and of health visitors from 39 to 76. The next Five Year Plan will provide for a steady stepping-up of the numbers that become available for service to the community.

It is appropriate to refer here to certain developments in health services which are bound to contribute a great deal to the health of the people as they become incrasingly organised and expanded. The Employees State Insurance Act, which was passed by Parliament in 1948, is now operating a medical care programme which will embrace during the next 18 months about two million industrial workers within its scope. It has been proposed that the inclusion of families of workers should be effected at an early date. The Act also provides for bringing within the scheme workers of all types, including commercial and agricultural labour. When these two developments are worked out in full, it seems probable that about 75 per cent of the total population of this country will be covered. Looking ahead only to the next five years it seems reasonably certain that at least 30 per cent of the urban population will be protected.

The approach by the Employees State Insurance Act towards the provision of a community health service is mainly urban in character although, in due course, the rural population will also be brought in. On the other hand, certain developments that are taking place are directly concerned with the rural areas. The Community Projects have started, within the areas they cover, an elementary form of preventive and curative health service which will undoubtedly be improved and strengthened along with a progressive rise in the economic status of the rural population.

The First Five Year Plan provides for the creation of maternal and child care centres in the rural areas and for the establishment of health units. Not all the money made available for these schemes has been utilised by the states, partly because initial difficulties in the implementation of large scale programmes have to be met. But there is not doubt that the policy of establishing a continuous chain of health units and of maternal and child care centres will be steadily pursued through coming years. These institutions may, in the beginning, be located in areas which are not covered by Community Projects, but the multiplication of the latter in due course, tend to absorb the former and thus create a health organisation which will provide protection to the farflung population of the countryside and outlying areas.

The medical care under the Employees State Insurance Act is based on contribution made by workers and by employees. The principle of self-help, which is stressed in this scheme, is sound and it tends to raise a sense of self-respect among the beneficiaries. Under the guidance of my Ministry a similar contributory scheme has been working for the past one year in Delhi for Central Government employees, the population covered, including families, being about to hundred and seventy thousands. I have no doubt that, with a steady rise in the income levels of the rural population, a similar system of contributions towards a medical care programme should be developed.

A socialist society rightly prizes its human resources as being far more important than its material resources. The full exploitation of the latter is indeed envisaged as an essential step to make life worthwhile for all. Such a society places Health and Education as services of supreme importance to promote the development of man to the fullest possible extent. This society stresses the principle that the medical care made available to the people should be in relation to the needs of the individual and not in relation to his ability to pay for such care. The health programmes that are being developed in the country, whatever their shortcomings may be in the immediate present, are intended to fulfil increasingly the application of this principle for the improvement of public health.

Rajkumri Amrit Kaur, India's Minister of Health, was elected President of the World Health Organisation and of the World Health Assembly in May 1950. In her address to the Fourth World Health Assembly delivered on May, 7, 1951 when she handed over charge to her successor Dr. Leonard Sheele, she brings out lucidly the value of international co-operation and of a unified effort in fighting disease and ill-health and building up a stable society in a tension ridden world. She pleads, for greater assistance to lesser favoured nations and more particularly the underdeveloped countries of South East Asia, which are the breeding grounds of many of the scourges of mankind.

ON INTERNATIONAL COOPERATION

"We must all hand together or assuredly we shall all hang separately." Benjamin Franklin at the Signing of the Declaration of Independence (July 4, 1876).

Although W.H.O. came into existence only four years ago, it is the inheritor of a long and fine tradition of international work. L'Office International d'Hygiene Publique started life nearly fifty years ago and has, within the 20th century, been actively concerned with the organisation and carrying out, on a cooperative basis among the nations, of quarantine measures which help to control the spread of epidemic diseases from one country to another through sea and air traffic, including large scale overseas pilgrimages. The Health Organisation of the League of Nations, the Pan American Sanitary Bureau and UNRRA have all worked actively in other spheres, which fact goes to show that the necessity of a common effort for the conservation of health of the peoples of the world has for sometime been in the minds of those responsible for international welfare. Nevertheless it was for W.H.O. to come into the picture and assume responsibility for the functions of these Organisations and weld all endeavour in the sphere of health into one. I think that we, who have served W.H.O. from its inception, can look back with satisfaction on a proud record of service during the very short time in which the Organisation has functioned and justly claim from the United Nations the certificate that though we are the youngest in years of her children we are perhaps the most advanced, both in thought and action.

I am sure history will record that in spite of trials and difficulties, in spite of wars and rumours of war which every country has witnessed throughout, and alas! continues to witness, the most significant human development has been in the field of social welfare. The world has been so narrowed down by the discoveries of science which have eliminated the obstacles of both time and distance, that it is impossible any longer for any one nation to live unto itself. Living unto oneself is not the best way for an individual to grow either physically, mentally or morally. The same law applies to the community, to society and to the world in general. Therefore, it was natural that thinking men should realise that there could be no happiness for the world until and unless we worked for or moved towards an integrated programme of international action for the promotion of human welfare. And in what sphere can this international action be more necessary than in the sphere of health? Health has often implied and still implies to many people nothing more than physical well-being and that well-being too depending not the quality and quantity of medical care and attention available. But the medical world has, I am glad to say, progressed far beyond this narrow outlook. Not only is the preventive side of medicine being stressed today even more than the curative side but it is recognised that there can be no physical well-being without mental and moral health. If we agree to this conception of health then I have no doubt that we can claim that the work of this Organisation is second to none of all the specialised agencies of U.N.O., if indeed it is not of prime importance.

A perusal of the Report for 1950 will tell us what further progress has been made during the year under review. In spite of severely restricted finances, WHO has during the past year been able to expand its services to Member States in addition to carrying on programmes launched in previous years, providing expert advisory services, and the ever-increasing activity in the Technical Services centred here at Geneva, including the setting up of new Expert Committees.

These are concrete examples of the practical services which WHO renders, and which it ought to be enabled to render on an ever-increasing scale.

But while we may rightly pride ourselves on such past achievements as we have to our credit we have also to be wise enough to see to it that our future development on right lines is ensured without let or hindrance. The W.H.O. as I have said before, has taken over the activities of some of the old Health Organisations and has done right in so doing. But there have come and are coming into being other agencies for advancing the cause of human welfare such as UNICEF, President Truman's Point Four Programme and the British Commonwealth Programme of development. It is obvious that wise use of the available funds and technical personnel is essential in order to ensure that these different agencies help to supplement each others' efforts do not create either unhelpful competition or overlapping of endeavour. This is particularly important as regards technical personnel. The number available is limited and a wise distribution of their services in a manner calculated to produce the maximum results is essential. Personally I would like all monies made available from Governmental or charitable sources for health work to be administered by WHO, the main specialised agency of the United Nations Organisation and where special sections already look after special activities. But human nature is human nature and those who give the money and those who have the money do somehow like to feel that they have a separate entity and full control. As a matter of fact, matters relating to health, education, nutrition and housing are so interlinked that it is only closely coordinated action by all different specialised agencies of the United Nations that can produce satisfactory results. It is gratifying to know that the basis for promoting work on effective and cooperative lines is being established with care. There are difficulties of course but with the necessary goodwill and understanding and tact on all sides there is no reason whatsoever why ways and means should not always be found to avoid friction and to forward hand in hand in ajoint endeavour which is fraught with such immense benefit to humanity. The responsibility that lies on WHO and all other agencies working in a great cause is heavy, and clear thinking and wise action in the immediate future are a definite essential for success because ours must be an enduring organisation. Short-term programmes cannot work miracles and we must plan for the time we will have to shoulder, through the regular WHO Budget, the full burden of the obligations laid on us by our Constitution. A long-term view is essential so that we may build surely.

A matter of considerable importance is decentralisation, a principle which was accepted at the First World Health Assembly and which has been given practical effect to in the shape of three Regional and three Nuclear Headquarters. I am proud of the fact that it was India's forceful plea for the formation of Regional Headquarters that made WHO take a step which, in the initial stages, required courage and faith. The wisdom of that step has been amply justified. I venture to say, speaking for my country and my Zone that it is the practical work carried on in our region from the very beginning that has found for WHO a warm place in the hearts of our people. Time and again when our Government is unable to undertake a health programme because of financial stringency the representatives of the people almost instinctively ask whether WHO cannot step into the breach. In any event, with the widely differing needs of different countries and with their varying grades of development, Who can hope to develop its activities properly only on the basis of an increasing delegation of power and responsibility to the Regional Bureaus. It may well be that we even have to revise the policies which have governed our programme planning in the light of recommendations from Regional Committees.

A pressing need of many countries is to find some way of overcoming difficulties in obtaining basic supplies and equipment for health work. Until this problem is solved many of the underdeveloped countries feel that they will not be able to derive full benefit from the WHO advisory and demonstration services. The action of WHO therefore in offering to assist governments in setting up plants for the manufacture of essential requirements such as DDT and Penicillin is very welcome. All possibilities of assisting worthwhile national health programmes must be examined and budget provision made for help in obtaining essential supplies. Speaking again for the Headquarters of the South East Asia Zone I can say with first-hand knowledge that the activities have extended during the three years of existence and with beneficient results. Its latest publication gives a clear picture of its set up and shows how within a brief period the Organisation has been actively engaged in combating malaria, tuberculosis. V.D., cholera and plague, has assisted in building up material and child welfare and nursing service, has had a fellowship programme and supplied medical literature, teaching and other equipment and supplies. This speaks volumes for the extent of the services rendered by WHO to the countries in this region. It would be unfair not to mention here the generosity and willing cooperation of UNICEF in all these programmes.

All this however goes to show that the world, and in particular the world of the underdeveloped countries is pining for more programmes and more help and cannot have the aid simply because of the unsatisfactory budgetary position of this fine Organisation. It is hard, indeed impossible, for all humanitarians to understand why WHO cannot have even a paltry 5 million dollars more with which to serve sick and suffering humanity. Countries labouring under the cruel burden of hunger and disease are breeding grounds for social unrest. If the man in the street can have a healthy environment, enough to eat, enough to clothe himself with, shelter over his head, employment, leisure and an all-round security of life there never will be war. But in a world which is so beautiful, where the sun, the moon and the stars, mountains and valleys, seas, rivers and lakes, forests, rich fields and pasture lands are ready to give to man of their country, it is indeed a tragedy that we have not yet found a way whereby to live at peace with our fellow men. And unless and until we can bury the grim spectre of war we shall continue to be starved for funds for what are the victories of peace. Nevertheless our efforts to serve wherever we can may not end for there is never any room for despair and the dark clouds that over-shadow our skies today can and must be dispelled by the fulfilment on our part of the pledge to serve one another. Our work is a precious heritage which we may not forsake and a positive factor for overcoming the root causes of conflict whether between governments and peoples or between nations. For ours is a peacetul yet unremitting battle against all that makes for armed warfare.

I therefore appeal to delegates when considering the Budget to raise it sufficiently so that the Organisation may at least be enabled to maintain its activities at a reasonable level. Are we to be paralysed because we cannot raise a couple of million more dollars? I sincerely hope not.

I regret the Health Stamp campaign which I advocated last year as means not only of augmenting the financial resources of WHO but also of securing the goodwill and sympathy of every individual in every country has not made any progress. I would ask this august assemblage to consider whether we may not encourage this campaign or discover some other means whereby we may promote the development of an annual programme which would mobilise public support on a wide scale for the beneficent activities of WHO.

The extra amount will make all the difference between a programme that is satisfactory and one which is unsatisfactory. It may be forgotten that inevitably any curtailment of the regular Budget falls most heavily on the demonstration and advisory services which we render to member States—that is to say on the very activities which are our most practical and valuable contributions to world health and by which we will eventually stand and grow or fail. Friends, there can never, there must never be failure in a high endeavour.

I thank you for the kind cooperation I have received from all of you and for your patient hearing. I hand over my office to Dr. Leonard A. Sheele in the full confidence that he will serve the Organisation with all his ability and with single-eyed devotion to the cause which we have espoused as our own and which is so vital for world peace and prosperity.

The abiding interest that Rajkumari Amrit Kaur has in the Child Welfare movement has resulted in her introduction of many schemes of maternal and child welfare during her tenure of office as Health Minister in the Government of India.

In the following address to the First Planary session of the International Study Conference on Child Welfare, delivered on December 6, 1952, Rajkumari Amrit Kaur brings out with clarity the various aspects of Child Welfare schemes and the problems of implementation.

ON CHILD WELFARE

Oh father and mother, if buds are nip'd
And blossoms blown away,
And if the tender plants are strip'd
Of their joy in the springing day,
By sorrow and care's dismay,
How shall the summer arise in joy,
Or the summer fruit appear?
Or how shall we gather what grief destroy,
Or bless the mellowing year,
When the blasts of winter appear?

. . . .William Blake . . . . in "The Schoolboy".

The promotion of child welfare is a problem of fundamental importance to the individual family and, through the family, to the nation. The children of a community form its most previous asset and the care and attention bestowed on furthering in every way the well-being of children and on their proper growth, physical, emotional and social, form a true index of the cultural and spiritual standards which the community has been able to establish for itself.

The children of today are the adults of tomorrow and, if the future of mankind is to witness and expanding era of social achievements, we must promote the happiness of all and eliminate, as far as may be possible, not only the fears, hatreds and ugly competition for material possessions that have led to two successive world wars in our life-time, with their untold tale of miseries, but also the lengthening shadow of an even grimmer and more destructive global conflict. To achieve this goal, the one basis on which constructive work should be centred is to create and enlarge opportunities for enabling children to grow up into healthy men and women, emotionally stable and free from the cramping influence of parochial and national prejudices. It, therefore, becomes the duty of all States, through purposeful effort, to encourage the flow of all national energies to the manifold tasks of improving the health and welfare of the children of the world.

A comprehensive programme of child care has its several aspects. Starting first in the home and expanding later into the outer world where community effort must provide for the welfare of pre-school children, of the school-going population and of adolescents with their many problems of psychological and social adjustment which begin to come into prominence as their personality develops under the influence of growing sexual maturity. Of these successive phases of development the most significant part is perhaps the early period of infanthood and childhood when home influence expresses itself most profoundly in shaping the future of the individual. It is here that parents can and should play their part and the extent to which they will be able to fulfil their role wisely and well will depend largely on the manner in which they have been educated to understand the true purpose of marriage, their children's needs and how to meet them. They should know the essential elements of physical care of children, including the basic principles underlying their development. They should be able to assist their children in the proper evolution of their emotional reactions to the continuous stream of physical, mental and social stimuli acting on them. No parent will be able to fulfil these functions without acquiring first the requisite knowledge and, secondly, without attaining that degree of self-discipline necessary to enable him or her to see the child's problems clearly and objectively and to offer help to solve them with understanding and sympathy. All too often the father and mother are tempted, in their dealings with their child, to seek relief for their personal emotional tensions, arising from excessive attachment, from undue fear and anxiety for the child's safety or from outbursts of temper which they are unable to control. What the child requires most in the home is an atmosphere of encompassing love and understanding, which gives him an assurance of security and helps to promote this growth on sound lines. Fear, anger, jealously are patterns of emotional behaviour which easily develop in the child, and the task of the wise parent should be to enable him to overcome these as far as may be possible. The cultivation of affection and consideration for all those around him, including animals, is another important contribution to the child's emotional development on healthy lines. Curiosity or the desire to extend his range of knowledge and experience in the expanding world personal contacts which his daily life brings to him is a healthy trait which requires to be developed in the child with care and with a sympathetic understanding of his limitations. Many questions that the child may ask about sex or religion may not be easy to answer, but an attempt should be made in every case to answer him simply but truthfully and in a straight forward manner. Successful parenthood will require that the father and mother should educate themselves continuously in order to meet intelligently the growing needs of their child and that the atmosphere of the home should be built up in a process of mutual adjustment, which places the health and welfare of their offspring as their primary concern. A child-welfare programme can therefore exert, if developed on proper lines, a profound influence for raising the standard of life and for promoting happiness in the home as well as in the larger national and international spheres. Apart from the fact that natural love prompts us to treasure our children as our most precious assets, the wider considerations to which I have briefly referred should, I submit, form a powerful motive force to strengthen and advance the child-welfare movement in every part of the world.

Proper physical care of the child, including his food, clothing, housing and home nursing, is the basis on which his future bodily and mental development will very largely depend. In the mother's womb nature has provided an ideal place where the growth of the foetus is effectively protected against changing weather conditions outside and nourishment is made available in easily assimilable form. On entering the world, the infant faces a totally different environment and is exposed to a wide variety of physical conditions including the possibility of risk of infection from time to time. To protect the child from the harmful impact of such adverse conditions and to help him to grow properly require sound mothercraft and the task of teaching the expectant mother to learn how to play her part as a parent is an essential function of the child welfare programme. Moreover the health of the child is also influenced largely by the health of the mother during pregnancy and an intelligent understanding of the hygiene of pregnancy is a very important part of the training to be imparted to the expectant mother. In this programme of instruction the physical needs of the infant, including food, clothing, hygienic home conditions and continuous care to protect him from adverse environmental influences, require the fullest possible emphasis. Such education has to be carried out in the home and in the child welfare centre. Apart from advice, visual demonstration of what should be done is of the utmost importance. Indeed I look upon the child welfare movement as a vital programme of education in which, with the child as the focus of attention, the community and parents, in particular, may be helped to develop their responsibility to promote conditions most favourable to social well being.

And here I would like to stress a point that is very often apt to be forgotten. To us, as a rule, the child only comes into being when he is born whereas, in reality, the parents should be alive to his existence from the moment he is conceived in his mother's womb. The procreation of children is a sacred task entrusted to man by God or Nature, or whatever any one may like to name the 'Unseen'. If the child is conceived in love and with the full sense of responsibility which parenthood demands of man and woman, he will be something which will inherently command the care and devotion which should be his. The thoughts the mother thinks while he is in her womb, indeed the way the parents, not only the mother, conduct themselves while he is being nourished even before birth will have a great bearing on his character.

We live in an age where the problem of birth control is a vexed problem for the entire world and especially for poor and over populated countries like ours. Nature has provided man with the power for full control over his physical senses. That he sometimes or, indeed, very often becomes their victim rather than their master is his own fault, whereby untold suffering is entailed. If the responsibility of parenthood were to be correctly understood as a sacred trust and self-control so regulated that no more babies were produced than could be properly looked after, not only would the problem of population control be easily solved but the children brought into the world would *ipso-facto* be ideally happy and fine specimens according to the best standards of eugenics.

Child development and the basic principles of education in the home is another important subject. The child is, at the beginning, entirely dependent on the mother even for his nourishment, while her natural affection for her off-spring provides her with that deep-seated satisfaction which is adequate reward for all the care and attention she bestows on him. Physical and emotional satisfactions, arising from the daily contacts between the child and the parents, help to create that trust and understanding between them, which will form a guarantee towards the harmonious development of home life. Thus the proper approach to the development of parent-child relationship is the basic principles of give and take. Parents must, from the beginning, recognise this principles as of fundamental importance. If they do so there will be no need for the exercise of parental authority for extracting obedience from their children; parental advice will be accepted and acted upon in a spirit of understanding and goodwill.

As the child grows older the task of the parents is to enable him to become increasingly self-reliant. Thus he should be able to feed and dress himself and in other ways also to take care of himself. Such education, if it is to be successful should be pursued with adequate patience by the parents and with a clear understanding of the child's mental and physical limitations. It is a process of helping the child to grow and to develop his faculties on lines best suited to his innate qualities. An atmosphere of understanding and full cooperation between the patents is essential if such child development is to proceed properly.

Another important subject is the role of health workers and health services in educating parents and the assistance that can be given in such education by voluntary or semi-trained personnel. Health workers and health services have a predominant part to play in this field. Instruction to the mother in the hygiene of pregnancy and in mothercraft is essential. The young mother needs to be told by advice and actual demonstration how to look after the physical needs of her infant and what precautions are to be taken during periods, such as teething, to enable the young one to get over its early troubles. Both parents should receive advice regarding the ways in which they can help towards promoting the proper emotional development of their off-spring. Much of the instruction that requires to be given falls within the field of health. Child welfare centres and domiciliary visits by health workers like public health nurses, health visitors and midwives must together provide for this programme of educating the parents in the art and practice of child care.

At a later stage, during the pre-school age and the school going period, nursery and elementary schools will also come into the picture as centres of such instruction. Here the scope for social education of the child widens greatly. The boy or girl enters a larger world than that provided so far by the home environment and adjustment becomes necessary not only to the discipline of the school but also to the needs of the daily contacts with other children. The extent to which education at home has helped the child to accept gladly disciplinary control and to adjust his own wishes and inclinations to those of others in the family will determine largely the manner in which he will react to the new environment which the school provides. Teachers will, of course, have to take a prominent part in guiding the pupil towards his proper social adjustment, but they must not forget that the major part of the student's time will continue to be spent outside the school and that in the circumstances, the active participation of parents in such training must continue to be of value. The contribution that educational services and organizations can make towards helping parents to take an intelligent part in the improvement of child-welfare is great. Every attempt should be made, through specially arranged meetings, to interest parents in the work of different institutions such as nursery, elementary and vocational schools. The school doctor and nurse will be able to secure correction of many of the defects they find in the mode of life of the child only if they can obtain the cooperation of the parents to accept and follow the advice given by them. Psychological mal-adjustments of child may often have their root cause in the home environment and here again the emphasis should be on preparing the parents to recognise the defects that exist and to rectify them as much as they can.

The vast programme of educational effort in the home and in the school, to which I have referred in this short address, can hardly be undertaken successfully without the development of appropriate community services on an adequate scale. Governments, as the main agents for promoting the health and welfare of the people, should take primary responsibility for the organisation and maintenance of such services. But voluntary effort has also its own due share of contribute. Voluntary agencies are to a large extent unhampered by the many restrictions that surround governmental procedure and therefore in undertaking pioneering work in new fields of social activity, they are in a position of advantage in comparison with government departments. But the latter have more resources in funds and in trained personnel for technical guidance. Therefore, it is of mutual advantage for Governments and voluntary agencies to cooperate freely in the tasks they undertake and to work out their programmes in a manner designed to make their contributions, to the scheme of child welfare, complementary to one another. In all such schemes the question of employment of semi-skilled personnel will arise where adequate numbers of skilled workers are lacking. Semi-skilled workers can and should be employed; but their limitations would be recognised and it is necessary to provide that they function under the direction of well-trained workers in their respective fields of activity.

I am tremendously jealous when I go abroad and see what facilities are available for children in the advanced countries of Europe. We are beginning from scratch, as it were, in every sphere and with our limited resources of both money and workers, progress seems to be desperately slow. Nevertheless we are aware of the need for tackling this important problem and therein lies every reason for hope and no cause for despair.

Rajkumari Amrit Kaur undoubtedly has vision, and it is her vision coupled with a sense of the practical and an ability and persistence so essential for turning visions into realities, that gave practical shape to her dream of a National Institute for post-graduate and collegiate studies which could set the pattern of medical education and research in India. Even financial stringency could not and did not deter her from trying to attain her set objective of founding the All India Institute of Medical Sciences of the management of which she is the Chairman. Great credit accrues to the New Zealand Government who made Rajkumari's dream come true by donating one million pounds sterling towards the project which on completion will have cost about £ 5.5 million. Mr. Watts, who laid the foundation stone of the Institute and is mentioned in Rajkumari's address at the ceremony held on April 4, 1952, was the Health Minister of New Zealand when the million pound gift was sanctioned by his Gvoernment.

A DREAM COME TRUE

"He whom a dream hath possessed
Knoweth no more of doubting.
And never comes darkness down, but
He greets a million morns."

Shaemas O'Sheel
in "He Whom a Dream Hath Possessed"

After the verb "to love" "to help" is
the most beautiful verb in the world.

Baroness Bertha von Suttner.

I do not know when I have felt so happy as I do today. Ever since I was called upon to serve the cause of health, it has been one of my ardent desires to bring into being an Institute which would not only provide first class post-graduate training to our medical personnel in their own environment and afford facilities for the highest type of research in the extensive field which our country offers but which would also set and maintain high standards of medical education and, above all, inspire in our trained personnel that lofty idealism without which those who adopt the noble profession of ministering to humanity cannot really rise to their full stature.

The hand of financial stringency has laid on none more heavily than it has on schemes of expansion in the sphere of health. Alas! It is almost an accepted axiom the world over that schemes that contribute to material prosperity must always receive first priority. Social services, therefore, such as health and education are apt to receive almost stepmotherly treatment, as it were. And yet, if we pause to think, we ought to realise that prosperity and contentment should be weighed in terms of human rather than material values. In other words, there cannot really be any prosperity without physical and mental well being. If we neglect the health of a nation we do so at grave peril to ourselves.

There is no gainsaying the fact that the level of health in our country, indeed in the whole of the South Asian zone, is at a low level. We here have neither the institutions nor the personnel to give adequate aid and relief to the people, most of whom live in rural areas. At the same time we do not want to, indeed we dare not lag behind the advanced countries of the world, where such dynamic progress has, of recent years, been made in modern medicine.

I would like here to stress some points of the scheme on which I personally feel very strongly.

First, this is to be an All-India Institute in the real sense of the term. Its branches will gradually come into being all over India. It is essential not only to lay down a uniform standard of medical education for the entire country, but also to create within all limbs of the medical profession a feeling that they do not belong to any particular State. The medical students, the nurses, the research scholars and the auxiliary personnel who will receive training both in urban and rural areas under the aegis of this Institute will be drawn from all over India on the basis of merit only. Medicine, like every other science, indeed more than any other, is the servant of mankind and transcends all barriers of race or clime. Wherever we need the services of medical personnel from abroad we shall not hesitate to welcome their collaboration and their help in our endeavour.

Further, it is my firm belief that the home environment of a person, the conditions under which he has been working and the extent of mal-adjustment that exists in his relations with his family and members of the community are contributory factors towards ill-health and it is therefore eminently desirable that a study of social pathology in a broad sense of the term should receive every bit as much emphasis as the study of clinical pathology. Such changes as are necessary in the prese[illegible] medical curriculum to enable students to acquire this wider background of health and disease will, I hope, be made an essential part of the undergraduate teaching offered by the Medical College associated with this All India Institute.

There is no doubt that we, as all progressive countries are doing or have done, must accept the idea that adequate health protection is one of the 'national minima' which every citizen has a right to expect and that for the attainment of this objective we must move towards the establishment of a socialised medical service. The doctor of the future must therefore himself be imbued with the proper social outlook while, in its turn, the State must remunerate him adequately for his services. I trust the atmosphere which the All-India Medical Institute will develop will help to emphasise the role of Medicine as a social service to the community and not merely as a profession. Professor Sigerist, a well-known authority on the History of Medicine has rightly said :

"The scope of medicine has indeed broadened. There is today hardly a field of human endeavour that does not require the physician's advice at some time or other. We begin to perceive an outline of a new physician, scientist and social worker, prepared to cooperate in team work and in close touch with the people he serves; a friend and leader, he will direct his efforts towards the prevention of disease and become a therapist when prevention has broken down—the social physician protecting the people and guiding them to a healthier and happier life".

Well–I like to envisage the doctors, research workers, students, nurses and all auxilliary personnel connected with the All India Medical Institute as men and women fitting with ease into the pattern of the India, may I say the world, of our dreams.

Finally, may I, Mr. Watts, before I ask you to lay the foundation stone of this Institute, request you to convey to the Government of New Zealand the sincere thanks of our Government and in particular of myself and my colleagues in the Central Ministry of Health for their generosity? Without the munificent aid of a million pounds which they are giving it would not have been possible for us to start on this venture. More than this I would like you to convey to the people of your country the happiness we fell at the closer cooperation and better understanding that such aid must necessarily bring about between us. We live in a world where so much sorrow and anxiety are caused to mankind by reason of the clouds of mistrust and suspicion which darken our horizon. I am sure it is only by lending a helping hand where help is needed and by cooperation in humanitarian endeavour that we can hope to dispel this tragic gloom. The Colombo Plan is one such joint endeavour and we are indeed happy to cooperate with all the countries of the commonwealth in trying to promote human welfare.

It is said that it is the privilege of youth to dream dreams. I may be said to have erred by having dreamt at my age a dream. But I am glad I did and I am thrilled today at the prospect of its early fulfilment. To you personally, Mr. Watts, my and my colleagues' heartfelt thanks are also due in full measure for your kindness in coming here today and consenting to join in this ceremony. It augurs well for us that a representative of the Government who have made this gift should be closely associated in laying the first brick of an edifice from which the cause of health in India should derive lasting benefit. Moreover, as Minister of Health of your own country not so very long ago, I am sure you will not cease to take an abiding personal interest in this Institute. I hope its development will satisfy not only us but also the New Zealand Government. Your greatest reward, however, will lie in the silent gratitude of the thousands who will learn how to serve and those to whom the workers of this Institute will minister in their hour of need.

India has made a determined essay into the field of social security by introducing many new schemes two of which relate to health insurance which is so necessary for a country in which there is so much of poverty and ill-health. In a broadcast talk to listeners in South East Asia and Africa transmitted by the All India Radio's New Delhi Station on February 5, 1955, Rajkumari Amrit Kaur deals with the Central Government Employees' Contributory Health Service Scheme and the All India Employees' State Insurance Scheme.

INSURING PEOPLES' HEALTH

"A decent provision for the poor is the true test of civilization."

Samuel Johnson
from Boswell's Life of Dr. Johnson.

I am glad that I have this opportunity to speak to the people of (the South East Asia Zone) and to tell them about certain plans which we are developing for the improvement of public health in India. All our countries have certain common handicaps which include a relatively low standard of living, a high degree of illiteracy among the people and imperfectly developed communications. We have at the same time the advantage of possessing potential resources of a high order, which await development. I consider it eminently desirable that we in the undeveloped countries of Asia and Africa should exchange freely our views and experiences so that we may derive mutual benefit from the successes and failures we meet with in our efforts to improve the health and welfare of our people. It is with this object in mind that I shall refer briefly today to two health programmes which we are promoting for certain classes of people. They are the medical insurance scheme a pilot venture, which will cater, in the first instance, to those are employed in Delhi by the Central Government and an Employees State Insurance scheme for industrial labour throughout the country.

In the first place let me state that, in developing such schemes, we lay great emphasis on the beneficiaries paying a contribution towards the medical services they secure. Such contribution is graded in relation to the income of each individual, but the fact that no one should be exempted from payment is stressed. It is good, in my opinion, to make people learn that the acceptance of charity lowers the moral stature of the individual while, on the other hand, the willing acceptance of a share of the cost helps to create and maintain a sense of self-respect and promotes the desire to participate freely in a cooperative endeavour for mutual benefit. We have therefore insisted that, in both schemes, all the beneficiaries shall pay in accordance with their income. At the same time we realise that the medical care made available to each patient should be in relation to his actual needs and not in relation to the amount he pays towards the scheme. The volume and quality of service given to patients are the same among all classes of people under both schemes.

The Central Health Ministry administers the medical care programme for government servants and their families. It includes outpatient service, home visits where they are required and facilities for hospitalisation.

When India became independent in 1947 the medical care programme for government servants excluded the lowest paid among them from the benefits of any medical care or relief while for the highly paid staff and their families all the services were free. We have now included all categories of government servants in the medical care programme and have provided, as already pointed out, the same amount of medical attention to all in spite of differences in their contributions towards the cost of the scheme.

The intention is that, as soon as it has been established that the scheme is able to work on an efficient basis, similar programmes of medical care should be created in places like Bombay, Calcutta and Madras where relatively large numbers of Central Government servants are employed. An interesting feature of this scheme is that the doctors employed by Government are whole-time employees and, contrary to the usage hitherto, are not allowed any private practice. Their emoluments are therefore much higher than they would be if it were otherwise. It is being increasingly felt that doctors who are not free from the burden of earning enough for their needs outside their working hours are naturally unable to give that attention to each individual patient which is his due.

This is only the beginning of what we hope will prove to be an object lesson to other classes of people. Big commercial firms, plantations and State enterprises employing labour can either come into the government scheme, if they are suitably situated, on payment of charges on an agreed basis, or they can start similar services, the experience gained by government organisations being a guide to them towards the creation of their own programmes. When a reasonable number of such schemes become established it will be time for legislation to be undertaken in order to ensure that these medical organisations are maintained on proper lines.

The Employees' State Insurance Scheme is a more comprehensive programme which is intended to cover, in due course, workers of all types in the country and their families. The medical services provided for these workers include outpatient treatment in dispensaries, home visits by the doctor to such patients as are unable to attend these dispensaries and facilities for hospitalisation. As a preliminary step about 2.5 million industrial workers have already been included and, in another six months, practically the whole industrial population will secure the medical benefits provided for under the scheme. It is interesting to mention here that 80% of the expenditure on this scheme is borne by the Central and State Governments and the Employers and only 20% by the workers. The States are responsible for the running of the scheme. Some have chosen to employ private practitioners on part time payment and others have engaged whole-time employees. It will be interesting to see which works out best in practice. Government has power to and I trust will in the near future be able to extend its operation to the families of workers. Moreover, the term worker can also be extended so as to include every type of employee, including agricultural labour. When this extension of the term is completed and when families of workers also begin to share the medical care available under the scheme, about 80 per cent of the total population of the country will have been brought under the health insurance programme for workers. In the meantime other forms of health service, which are being established in the rural areas under the community projects, will have expanded both in respect of coverage of population and in the quality and volume of medical service. What I envisage is a gradual convergence of the two types of health services towards a unified national health organisation offering protection to all, on the basis of a contribution from the beneficiaries.

The problems that we face in this country are immense and, in relation to their magnitude, our present resources in trained personnel and funds are wholly inadequate. But we are undaunted and are going ahead with our plans to develop our natural health and to apply it to promote the welfare of our people. We in the present generation, can at best hope to be able to lay the foundation of future progress on sound and enduring lines. If we are able to do that, we shall hand on to the succeeding generations the task of building the superstructure of national welfare with the confidence that the years as they go by will see an era of steady progress and increasing prosperity in which all the people will share.

7

Role of Central Council of Health

"Men are never so likely to settle a question rightly as when they discuss it freely."

Lord Macaulay
in Southey's Colloquies.
(January 1830)

The first Meeting of the Central Council of Health was held at Hyderabad on 29th January, 1953. In her inaugural address Rajkumari Amrit Kaur outlined the necessity for close collaboration between the Central and the State Governments which was essential for building up the health of the nation.

I consider this to be a memorable occasion which may well be remembered in the years to come as an important milestone in the building up of the Health Services of this vast and needy land or ours. You and I are colleagues in a great venture and it is our bounden duty to see to it that all we do at this critical juncture in the life of the country is done on the basis of voluntary and mutual co-operation between the Union and State Governments and between the State Governments themselves for this is the only way to ensure progress on right lines.

The immensity of our task in fully known to you and you are also equally conscious of our severe limitations and handicaps. In order to meet difficulties man has at all times to resort to his ingenuity and derive inspiration from a firm determination to forge ahead inspite of obstacles. To this end we must approach our problems with a new confidence and fresh optimism. Neither the magnitude of our task nor its complexity should make us feel either despondent or helpless. Indeed the difficulties, perplexities and complexities of the situation may not be allowed to act as deterrents but rather made to serve as added incentives to increased effort. I myself am confident that with patience, fortitude, determination and, what is very important, careful and realistic planning, we can and will in due course solve our problems with the same success as they have been solved in the other more advanced countries of the world.

In facing the herculean task before us, we have obviously to rely more and more on each other. The health of the nation is a national asset. The problem has to be solved on an all-India basis. It is, therefore, to promote concerted action and co-operative effort that this Council has been set-up.

Though its establishment is the immediate outcome of the recommendations of the Third Health Ministers,' Conference held in 1950, the underlying idea is not new. The Government of India, even under the old regime, before Public Health became a Transferred Subject, not infrequently convened conferences of public health and medical experts. This healthy practice was not discarded with the advent of provincial autonomy and a Central Health Board was constituted in 1921 to advise the Central and State Governments. Though this, unfortunately, ceased to function in 1923 owing to financial stringency, the need for periodical consultation and exchange of views, as the result of varying experience, became more and more apparent and it was felt that neither the Government of India nor the Provincial Governments could adequately fulfil their responsibilities in the domain of public health without periodically taking counsel with one another. The Government of India, therefore, considered it necessary to provide suitable machinery for such consultation.

The then Viceroy of India, while addressing the Indian Legislature on September 21, 1936, announced the establishment of a Central Advisory Board of Health with a view to evoke an adequate measure of central and provincial co-operation and, in due course, to provide Federal India with a valuable forum for discussion and formulation of health policy. This Central Advisory Board of Health came into being in 1937 and held five –meetings during the period 1937-43. The Interim Government, soon after its formation, followed up the practice in a slightly different form and convened a Conference of Health Ministers of all States in October, 1946. Since achieving our Independence two more Conferences of the State Health Ministers have been held in August 1948 and August-September 1950. These conferences were, however, held on an *ad hoc* basis, and it was considered necessary to replace such periodical conferences by a permanent statutory body under the aegis of which a broad programme of co-ordinated action in the field of health could be gradually built up. The constitution of such a forum had also been recommended by the Health Survey and Development Committee. It is, therefore, the cumulative effect of all these factors which is really responsible for the establishment of this Council.

In a personal communication to all members I forwarded a printed compendium of the resolutions that have been passed at the five meetings of the Central Advisory Board of Health and the three Conferences of State Health Ministers. In forwarding this Compendium I had perforce to point out that many of these resolutions still remain unimplemented; but I do venture to express the hope that the recommendations made by this Council will have a better fate and that we will all attach to them the sanctity they deserve. It goes without saying that any resolutions that are passed by a representative and responsible body like ours have to be actively pursued and I am sure I can count on the full support of every member in this respect.

Under our present constitution, in respect of the subject of Health, the direct responsibility of the Central Government, compared to that of the State Governments, is very different and restricted only to certain spheres. The main functions in regard to the promotion of health of the people such as the provision of remedial and preventive care, environmental hygiene and health education are quite rightly the responsibility of the States. Even in the wide field of concurrent activities in which central legislation can lay down the pattern for the country as a whole, the responsibility for the implementation of the provisions of such all-India legislation will still rest with the States. I would like to make it perfectly clear that there is absolutely no intention on the part of the Central Government to infringe in any way whatsoever on the autonomy of the State Governments. Nevertheless, the Central Government has also a very important role to play and I sincerely hope that this Council will provide the medium through which the Centre can discharge that obligation and promote the much-needed co-operation between itself and the different units forming the Union, so as to achieve a progressive improvement of the health and welfare of the country as a whole.

The functions of the Council have been deliberately left broad enough to give it every opportunity of development on the lines dictated by its experience, so that this Body shall become a live and active organisation. It is now for you, to help its growth and development and impart to it the required vigour.

We live in difficult but stirring times. No one activity of the Government can be separated from the other. Standing, as we do, on the threshold of entrance into the India of our dreams, everything has top priority. We may not wait for our big projects to fructify before we begin to cater for health and education. These are nation-building activities without due attention to which no real progress can be expected. I often wish economists would sometimes turn their attention to human values instead of always dwelling on standards of life in purely material terms. The health of the nation—in particular of its children and youth—is its most priceless asset.

The Fifth Meeting of the Central Council of Health was held at Ranchi (Bihar) on December 14, 1956. In her opening address Rajkumari Amrit Kaur gave a brief review of the progress made in the implementation of the recommendations of the Council, and an account of other important developments connected with health. She also referred to the salient features of the Second Five Year Plan in the domain of health and medical relief. Here she analyses the achievements of the immediate past and future trends.

I am glad to report that there has been good progress in many fields and some notable developments have taken place since we last met. The magnitude of our task is, however, so great and there is so much that remains to be done that whatever success we might have achieved should only act as a fillip to much greater effort in the future. We cannot afford to be jubiliant or even complacent.

The targets laid down for nursing and ancillary personnel at the end of the second Five Year Plan are 31,000 nurses, 32,000 midwives, 2,500 health visitors and 41,000 nurse-dais and dais.

Against this target the number available at present is 17,000 nurses, 21,000 midwives, 1,200 health visitors and 6,826 nurse-dais and approximately 10,000 dais. We must, therefore, intensify our training programme to overcome this shortage.

The Centrally aided training schemes for the training of health visitors and auxiliary nurse-midwives which started in the First Five Year Plan are to be continued in the Second Plan. Provision has been made to train 1,600 health visitors, 6,000 auxiliary nurse-midwives and 36,000 dais in the Second Five Year Plan period. I hope all State Governments will fully avail themselves of this assistance so that the targets we have set can be reached.

Two new courses have been started this year by the Government of India with the help of W.H.O., a course for midwife tutors at the College of Nursing, Delhi, and a course in Psychiatric Nursing at the Institute of Mental Health, Bangalore. Four refresher courses for nurses and midwives were also conducted with the assistance of W.H.O. and UNICEF. A course for Public Health Nurses has also now been established in Madras.

One of the recommendations of the Nursing Committee was that training in public health should be integrated in the basic course for nurses and midwives, so that all nurses and midwives are trained for domiciliary as well as institutional services. As this type of training is yet comparatively new, the Central Government has made provision for a pilot scheme to be introduced in ten training centres. The Government of India have also under consideration a somewhat modified scheme to give assistance to another 30 training centres to train an increased number of nurses and integrate public health training in the nursing and midwifery course.

The Health Programme in the Community Project Development Areas is now forging ahead though there are still numerous difficulties to be surmounted. Community Development is now one of the most important items in our national programme. In view of its importance the Community Projects Administration has been elevated to the Ministry of Community Development. Community Development personnel will now constitute the largest single body of government workers. As most of these workers have to serve on a multipurpose basis including health, the bulk of the rural population can be reached effectively through these workers for the purpose of disseminating health education amongst the masses. Evidently, the utility of the village-level worker in the improvement of environmental sanitation has not been sufficiently realised. Special attention is however necessary for the orientation of the training of village-level workers in the fundamentals of public health and environmental sanitation in the Extension Training Centres. The village level worker is in day to day touch with the people and has been specially trained in the methodology of approach to the people to seek their acceptance of new ideas and skills for the improvement of health and prevention of disease.

In rural areas environmental sanitation work has been lagging behind other programmes. Especially in the construction and use of sanitary latrines. To aid in determining the reasons for this and to help find solutions of the problems with the generous assistance from the Ford Foundation, a Research-cum-Action Project has been undertaken based on the same three centres involved in the orientation programme where studies are now being conducted along six main lines. It is not however contemplated that the small research-cum-action teams which are working in the three centres either can or should try to carry out all these lines of investment unaided. The tremendous job must be thought of in long-range terms and as the work of many people and of many agencies.

When the Programme was inaugurated it was calculated that each unit would be able to protect a population of one million. Recent experience has, however, shown that with the present composition of these units this is not always possible. In certain areas, therefore, the staff has to be augmented, additional transport is required and the quantity of D.D.T. supplied has to be increased. The position is being reviewed and necessary steps will be taken to make this control programme fully effective in every part of the country. The active operational phase of the programme has now been increased from 3 to 5 years and it is to be continued during the Second Five Year Plan period.

A control programme of this nature will be very expensive if it is to be continued indefinitely. It is, therefore, necessary that we should consolidate the success that has been so far achieved in reducing the incidence of malaria and, by further intensifying our efforts, pave the way for the complete eradication of this infection which in the past has wrought such havoc on our rural population. Apart from economic considerations there are other reasons for shifting the emphasis from control to eradication. It has been reported that Malaria carrying mosquitoes in different parts of the World have started showing resistance to D.D.T. Fortunately, such resistance has not so far been reported in India and as it ordinarily takes a few years for such resistance to develop, we should put in an all-out effort to completely eradicate malaria within the next few years. International and bilateral agencies are now also taking a keen interest in the eradication of this infection. The Technical Co-operation Mission of the U.S.A., which has already given us munificent assistance in our control programme. We are very hopeful of getting substantial assistance from this source if we venture to embark on such a programme. The W.H.O. have also been laying great stress on the eradication of malaria throughout the world and have created a special fund for the purpose. Our neighbours in the South East Asia Region too are embarking on complete eradication programmes in their respective areas. We cannot afford to lag behind and, I am glad to report, that an eradication programme, prepared by the Malaria Institute of India is now under examination in consultation with the Planning Commission.

The National Water Supply and Sanitation Programme has gained considerable popularity and all the State Governments have forwarded a large number of both urban and rural schemes. The progress made in the implementation of this programme has not, however, been upto expectation. The main reasons for the slow progress are lack of trained personnel and inadequate supply of equipment. To overcome the shortage of trained personnel provision has been made in the Second Five Year Plan period for the training of Engineers, Overseers, Water-works Operators and Sanitary Inspectors. An agreement has been signed with the Government of U.S.A. for large quantities of equipment and materials to be distributed to various State Governments. With the re-organisation of States it should now be possible for each State to have a full fledged Public Health Engineering Organisation. To achieve effective co-ordination I must again emphasize the need to place this organisation under the State Health Departments.

The mass B.C.G. Campaign had made excellent progress upto about April, 1955. The main reasons for deterioration since then are the unsatisfactory conditions of service for B.C.G. Staff and inadequate publicity. I would therefore, urge on all State Government to improve the conditions of this staff and also arrange for adequate publicity so as to intensify the mass B.C.G. vaccination programme in their respective areas.

Apart from B.C.G. Vaccination which was undertaken as a national programme, until recently there has been no co-ordinated policy for tuberculosis control in the country as a whole. In the First Five Year Plan a scheme giving certain priorities for tuberculosis control in the various States was indicated, but most States were carrying out a policy of their own. The tuberculosis control schemes included in the Second Five Year Plan are, however, being now developed into a National Tuberculosis Programme. Treatment and Study Centres and subsidiary Centres have already been established in the various States. The Subsidiary Centres provide only mass treatment of all cases of leprosy including early cases detected through examination of contacts. The Study and Treatment Centres, on the other hand, in addition to such mass scale treatment with sulphones carry out detailed studies of the epidemiology of the disease and also assess scientifically the results of sulphono thercapy.

A Central Leprosy Teaching and Research Institute has been established at Tirumani in Madras State in association with the Lady Willingdon Leprosy Sanatorium, Tirumani, and the Silver Jubilee Children Clinic for Child Leprosy, Saidapet. An autonomous Governing Body for the Institute has been set up.

Health Education is now assuming much greater importance. The plans for the building of the Central Health Education Bureau have been finalised and it is expected that the building including a museum will be completed within a year or so. The activities of this Bureau have been hampered due to lack of qualified staff. Many State Governments have submitted plans for the establishment of Health Education Bureaus in their Health Departments under the Second Five Year Plan. Though originally these schemes could not be included in the Plan, steps are now being taken to make the necessary provision subject to certain readjustments. W.H.O. and T.C.M. are showing an active interest in this subject and are providing technical experts, fellowships and equipment. A short training course for Health Educators has already been instituted at the All India Institute of Hygiene and Public Health, Calcutta. This has been quite popular with the State Governments. Arrangements are now almost complete to institute a longer course for Health Education Specialists who, completion of the training, can assume leadership in this particular field in their respective States. It is for the State Government now to select suitable trainees. The art of education being more important than purely technical knowledge, it would be advantageous to select suitable persons from amongst teachers and give them training in health education.

The Maternal and Child Health Project at the All India Institute of Hygiene and Public Health is now practically complete. Most of the buildings have been constructed and both the Urban and Rural Training Centres are functioning. The training facilities of the Institute are now being fully utilised. Difficulty is, however, still being experienced in filling certain posts in view of the dearth of suitably qualified persons. This Institute is unique of its kind in the East and I would suggest that Members of this Council should pay a visit to it at their convenience to personally acquaint themselves of the good work that is being done there and the training facilities that it offers.

Medical education has been engaging the special attention of the Government of India and this Council. At its first meeting in 1953 the Council recommended uniforms standards of medical eduction and abolition of the Licenciate Course. Later at its third meeting, to counteract and deterioration in the standards of teaching that had been reported in certain institutions, the Council recommended the formation of an All-India Cadre for teachers in non-clinical subjects. This unfortunately no agreed solution has been found as yet. The only alternative, therefore, appears to be to give a subsidy to those State Governments who are prepared to increase the emoluments of their non-clinical teachers upto a certain minimum level. The proposal now under the active consideration of the Ministry of Health is for the grant of a subsidy of 50 per cent of the difference between the existing scales of pay in particular States and the scales of pay which are considered to be adequate to attract suitable candidates.

The recommendations of the Conference on undergraduate medical education held in New Delhi in November, 1955, were forwarded to all State Governments, Universities and the Indian Medical Council. The replies received so far are under examination in the Ministry of Health. Although there is a fair amount of general agreement with the recommendations made by the Conference, some States and Universities are finding it difficult to implement some of them. Such divergence of opinion is naturally to be expected but I am hopeful that in due course most of the recommendations of the Conference will be acceptable to all concerned.

The Second Five Year Plan includes provision for opening six more medical colleges in various parts of the country and the expansion of some existing institutions. With the collaboration of W.H.O., the Rockefeller Foundation and T.C.M., proposals regarding the improvement in some of the existing Medical Colleges are also under active examination. The existing upgraded departments for post-graduate education in various subjects have been working satisfactory and we are receiving more requests for the upgrading of some others.

The All India Institute of Medical Sciences has now been established under a special Act of Parliament. This institution will develop and demonstrate high standards of teaching in under graduate and post-graduate medical education in all its branches. It will bring together in one place, educational facilities of the highest order for the training of personnel engaged in different fields of activity. Its most important function will be to attain self-sufficiency in post-graduate medical education in India.

The All India Institute of Mental Health, Bangalore, which is affiliated to the University of Mysore, is making good progress and provides facilities for training for Diplomas in Psychological Medicine and Medical (Clinical) Psychology, each of two years' duration. Training for Psychiatric nurses is also provided. A scheme has been included in the Second Five Year Plan for further expansion of this Institute on the lines of the Maudsley Institute, London. The activities of the institute include research on various aspects of mental diseases and giving advice to State

Governments on the establishment of Child Welfare Clinics and Psychiatric Departments in teaching hospitals.

The Indian Council of Medical Research has now considerably expanded its activities. Time does not permit me to elaborate on the good work that is being carried out under the auspices of this organisation. In the past most of the work of the I.C.M.R. was connected with the study of epidemiology and the control of the major communicable diseases, e.g. plague, cholera, malaria, filariasis and leprosy. Such work has now been extended to include other communicable diseases, particularly tuberculosis and trachoma.

The fellowship programme sponsored by the I.C.M.R. in collaboration with the Rockefeller Foundation is making good progress. This fellowship programme has also helped in the promotion of research work in the various medical colleges. This is a very significant development up in the past there was little research activity in such institutions. Apart from the contribution which the medical colleges can now make towards the advancement of knowledge, such activity is bound also to have a profound influence upon the quality of teaching. To further encourage these activities it is now proposed to have more search units located in various medical colleges particularly for research on drugs, therapeutic trials, investigation of cardiovascular diseases etc. Such units can also undertake research in certain indigenous drugs and can well assist in the development of the drug industry in the country.

The Nutrition Research Institute, Conoor, has continued to do useful work in connection with protein malnutrition in infants and children and finding cheap vegetable protein substitutes. Studies on the growth and physical development of normal Indian children and control of specific nutritional diseases such as endemic goitre, lathyrism, fluorosis etc. are also in progress.

The Virus Research Centre at Poona has also considerably expended its activities and has done very useful work, particularly in connection with insect borne viruses. The Cancer Research Centres at Bombay and Calcutta are doing excellent work in connection with the incidence and etiology of Cancer.

This Council recommended at its Third Meeting the deputation of Junior Medical Officers from various States to serve as Short Service Commissioned Officers with the Army Medical Corps. Details regarding this proposal have now been worked out.

The question of the preparation of a National Formulary of Medicines has been engaging the attention of the Government of India for some time. As a result of the large scale use of costly patent and proprietary medicines, both imported and locally produced, the treatment of diseases has become very costly. This has also been responsible for raising the nation's drug bill and for the unwholesome practice of self medication. It is, therefore, necessary to prepare a National Formulary containing a list of certain essential combinations which only should be allowed to be imported or manufactured in the country. The Government of India have accordingly constituted a Committee to be known as the "National Formulary Committee". The Committee shall have the power to form sub-committees when required and also to co-opt experts as and when necessary on such sub-committees.

The Hindustan Antibiotics (Private) Limited, Pimpri, which is a State project in collaboration with W.H.O. and UNICEF has now started the manufacture of clinical products. A completely automatic filling line has been functioning there since March this year. The Bombay Bottling Plant is now also bottling the bulk pencillin manufactured at this factory is distributed through two selling agents, but government and other public institutions are supplied direct. The capacity of the factory at present is 1.5 million mega units per month. It is also proposed to produce Bicillin for which an agreement has been recently drawn up with an American firm. During the next Five. Year Plan it is proposed to increase the production of pencillin by 60 per cent and also to manufacture streptomycin.

The Hindustan Insecticides (Private) Limited, Delhi which is also a State project in collaboration with W.H.O. and UNICEF is producing D.D.T. according to schedule and the scheme to expand its capacity and to set up another plant is being actively pursued. The D.D.T. produced at this factory has fully proved its efficacy in the Malaria Control Programme.

The Council at its last meeting recommended that State Governments should issue necessary instructions for popularising in their respective areas the use of quinine in preference to other synthetics with a view to consume the accumulated government stocks. I am glad to report that most of the State Governments have issued such instructions. I consider this important because, in the event of any unfortunate international crisis arising, we will have to a large extent to fall back on our own resources in the treatment of malaria.

The Planning Commission in formulating its First Five Year Plan emphasised that "increasing pressure of population on natural resources (which must inevitably be limited) retards economic progress and limits seriously the rate of extension of social services so essential to civilised existence". The Commission therefore considered a population policy essential to planning. During the First Five Year Plan period efforts were primarily directed to the building up of an active public opinion in favour of family planning and the promotion of family planning advice and service on the basis of existing knowledge. At the same time, demographic as well as medical and biological studies were carried out.

A Family Planning Research and Programme Committee was set up to make recommendations to the Government of India regarding research schemes and experimental and other programmes relating to family planning and the nature and amount of assistance, if any, to be given to existing voluntary organisations in the field of family planning. The Committee made comprehensive recommendations, which were generally accepted by the Ministry of Health. A Family Planning Grants Committee was constituted to scrutinise and recommend applications for financial assistance for family planning and research.

The progress, as measured by the number of clinics opened during the First Plan, has not been very impressive but by making the people more conscious about the real need for family planning the ground has now been prepared to embark on a countrywide programme.

Due emphasis is being placed on research. A Contraceptive Testing Centre has already been established in Bombay. The search for cheap, simple, harmless, effective and acceptable contraceptives is in progress. Arrangements have been made with the Indian Council of Medical Research for undertaking medical and biological research schemes relating to family planning.

A high powered Family Planning Board has now replaced the previous committees at the Centre in order to effectively direct Family Planning Programmes. I would also suggest that the State Governments consider forming similar Family Planning Boards in the respective States. The success of the programmes depends largely upon the willing co-operation of the States and I earnestly hope that no efforts will be spared to expedite implementation of the various schemes envisaged in his programme.

I am happy indeed that representatives of the various International and Bilateral Agencies who so willingly co-operate with us are present here today. I take this opportunity to express by deep sense of gratitude to them for all the help they have given us in developing our health programmes during the last nine years. I am confident that such assistance will continue to be made available to us in the years to come.

8

The Assessment

RAJKUMARI AMRIT KAUR : INDIA'S FIRST CABINET MINISTER

—Hansa Mehta

It was years ago, when I was a student at Baroda College, that I first saw Rajkumari who came to Baroda with her parents, Raja and Rani Harnam Singh of Kapurthala. They were the guests of His Highness Maharaja Sayaji Rao Gaekwad of Baroda. I saw Rajkumari at the Resident's Garden party where she played tennis. Rajkumari was then known as Bibi Amrit Kaur. She was a great tennis player, and used to take part in tennis tournaments in Lahore. It was only in March 1931 that I actually met her. It was in Simla where I had gone to attend the meeting of the Standing Committee of the All India Women's Conference (AIWC). Rajkumari was then the Chairman of the AIWC Standing Committee. One of the resolution was that a deputation of the Standing Committee members be sent to the Viceroy. Lord Irwin, to urge him to include a woman in the delegation that was going to the Round Table Conference in London later that year. At the Conference, Gandhiji was the sole representative of the Indian National Congress, and the AIWC wanted Sarojini Naidu, President of AIWC, to represent the Indian Women. Rajkumari led the delegation to the Viceroy. I was in the delegation as the Vice-President of AIWC. Our proposal was agreed to by the Viceroy, and Sarojini Naidu attended the Round Table Conference as the representative of Indian Women. Besides her there were two other women but they were nominated by the Government of India (Smt. Subarayan and Begum Shah

Nawaz).

It was about this time that Rajkumari joined Gandhiji, which association lasted until Gandhiji's death. Although having been brought up in a princely family and being used to luxurious living, Rajkumari went to live in Gandhiji's Ashram at Sevagram where living conditions were simple and rigorous. She looked after Gandhiji's correspondence along with Mahadev Desai. She continued to be associated with AIWC taking active part in its deliberations, and become its President in 1937. She was also the Chairman of the All India Women's Education Fund Association, as also of the Executive Committee of Lady Irwin College. Rajkumari was an able chairwoman. I had the pleasure of working with her on many occasions. We were members of the Sub-committee on Fundamental Rights of the Constituent Assembly where we strongly advocated equal rights for women. It was thus a matter of great pride that Rajkumari become the first women Cabinet Minister of independent India in recognition of her own role in fighting for equal rights for women, as well as in recognition of the contribution the women of India had made to the national freedom movement. It was thus a matter of great pride that Rajkumari became the first woman Cabinet Minister of independent India in recognition of her own role in fighting for equal rights for women, as well as in recognition of the contribution the women of India had made to the national freedom movement.

RAJKUMARI AMRIT KAUR : THE MAKING OF A LEADER

—Lakshmi N. Menon

It was indeed a strange encounter. The venue was Lahore, occasion the annual session of the All India Women's Conference. The President of the session was none other than the distinguished Doctor and social worker from Madras, Dr. Muthulakshmi Reddy. I was an active member of the conference having attended all the session since the second one held at Delhi in February, 1928. The Session was also an important landmark because the session was not presided over by a Begum or Rani. Maharani Chimanbai Gaekwad of Boarda known for her forward looking ideas about women's status, lit the Bhadra Deep, on the occasion of the launching of the conference. The second session which was held in Delhi was presided over by the Begum mother of Bhopal, another distinguished and progressive social revolutionary in her ideas about women's progress and status. The Patna conference was presided over by Rani Lalitkumari of Mandi. Now at Lahor, the mantle had fallen on a professional woman of eminence and it seemed that the wind of change was slowly setting in.

Delegates to the first session at Pune who doubted whether the seed will sprout at all were pleasantly surprised to see it developing into a sapling. At the Delhi Session presided over by the Begum mother of Bhopal, it was the Vicereine Lady Irwin who inaugurated the session and the idea of Home Science College, now the Lady Irwin College of Home Science was thought of then as something different. However, the college has become a pioneering Institution giving a new direction to women's education.

At the Lahore Conference we moved a number of resolutions. I was asked to move one of Swadeshi. I was then, as now, an ardent advocate of Swadeshi and I was enthusiastically preaching swadeshi and said that only in India speaking about swadeshi is interpreted as anti government; the Queen of England made an appeal that the ingredients of the Christmas cake should be those produced in the Commonwealth countries. I had hardly finished that sentence when somebody from behind in clipped English accent said "she is talking politics." Infuriated, I said, "Not politics but economics." Turning around I saw a delicate looking slender woman rather fashionably dressed bearing the indelible mark of foreign schooling. I was told that she was the daughter of Raja Harnam Singh of Kapurthala who because of his conversion to Christianity lost the right to the gaddi.

Rajkumari Amrit Kaur become a member of the Conference. We had many occasions to meet, write to each other on problems and work together. In those days the President was only a titular head, the day-to-day work was the responsibility of the Chairman. She became the Chairman before she was elected President. She was an excellent Chairman, bringing in her interventions both efficiency and refinement of manner and behaivour and dignity of her unmistakable position. We exchanged notes and views during the Lothian Committee interviews. We had planned that the Conference should press for universal adult suffrage for the simple reason that any prescribed qualification would militate against giving adequate representation to women. In fact, any qualification will act as a disqualification as women cannot claim property or education as most of them had neither education nor rights in property. She took serious and sincere interest in both education and franchise. Perhaps the expansion of women's franchise by lowering the educational qualification and the introduction of wifehood, qualification might have been due to the persistence of the conference representatives.

The motto of the conference 'Bhktya ma abhijani' from the Bhagawat Gita was suggested by her or through her efforts. I was editor of the Roshni, I think the name was suggested by her if I remember right. Rajkumari gave me unstinted support and was a regular contributor. During the war our little journal was subjected to censorship. It was printed and published in Lucknow where I was staying. I used to go to the press to see the progress of printing. Invariably the publisher, a kindly old Anglo-Indian gentleman will show me sentences so affectionately drafted by us completely blacked out, to our dismay . . . Perhaps it was to be expected, war time habit in the name of security.

While in the conference she joined Gandhiji at Sevagram as one of his secretaries. She had a beautiful handwriting, woll formed, steady, clear and forceful. Her voice was well modulated and pleasant to listen to. She had to course changed. It was no longer the fashionable lady who though speaking for swadeshi was politics. She look to Khadi, cut her hair short, plunged headlong into the national movement, became a close associate of Gandhiji.

After Independence she became the first Health Minister of Free India. As Health Minister she did many thing for the health of the nation and welfare of women and children. I remember particularly the introduction of the BCG vaccine programme to control tuberculosis and many other innovative programme which with the lapse of time became a part of our national health policy such a family planning, eradication of small pox, malaria, training of nurses, health workers, etc. I do not know whether she had any difficulty in reconciling Gandhian ethics and modern medicines. That she was followed, after an interval, by another

Gandhian Dr. Sushila Nayar might have made things easier for all. Before she died she gave her beautiful house, 'Manorville' as a gift to be used as a holiday home for nurses. She remained a true Christian and was an activist in the YWCA. When she was Minister for health she asked me for lunch and as I was about to leave she asked me to become a member of the YWCA which I promptly did.

Such was Rajkumari, Patron of the AIWC, President of the National YWCA and active Patron and supporter of many institutions for the good of the nation specially for the welfare of children. I am sure she will live for ever in the memory of those who shared her ideals and worked with her. Indeed our motherland is blessed in having such daughters to serve her.

She died in 1964. It was great loss to our countrymen who mourned it with much concern, anxiety and sympathy. People, greatly praised her sacrifices during the freedom movement and thereafter, as Health Minister and as a staunch social worker and dedicated Gandhian and Parliamentarian.

Bibliography

Unpublished and Published Sources

A.I.C.C. Papers, 1920-22.

Debates, House of Commons, 1920-22.

Debates, Legislative Assembly, 1920-22.

Home Political Records, 1920-22, available in the National Archives of India, New Delhi.

Selected Works of Jawaharlal Nehru, vols. I and II, (edit.) S. Gopal.

The Collected Works of Mahatma Gandhi, relevant volumes.

Young India, relevant volumes.

Private Papers

Chelmsford Papers

Gandhi Papers

Jawaharlal Nehru Papers

Motilal Nehru Papers

Reading Papers

Sapru Papers

Oral History Interviews Available in Nehru Memorial Museum and Library, New Delhi.

Smt. Vijay Lakshmi Pandit.

Smt. Renuka Ray.

Newspapers

Amrita Bazar Patrika

The Hindu

The Hindustan Times

The Searchlight

The Tribune

Times of India

Indian Journals

Bengal : Past and Present

India Quarterly

Indian Economic and Social History Review

Journal of Indian History

South Asian Studies

Studies in History

The Indian Historical Review

The Indian Journal of Political Science

The Panjab : Past and Present

The Quarterly Review of Historical Studies

Foreign Journals

Asian Affairs

Bulletin of the School of Oriental and African Studies

Journal of Contemporary History

Journal of South-East Asian Studies

Modern Asian Studies

New Zealand Journal of History

Pacific Affairs

Pacific Historical Review

South Asia

The Australian Journal of Politics and History

The Journal of Asian Studies

The Journal of Commonwealth and Comparative Politics

The Journal of Imperial and Commonwealth History

The Journal of Modern History

Secondary Works

Abbot, G.F., *Turkey in Transition,* London, 1909.

Abbot, G.F., *Select Writings and Speeches of Maulana Muhammad Ali,* Lahore, 1944.

Aga Khan, *India in Transition,* London, 1918.

Agarwal, Amar Narain, *Gandhism : A Socialistic Approach*, Allahabad, 1944.

Agarwala, M.M., *The Hindu-Muslim Riots : Their Causes and Cures*, Lucknow, 1944.

Aiyar, R.P. and Bhandare, L.S., *The Congress Caravan : The History of the Indian National Congress and of India's Struggle for Swaraj, 1885-1945*, Bombay, 1945.

Alexander, Horace, *Social and Political Ideas of Mahatma Gandhi*, Delhi, 1949.

Ali, Ameer Syed, *The Spirit of Islam*, London, 1935.

Ali Brothers, *For India and Islam*, Calcutta, 1922.

Ali, Muhammad, *Freedom of Faith and its Price*, London, 1919.

——, *My Life—A Fragment*, Lahore, 1946.

Ali, Zaki, *Islam in the World*, Lahore, 1947.

Amery, L.S., *India and Freedom*, London, 1942.

Andrews, C.F., *How India Can Be Free*, Madras, 1921.

——, *The Indian Problem*, Madras, 1921.

——, *The Meaning of Non-Cooperation*, Madras, 1923.

——, *Mahatma Gandhi at Work*, New York, 1931.

——, *Mahatma Gandhi's Ideas*, London, 1949.

Anjaria, J.J., *Essays on Gandhian Economics*, Bombay, 1945.

Appadorai, A., *Dyarchy in Practice*, London, 1937.

Arberry, J. and Landau Rom, *Islam Today*, London 1942.

Argov Daniel, *Moderates and Extremists in the Indian Nationalist Movement, 1883-1920*, Bombay, 1961.

Arnold, Thomas W., *The Caliphate*, Oxford, 1924.

Asaf Ali, M., *Constructive Non-Cooperation*, Madras, 1921.

Asquith, *Memories and Recollections*, vols. I and II, Boston, 1923.

Athalye D.V., *The Life of Mahatma Gandhi*, Poona, 1923.

Ayengar, A.S., *All Through the Gandhian Era, Indian, 1915-50*, Bombay, 1950.

Azad, Maulana Abul Kalam, *India Wins Freedom*, Delhi, 1959.

Aziz, K.K., *Britain and Muslim India*, London, 1963.

Baksh, S. Khuda, *Caliphate*, Lahore, 1954.

Bakshi, S.R., *British Diplomacy and Administration In India, 1807-13*, Delhi, 1971.

——, *Simon Commission and Indian Nationalism,* Delhi, 1977.

——, *Ranjit Singh and Charles Metcalfe,* Delhi 1980.

——, *Gandhi and Salt Satyagraha,* Delhi 1981.

——, *Bhagat Singh and His Ideology,* Delhi 1981.

——, *Jallianwala Bagh Tragedy,* Delhi 1982.

Bamford, P.C., *Histories of the Non-Cooperation and Khilafat Movements,* Delhi, 1974.

Bandyopadhyaya, J., *Social and Political Thought of Gandhi,* Calcutta, 1969.

Banerji, Nripendra Chandra, *Gandhism in Theory and Practice,* Madras, 1923.

Banerji, R.C., *The Story of the Khilafat,* Jessore, 1922.

Banerjea, S.N., *A Nation in Making : Being the Reminiscences of Fifty Years of Public Life,* London, 1925.

Barkatullah, Mohammad, *The Khilafat,* London, 1924.

Barns, Margarite, *India : Today and Tomorrow,* London, 1937.

Basu, Aparna, *The Growth of Education and Political Development in India, 1898-1920,* Delhi, 1974.

Bayly, C.A., *The Local Roots of Indian Politics, Allahabad, 1880-1920,* Oxford, 1975.

Besant, Annie, *How India Wrought For Freedom,* Madras, 1915.

——, *The Birth of New India,* Madras, 1917.

——, *Gandhian Non-Cooperation or Shall India Commit Suicide?* Madras, 1920.

——, *Shall India Live or Die?* Madras, 1925.

——, *India : A Nation,* Madras, 1930.

——, *India : Today and Tomorrow,* London, 1937.

——, *India Bond or Free,* Adyar, 1939.

——, *Speches and Writings,* Madras, n.d.

Besterman, Theodore, *Mrs. Annie Besant : A Modern Prophet,* London, 1934.

Bevan, Edywn, *Indian Nationalism : An Independent Estimate in India,* Delhi, 1966.

Bhagwan Das, *The Meaning of Swaraj or Self-Government,* Banaras, 1921.

——, *The Philosophy of Non-Cooperation,* Madras, 1922.

Bipan Chandra, *Rise and Growth of Economic Nationalism in India*, Delhi, 1966.

——, *Nationalism and Colonialism in Modern India*, Delhi, 1979.

Birla, G.D., *In the Shadow of the Mahatma : Personal Memoirs*, Bombay, 1968.

Bisheshwar Prasad, *Bondage and Freedom : A History of Modern India, 1707-1947*, vol. II, *Freedom, 1858-1947*, Delhi, 1979.

Bolitho, Hector, *Jinnah : Creator of Pakistan*, London, 1954.

Bondurant, Joan. V., *Conquest of Violence : The Gandhian Philosophy of Conflict*, London, 1959.

Bose, Nirmal Kumar, *Studies in Gandhism*, Calcutta, 1962.

Bose, Nirmal Kumar, and Patwardhan, P.H., *Gandhi in Indian Politics*, Bombay, 1967.

Bose, Subhas Chandra, *The Indian Struggle, 1920-42*, New York, 1964.

Brailsford, Henry Noel, *Rebel India*, New York, 1931.

——, *Subject India*, New York, 1943.

Brecher, Michael, *Nehru : A Political Biography*, London, 1959.

Bright, J.S., *The Himalayan Blunders of Mahatma Gandhi*, Lahore, 1946.

Brockway, A. Fenner, *Non-Cooperation in Other Lands*, Madras, 1921.

——, *The Indian Crisis*, London, 1930.

Brown, Judith M., *Gandhi's Rise to Power : Indian Politics, 1915-1922, London*, 1972.

Bryant, John Forbes, *Gandhi and Indianisation of the Empire*, London, 1924.

Buch, M.A., *Rise and Growth of Indian Liberalism*, Baroda, 1938.

——, *Rise and Growth of Indian Militant Nationalism*, Bombay, 1940.

Caveeshar, Sardul Singh, *India's Fight for Freedom*, Lahore, 1936.

Chakravarty, Amiya, *Mahatma Gandhi and Modern World*, Calcutta, 1945.

Chatterjee, B.C., *Gandhi and Aurobindo*, Calcutta, 1967.

Chatterjee, Dilip Kumar, *C.R. Das and Indian Naitonal Movement*, Calcutta, 1956.

Chatterjee, Jogesh, *The Search of Freedom*, Calcutta, 1967.

Chatterjee, Nandlal, *India's Freedom Struggle*, Allahabad, 1958.

Chesney, George, *Indian Policy : The System of Administration*, Delhi, 1976.

Chintamani, C.Y., *Indian Politics Since the Mutiny,* Allahabad, 1947.
Chirol, Valentine, *Pan-Islamism,* London, 1906.
——, *India : Old and New,* London, 1921.
——, *India,* London, 1926.
Cole, F. Seymour, *India Should Know Turkey,* Bombay, 1943.
Coupland, R., *The Indian Problem, 1833-1935,* London, 1942.
——, *The Goal of British Rule in India,* London, 1948.
Craddock, Reginald Henry, *The Dilemma in India,* London, 1920.
Crozir, Frank Percy, *A Word to Gandhi : The Lesson of Ireland,* London, 1931.
Curtis, L., *Dyarchy,* Oxford, 1920.
Das, C.R., *India for Indians,* Madras, 1921.
Das, M.N., *The Political Philosophy of Jawaharlal Nehru,* London, 1961.
——, *India Under Morley and Minto,* London, 1964.
——, *Indian National Congress Vs. The British, 1885-1918,* Delhi, 1978.
Datta, K.K., *History of the Freedom Movement in Bihar,* Vol. I, *1857-1928,* Patna, 1957.
Desai, A.R., *Social Background of Indian Nationalism,* Bombay, 1959.
Desai, Mahadev, *The Story of Bardoli,* Ahmedabad, 1957.
Dhawan, Gopinath, *The Political Philosophy of Mahatma Gandhi,* Ahmedabad, 1946.
Digby, William, *Prosperous British India,* London, 1901.
Diwakar, R.R., *Satyagraha : Its Technique and History,* Bombay, 1946.
——, *Satyagraha in Action,* Calcutta, 1949.
——, *Satyagraha : The Power of Truth,* Illinois, 1948.
Doke, Joseph, *M.K. Gandhi : An Indian Patriot in South Africa,* Madras, 1919.
Duncan, Ronald, *Select Writings of Mahatma Gandhi,* London, n.d.
Dutt, K. Iswara, *Congress Cyclopaedia,* vol., I, Delhi, n.d.
Dutt, K.N., *Landmarks of the Freedom Struggle in Assam,* Gauhati, 1958.
Dutt, R. Palme, *India Today,* Bombay, 1949.
Dutt, Ramesh Chandra, *The Economic History of India in the Victorian Age,* vol II.
Dwarkadas, Kanji, *India's Fight for Freedom, 1913-1937,* Bombay, 1966.

Edib, Halide, *Conflict of East and West in Turkey,* Delhi, 1935.

Elwin, Harry Verrier Holman, *Mahatma Gandhi,* London, 1932.

Fischer, Louis, *The Life of Mahatma Gandhi,* New York, 1950.

——, *The Essential Gandhi,* London, 1963.

Fraser, Andrew, *Among Indian Rajahs and Ryots,* London, 1911.

Fuller, Bampfylde, *The Empire of India,* London, 1913.

Fuller, J.F.C. *Indian in Revolt,* London, 1931.

Gallagher, J., Johnson, G., and Seal, A., (ed.), *Locality, Province and Nation : Essays on Indian Politics, 1870-1940,* Cambridge, 1973.

Gandhi, M.K., *An Autobiography or The Story of My Experiments with Truth,* Ahmedabad, 1958.

——, *Hind Swaraj,* Madras, 1921.

——, *Swaraj in One Year,* Madras, 1921.

——, *Communal Unity,* Ahmedabad, 1948.

——, *Non-Violence in Peace and War,* Ahmedabad, 1942.

——, *Economics of Khadi,* Ahmedabad, 1941.

——, *Constructive Programme : Its Meaning and Place,* Ahmedabad, 1948.

Ghose, P.C., *Mahatma Gandhi As I Saw Him,* Delhi, 1968.

Ghose, Shankar, *Political Ideas and Movements in India,* Calcutta, 1975.

Gokhale, G.K., *Speeches,* Madras, 1916.

Gopal, Ram, *Indian Muslims : A Political History, 1858-1947,* Bombay, 1959.

——, *How India Struggled for Freedom,* Bombay, 1967.

Gopal, S., *British Policy in India, 1858-1905,* London, 1965.

——, *Jawaharlal Nehru : A Biography,* Vol., I, London, 1975.

Gordon, Leonard, A., *Bengal : The Nationalist Movement, 1879-1940,* Delhi, 1974.

Gour, H.S., *The British Impact on India,* London, 1965.

Gregg, Richard B., *Psychology and Strategy of Gandhi's Non-violent Resistance,* Madras, 1929.

——, *Economics of Khaddar,* Ahmedabad, 1946.

Griffths, P.J., *The British Impact on India,* London, 1965.

Gupta, Nagendranath, *Indian Nationalism,* Bombay, 1946.

——, *Gandhi and Gandhism,* Bombay, 1948.

Gwyer, Maurice and Appadorai, A., *Speeches and Documents on the Indian Constitution, 1921-47,* Vol. I, London, 1957.

Hamper, D.A., *John Morley, Liberal Intellectual in Politics,* London, 1968.

Hasan, Mushirul, *Nationalism and Communal Politics in India, 1916-28,* Delhi, 1974.

Hitti, Phillip K., *The Arabs,* London, 1960.

Holmes, John Haynes, *Gandhi Before Pilate : A Sermon on the Indian Revolution,* New York, 1930.

Horne, E.A., *The Political System of British India,* Oxford, 1922.

Horniman, B.G., *Amritsar and Our Duty to India,* London, 1920.

Houghton, Bernard, *The Issue in India,* Madras, 1922.

——, *Realities of Today,* Madras, 1923.

Hoyland, John S., *The Case for India,* London, 1929.

——, *Indian Crisis : The Background,* London, 1943.

Hull, William Isaac, *India's Political Crisis,* Baltimore, 1930.

Hunter, W.W., *The Indian Musalmans,* London, 1972.

Husain, Azam, *Fazl-i-Husain : A Political Biography,* Bombay, 1946.

Hyde, H. Montgomery, *Lord Reading,* London, 1967.

Hyndman, H.M., *The Awakening of Asia,* London, 1919.

Iyenger, C.S. Ranga, *India in the Crucible,* London, 1927.

——, *How To Lose India,* Lahore, 1935.

Jayakar, M.R., *The Story of My Life, 1873-1922,* vol. I, Bombay, 1958.

Jha, Shiva Nand, *A Critical Study of Gandhian Economic Thought,* Agra, 1961.

Iyer, Raghavan, N., *The Moral and Political Thought of Mahatma Gandhi,* London, 1978.

Kabir, Humayun, *Muslim Politics, 1906-42,* Calcutta, 1943.

Kamath, M.S., *The Home Rule League,* Madras, 1927.

Karmarkar, D.D., *Bal Gangadhar Tilak : A Study,* Bombay, 1956.

Karve, D.G., and Ambedkar, D.V., (ed.), *Speeches and Writings of Gopal Krishna Gokhale,* vol. II, Bombay, 1966.

Kaura, Uma, *Muslim and Indian Nationalism : The Emergence of the Demand for India's Partition, 1928-40,* Delhi, 1977.

Kaushik, P.D., *The Congress Ideology and Programme, 1920-47,* Delhi, 1964.

Keer, Dhananjay, *Lokamanya Tilak : Father of our Freedom Struggle,* Bombay, 1958.

——, *Mahatma Gandhi : Political Saint and Unarmed Prophet,* Bombay, 1973.

Keith, A.B. (ed.) *Speeches and Documents on Indian Policy,* Vol. II, London, 1922.

Kenworthy, J.W., *India : A Warning,* London, 1931.

Kidwai, Shaikh Mushir Hasan, *Pan-Islamism,* London, 1908.

Kohli, M.S., *Mahatma Gandhi's Confessions,* Lahore, 1943.

Kohn, Hans, *A History of Nationalism in the East,* New York, 1929.

Koss, Stephen, E., *John Morley at the India Office, 1905-1910.* Yale University Press, 1969.

Kripalani, J.B., *The Gandhian Way,* Bombay, 1946.

——, *Gandhi : His Life and Thought,* Delhi, 1970.

Krishnamurti, Y.G., *Gandhi Era in World Politics,* Bombay, 1943.

Kumarappa, J.C., *Gandhian Economic Thought,* Bombay, 1931.

Kurup, T.C.K., *Gospel of Gandhi,* Madras, 1921.

Lajpat Rai, *The Political Future of India,* New York, 1919.

——, *India's Will To Freedom :Writings and Speeches On The Present Situation,* Madras, 1921.

——, *Ideals of Non-Cooperation and Other Essays,* Madras, 1924.

Lal Bahadur, *The Muslim League : Its History, Activities and Achievements,* Agra, 1954.

Lawtom, Lancerton, *Empire of the East,* Part II, London, 1912.

Lovett, Verney, *A History of the Indian Nationalist Movement,* London, 1920.

Lucas, Charles, *The Empire at War,* London, 1921.

Mackenzie, Brown, *Indian Political Thought from Ranade to Bhave,* Berkeley, 1961.

MacDonald, J. Ramsay, *The Government of India,* London, n.d.

Macnicol, Nicol, *The Making of Modern India,* London, 1924.

Mahmud Ahmad, *Non-Cooperation and Islam,* Lahore, 1921.

——, *Indian Problem and its Solution,* London, 1926.

Mahmud, Syed, *The Khilafat and England,* Patna, 1922.

Majumdar, R.C., *Three Phases of India's Struggle for Freedom,* Bombay, 1961.

——, *History of Freedom Movement in India,* vol. III, Calcutta, 1963.

Malhotra, P.L., *Administration of Lord Elgin in India, 1894-99,* Delhi, 1979.

Mary, Countess of Minto, *India, Minto and Morley, 1906-10,* London, 1934.

Masani, R.P., *Dadabhai Naoroji : The Grand Old Man of India,* London, 1939.

Mathur, J.S., *Essays on Gandhian Economics,* Allahabad, 1960.

Mazumdar, H.T., *Gandhi : The Apostle,* Chicago, 1923.

——, *Mahatma Gandhi : Peaceful Revolutionary,* New York, 1952.

Mehrotra, S.R., *India and the Commonwealth, 1885-1929,* London, 1965.

——, *Towards Indian Freedom and Partition,* Delhi, 1979.

Menon, P.K.K., *The History of Freedom Movement in Kerala, 1885-1938,* vol. II, Trivandrum, 1972.

Meston, Lord, *India and the Empire,* London, 1924.

Mishra, D.P. (ed.), *The History of Freedom Movement in Madhya Pradesh,* Nagpur, 1956.

Mitra, S.M., *Indian Problems,* London, 1908.

Mody, H.P., *The Political Future of India,* London, 1908.

Montagu, E.S., *An Indian Diary,* London, 1930.

Moon, P., *Gandhi and Modern India,* London, 1968.

Moore, R.J., *The Crisis of Indian Unity,* Oxford, 1964.

Moraes, Frank, *Jawaharlal Nehru : A Biography,* New York, 1956.

Mukerjee, H., *India Struggles for Freedom,* Bombay, 1946.

——, *Gandhiji : A Study,* Calcutta 1958.

Naik, V.N., *Indian Liberalism,* Bombay, 1945.

Nair, C. Sankaran, *Gandhi and Anarchy,* Madras, 1922.

Namboodiripad, E.M.S., *The Mahatma and the Ism,* Delhi, 1958.

Naoroji, Dadabhai, *Poverty and Un-British Rule in India,* Delhi, 1962.

——, *Speeches and Writings of Dadabhai Naoroji,* Madras, n.d.

Narayan, Shriman, *The Gandhian Plan of Economic Development of India,* Bombay, 1944.

Nariman, K.F., *Whither Congress,* Bombay, 1933.

Nehru, Jawaharlal, *An Autobiography,* London, 1936.

——, *Glimpses of World History,* Bombay, 1945.

——, *The Discovery of India,* Calcutta, 1946.

——, *A Bunch of Old Letters,* Bombay, 1960.

Nevinson, Henry W., *The New Spirit in India,* Delhi, 1975.

Nomon, Mohammed, *Rise and Growth of All India Muslim League,* Allahabad, 1941.

——, *Muslim India,* Allahabad, 1942.

Nundy, Alfred; *Indian Unrest, 1919-20,* Dehradun, 1921.

O'Dwyer, Michael, *India As I Knew it, 1885-1925,* London, 1925.

Pal, B.C., *The Spirit of Indian Naitonalism,* London, 1910.

——, *Nationality and Empire,* Calcutta, 1916.

——, *Non-Cooperation : Four Lectures,* Calcutta, 1920.

——, *Swaraj : The Goal and Way,* Madras, 1921.

——, *Swadeshi and Swaraj,* Calcutta, 1954.

Pande, B.N., *Nehru,* Delhi, 1977.

Panikkar, K.M., *The New Empire,* London, 1934.

Pardaman Singh, *Lord Minto and Indian Nationalism, 1905-1910,* Allahabad, 1976.

Parmanand, Bhai, *The Story of My Life,* Lahore, 1934.

Pavate T.V., *Bal Gangadhar Tilak,* Ahmedabad, 1958.

Patil, V.T., *Nehru and the Freedom Movement,* Delhi, 1977.

Paul, K.T., *The British Connection With India,* London, 1927.

Payne, Robert, *The Life and Death of Mahatma Gandhi,* London, 1969.

Polak, H.S., and others, *Mahatma Gandhi,* London, 1949.

Pole, D., Graham, *I Refer to India,* London, 1929.

——, *India in Transition,* London, 1932.

Prabodh Chandra, *Sixty Years of Congress,* Lahore, 1946.

Pradhan, R.G., *India's Struggle For Swaraj,* Madras, 1930.

Prasad, Rajendra, *Satyagraha in Champaran,* Ahmedabad, 1949.

——, *Autobiography,* Bombay, 1957.

——, *At the Feet of Mahatma Gandhi,* Bombay, 1961.

Price, Clair, *The Rebirth of Turkey,* New York, 1923.

Pylee, M.V., *Constitutional Government in India,* Bombay, 1965.

Raju, J.B., *A Critical Study of the Non-Cooperation Movement,* Nagpur, 1920.

Ram Rattan, *Gandhi's Concept of Political Obligation,* Calcutta, 1972.

Ramachandran G., *Promotion of Gandhian Philosophy,* Mysore, 1966.

Rao, C.V.H., *Civil Disobedience Movement in India or The Indian Struggle for Freedom,* Lahore, 1946.

Ray, Prithwis Chandra, *Life and Times of C.R. Das,* Calcutta, 1927.

Reading, Marquess of, Rufus Issacs, *First Marquess of Reading.* vols. I and II, London, 1945.

Reynolds, Reginald, *The White Sahibs in India,* London, 1937.

Rivelt, Kenneth, *Economic Thought of Mahatma Gandhi,* Delhi, 1959.

Ronaldshay, Earl of, *The Life of Lord Curzon,* London, 1928.

Roy, M.N., *One Year of Non-Cooperation from Ahmedabad to Gaya,* Calcutta, 1923.

——, *The Future of Indian Politics,* London, 1928.

Rutherford, V.H., *Modern India : Its Problems and Their Solution,* London, 1927.

Ruthnaswamy, M., *The Political Philosophy of Mr. Gandhi,* Madras, 1922.

Santhanam, K., *Gospel of Gandhi,* Bombay, 1967.

Sarkar, Sumit, *The Swadeshi Movement in Bengal, 1903-1908,* Delhi, 1973.

Shakir, Moin, *Khilafat to Pakistan,* Delhi, 1970.

Sharma, Bishan Swarup, *Gandhi As a Political Thinker,* Allahabad, 1956.

Sharp, Gene, *Gandhi Weilds the Weapon of Moral Power,* Ahmedabad, 1960.

——, *The Politics of Non-violent Action,* Boston, 1972.

Shridharani, K., *War Without Violence : A Study of Gandhi's Method and its Accomplishments,* New York, 1939.

Singh, Hira Lal, *Problems and Politics of the British in India,* Bombay, 1963.

Singh, Sita Ram, *Nationalism and Social Reform in India,* Delhi, 1968.

Sitaramayya, B. Pattabhi, *History of the Indian National Congress, 1885-1935,* vol. I, Delhi, 1969.

Smith, W.C., *Modern Islam in India,* Lahore, 1947.

Smith, W.R., *Nationalism and Reform in India,* London, 1973.

Speeches and Writings of Bal Gangadhar Tilak, Madras, n.d.

Sprat, P., *Gandhism An Analysis,* Madras, 1932.

Street, C.J.C., *Lord Reading,* London, 1926.

Swinson, Arthur, *Six Minutes to Sunset,* London, 1964.

Sykes, Frederick, *From Many Angles : An Autobiography,* London, 1942.

Tara Chand, *History of Freedom Movement in India,* vol. III, Delhi, 1972.

Tendulkar, D.G., *Mahatma : Life of Mohandas Karamchand Gandhi,* vols. II and III, Delhi, 1961.

Thomson, Edward, *The Reconstruction of India,* London, 1930.

Vaswani, T.L., *Non-Cooperation and National Idealism,* Calcutta, 1921.

——, *India in Chains,* Madras, 1922.

Wasti, Syed Razi, *Lord Minto and the Indian Nationalist Movement, 1905 to 1910,* Oxford University Press, 1964.

Wint, Guy, *The British in Asia,* New York, 1954.

Wolpert, Stanley A., *Tilak and Gokhale,* California, 1962.

Woodruff, Philip, *The Men Who Ruled India,* London, 1974.

Woolacot, J.E., *Britain's Record in India,* London, 1927.

——, *India on Trial,* London, 1929.

——, *India The Truth,* London, 1930.

Yajnik, Indulal K., *Gandhi As I Know Him,* Delhi, 1943.

Zakaria, Rafiq, *Rise of Muslims in Indian Politics*, Bombay, 1970

Index

Q

R

S

T